CIRCUMVENTING THE MIDDLE EAST CHOKEPOINTS

Infrastructure, Strategy and Geopolitics

CIRCUMVENTING THE MIDDLE EAST CHOKEPOINTS
Infrastructure, Strategy and Geopolitics

Edited by

Amit Ranjan
National University of Singapore, Singapore

Asif Shuja
Geopoconsult, UAE

NEW JERSEY • LONDON • SINGAPORE • BEIJING • SHANGHAI • HONG KONG • TAIPEI • CHENNAI • TOKYO

Published by

World Scientific Publishing Co. Pte. Ltd.
5 Toh Tuck Link, Singapore 596224
USA office: 27 Warren Street, Suite 401-402, Hackensack, NJ 07601
UK office: 57 Shelton Street, Covent Garden, London WC2H 9HE

Library of Congress Control Number: 2024021804

British Library Cataloguing-in-Publication Data
A catalogue record for this book is available from the British Library.

CIRCUMVENTING THE MIDDLE EAST CHOKEPOINTS
Infrastructure, Strategy and Geopolitics

Copyright © 2025 by World Scientific Publishing Co. Pte. Ltd.

All rights reserved. This book, or parts thereof, may not be reproduced in any form or by any means, electronic or mechanical, including photocopying, recording or any information storage and retrieval system now known or to be invented, without written permission from the publisher.

For photocopying of material in this volume, please pay a copying fee through the Copyright Clearance Center, Inc., 222 Rosewood Drive, Danvers, MA 01923, USA. In this case permission to photocopy is not required from the publisher.

ISBN 978-981-12-9469-3 (hardcover)
ISBN 978-981-12-9470-9 (ebook for institutions)
ISBN 978-981-12-9471-6 (ebook for individuals)

For any available supplementary material, please visit
https://www.worldscientific.com/worldscibooks/10.1142/13885#t=suppl

About the Editors

Amit Ranjan is a research fellow at the Institute of South Asian Studies, National University of Singapore. His latest books include the following: (with Ian Talbot) *Urban Development and Environmental History in Modern South Asia* (Routledge, London, 2023) and *Contested Waters: India's Transboundary River Water Disputes in South Asia* (Routledge, London and New Delhi, 2020). He is also the author of *India-Bangladesh Border Disputes: History and Post-LBA Dynamics* (Springer, Singapore, 2018). Amit has edited the following books: *India in South Asia Challenges and Management* (Springer, Singapore, 2019), *Partition of India: Postcolonial Legacies* (Routledge, London and New Delhi, 2019), and *Water Issues in Himalayan South Asia: Internal Challenges, Disputes and Transboundary Tensions* (Singapore, 2019). His papers, review essays, and book reviews have been widely published in journals, including *Asian Survey, Asian Affairs, Asian Ethnicity, Asian Journal of Comparative Politics, Economic and Political Weekly, India Review, Indian Journal of Public Administration, India Quarterly, Journal of Migration Affairs, Journal of the Indian Ocean Region, Round Table: The Commonwealth Journal of International Affairs, Social Change, Studies in Indian Politics, Society and Culture in South Asia, South Asia Research, Journal of Asian Security and International Affairs, Water History*, and *World Water Policy*.

Asif Shuja is Director of Geopoconsult, a geopolitics management consultancy based in Dubai. He was formerly a Senior Fellow with the Middle East Institute, National University of Singapore. His research focus includes Iranian domestic politics, the Iranian nuclear issue, Iran's foreign policy, and Iran's regional role. Asif was previously associated with the International Center for Strategic Studies, Abu Dhabi, as a non-resident fellow. His other research affiliations include the Indian Council of World Affairs and the Centre for Air Power Studies, New Delhi. He obtained his PhD on Iran's political power struggle from the Centre for West Asian (Middle East) Studies, Jawaharlal Nehru University, New Delhi. He has authored the book, *India-Iran Relations under the Shadow of the Iranian Nuclear Issue*. His wider area of interest is Gulf Security and Great Power Rivalry in the Middle East.

© 2025 World Scientific Publishing Company
https://doi.org/10.1142/9789811294709_fmatter

About the Contributors

Alam Saleh is a Senior Lecturer in Iranian Studies at the Centre for Arab and Islamic Studies at the Australian National University. Alam is also a Council Member of the British Society for Middle Eastern Studies (BRISMES) and Reviews Editor for the *British Journal of Middle Eastern Studies*. He received his PhD, MA, and BA from the School of Politics and International Studies at the University of Leeds. He is a Fellow of Higher Education Academy, and he has previously taught undergraduate and graduate courses on International Relations, Security Studies, and Middle East Politics at Lancaster, Exeter, Durham, Leeds, and Bradford Universities. Alam has also been engaged with policy practitioners and external professional bodies such as the UK Ministry of Defence, NATO, European Council on Foreign Relations, and has also consulted for Transparency International Defence & Security, UNICEF, and the BBC.

Atha Tahir is a PhD candidate at the National Institute of Pakistan Studies, Quaid-I-Azam University, Islamabad. He previously earned an MPhil degree from the same department in 2019, and an MSc degree in Gender Studies from the same university in 2016. He is currently serving as a lecturer in Social Sciences at Mir Chakar Khan Rind University, Sibi, Balochistan. His doctoral research examines political activism of the women of the fisherfolk community against mega projects in Gwadar, Pakistan. Atha has conducted extensive ethnographic fieldwork in Balochistan, and his work experience includes research positions focused viii *About the Contributors*

on communal displacement and vulnerable populations of mega-projects. He aims to produce scholarship that advances theoretical perspectives on gender, development, and social movements in Pakistan and South Asia.

Deepika Saraswat is an Associate Fellow at the West Asia Center, Manohar Parrikar Institute for Defence Studies and Analyses, New Delhi. Her research interests include Iran's geopolitics in the Middle East and Eurasia and interpenetration of religion and politics in postcolonial contexts. Her research project at MP-IDSA is on 'Iran's Asian Orientation: Quest for Status and Regional Cooperation'. Deepika has a PhD in Political Geography from Centre for International Politics Organisation and Disarmament, School of International Studies, Jawaharlal Nehru University, New Delhi. Earlier, she was a Research Fellow at the Indian Council of World Affairs (March 2018–October 2021). Her book titled *Between Survival and Status: The Counter-hegemonic Geopolitics of Iran* was jointly published by the Indian Council of World Affairs and Macmillan in January 2022. Her commentaries on Iran's geopolitics have appeared in the *National Interest, Lobe Log, The Indian Express, the Roundtable Journal*, and *LSE Blog* among others.

Eleonora Ardemagni is an expert on Yemen, the Gulf monarchies, and Arab military forces. She is an Associate Research Fellow (Yemen and the Gulf) at the Italian Institute for International Political Studies (ISPI) and a Teaching Assistant ('History of Islamic Asia'; 'New Conflicts') at the Catholic University of Milan. She is also an Adjunct Professor at the Graduate School of Economics and International Relations-ASERI ('Yemen: Drivers of conflict and security implications'). Former Gulf Analyst for the NATO Defense College Foundation (2015–2020) and Yemen contributor for The Armed Conflict Survey 2021, International Institute for Strategic Studies (IISS). She advised and produced studies on Security Sector Reform for the Office of the UN Special Envoy of the Secretary-General for Yemen (OSESGY-SSR Team). Her articles and essays also appeared in Carnegie Sada, Carnegie Middle East Center, The Arab Gulf States Institute in Washington (AGSIW), Middle East Institute, LSE Middle East Centre Blog, *International Studies* journal, *ORIENT-German Journal for Politics*, Economics and Culture of the Middle East, EUISS, POMEPS, RUSI, and the NATO Defense College. Latest publications: 'The Yemeni-Saudi Border: The Huthis and the Evolution of Hybrid

Security Governance', in A. Hamidaddin (ed.), *The Huthi Movement in Yemen. Ideology, Ambition and Security in the Arab Gulf*, KFCRIS Series-I.B. Tauris, Bloomsbury, 2022; 'Policing the Emirati nation: The politics of community-building', in W. Gueraiche-K.Alexander (eds.), *Facets of Security in the United Arab Emirates*, Routledge, 2022; 'Yemen's Defense Structure: Hybridity and Patronage after the State', *Journal of Arabian Studies*, 2020; 'Arab Gulf States: Expanding Roles for the Military', *Oxford Research Encyclopedia of the Military in Politics*, 2020; 'The Huthis: Adaptable Players in Yemen's Multiple Geographies', *CRiSSMA-Catholic University*, 2019.

Gürol Baba is currently an Associate Professor, Social Sciences University of Ankara, Turkey. Gürol Baba has his BA degree from Marmara University, Department of Political Science and International Relations. He had his MA degree from the Çanakkale Onsekiz Mart University, Graduate School of Social Sciences, and his MPhil and PhD degrees from the Australian National University, Canberra at the Research School of Humanities.

Mohammed Al-Hajri is a PhD candidate at the Department of Politics, Birkbeck, University of London. His research interests include the Arab–Asia studies, with a particular focus on Sino–GCC relations, the foreign policy of smaller Gulf states, International Political Economy, and port infrastructure politics. The PhD thesis looks at the dynamics of China–GCC relations and the impact of the Belt and Road Initiative (BRI) on port infrastructure in the GCC region. Al-Hajri has actively participated in various conferences focusing on Gulf studies. He has also written articles that are currently being reviewed for publication in reputable academic journals.

Nigel Li is a Singaporean who specialises in Russian foreign policy and geopolitical developments in Eurasia. He is a graduate of the Moscow State Institute of International Relations (MGIMO) and is currently pursuing his MA in Eurasian, Russian, and East European Studies at Georgetown University's Walsh School of Foreign Service. His commentaries have been published in the *Taipei Times*, *The Diplomat*, *Channel News Asia*, among others. In 2022, he published his first novel *Light is My Heart From a Cheerful Song* while in Moscow.

x *About the Contributors*

Roger Kangas is the Academic Dean and a Professor of Central Asian Studies at the Near East South Asia Center for Strategic Studies, a U.S. Department of Defense regional center. Previously, Roger served as a Professor of Central Asian Studies at the George C. Marshall Center for European Security in Garmisch-Partenkirchen, Germany, Deputy Director of the Central Asian Institute at Johns Hopkins University School of Advanced International Studies, Central Asian Course Coordinator at the Department of State's Foreign Service Institute, Research Analyst on Central Asian Affairs for the Open Media Research Institute in Prague, Czech Republic, and as an Assistant Professor of Political Science at the University of Mississippi. He has been an advisor to the Combatant Commands, NATO/ISAF, and various US government agencies on issues relating to Central and South Asia, Russia, and the South Caucasus. He has written refereed articles and book chapters, as well as lectured to a range of audiences, on these topics. He is also an Adjunct Professor at Georgetown University and a Visiting Fellow at the International Institute for Strategic Studies. Roger holds a B.S.F.S. in Comparative Politics from the Edmund A. Walsh School of Foreign Service at Georgetown University and a Ph.D. in Political Science from Indiana University.

Zakiyeh Yazdanshenas is Director of China-Middle East Project at the Center for Middle East Strategic Studies (Tehran), Iran. Her research focus is Iran's foreign policy. She tweets on @YzdZakiyeh.

© 2025 World Scientific Publishing Company
https://doi.org/10.1142/9789811294709_fmatter

Acknowledgements

This edited volume would not have been possible without the invaluable contributions of our esteemed authors. We extend our deepest gratitude to them for adhering to the timelines and delivering exceptional work.

We also wish to express our heartfelt thanks to our families, whose unwavering support and understanding have been a source of strength throughout this endeavour. There are no words sufficient to convey our appreciation for their invaluable role in our lives.

Lastly, we are grateful to the dedicated team at World Scientific Publishing, particularly the Desk Editors Sanjay Varadharajan and Nicole Ong, for their meticulous handling of the production process. Their professionalism and dedication have been instrumental in bringing this book to fruition.

© 2025 World Scientific Publishing Company
https://doi.org/10.1142/9789811294709_fmatter

Contents

About the Editors	v
About the Contributors	vii
Acknowledgements	xi
Introduction	xv

Part I   Chokepoints and Strait of Hormuz   **1**

Chapter 1   Maritime Chokepoints and Ocean Infrastructures
in Asia: Strategic Cooperation, Geostrategic Contests,
and Vulnerabilities   3
Amit Ranjan

Chapter 2   Comparative Strategies of the US, China, and India
on the Strait of Hormuz   31
Asif Shuja

Chapter 3   Russia in the Persian Gulf   47
Nigel Li and Roger Kangas

Part II   Ports of Duqm, Gwadar and Chabahar   **67**

Chapter 4   A Chokepoint of Asymmetric and Complex
Rivalry: The Port of Duqm   69
Gürol Baba

xiv *Contents*

Chapter 5	Gwadar: Geopolitics, Development, and Social Change in a Strategic Port City *Atha Tahir*	93
Chapter 6	Chabahar: Geoeconomic Hopes and Geopolitical Games *Deepika Saraswat*	119

Part III Regional and External Dynamics **141**

Chapter 7	The Strait of Hormuz and Iran's Active Deterrence Strategy *Alam Saleh and Zakiyeh Yazdanshenas*	143
Chapter 8	Comparing UAE and Oman *Beyond Hormuz* Security Strategies *Eleonora Ardemagni*	163
Chapter 9	The People's Republic of China Strategic Imperatives in Oman's Port of Duqm *Mohammed Al-Hajri*	181

Index 205

© 2025 World Scientific Publishing Company
https://doi.org/10.1142/9789811294709_fmatter

Introduction

More than 60% of the world's oil and petroleum products are transported via different sea routes. The bulk of such products is supplied from the Middle East countries to different parts of the world. During the supplying process, the goods have to pass via three significant chokepoints of the region — Suez Canal, the Bab-el-Mandeb Strait, and the Strait of Hormuz — making the narrow waterways critical to the global energy security. To secure an economic interest and geostrategic position in the gulf, the United States of America (USA), along with its European allies, has maintained a strong military presence in the region. In 1995, the USA reactivated its Fifth Fleet, which was deactivated in 1947.[1] This fleet looks at the affairs in the Persian Gulf, Red Sea, Arabian Sea, and parts of the Indian Ocean. In recent years, as the tensions between the major energy dependent powers have escalated, alternate routes have been discovered and infrastructures have been built to circumvent the three chokepoints of the Middle East. The circumvention is emphasised upon, as it is largely believed that in times of aggravation of conflict one or the other power may choke or try to choke the enemy's supplies, especially at the Strait of Hormuz. To evade the chance of getting choked, the major powers with the help of the Middle East countries are investing in port infrastructures, such as Duqm in Oman, Gwadar in Pakistan, and Chabahar in

---

[1] Schneller Jr., Robert J. (2007). *Anchor of Resolve: A History of US Naval Forces Central Command/Fifth Fleet*. Naval Historical Center, Department of the Navy, Washington. https://www.history.navy.mil/content/dam/nhhc/browse-by-topic/War%20and%20Conflict/operation-praying-mantis/AnchorOfResolve.pdf, pp. 41–42.

xvi *Introduction*

Iran. The three new ports are likely to play a prominent role and may turn as new chokepoints in the Persian Gulf and Arabian sea.

At present, the major powers are rivalling over the connectivity routes and contesting to develop new projects which benefit them. The rivalry over connectivity increased multiple times mainly after the Chinese President Xi Jinping came out with his One Belt, One Road (called Belt and Road Initiative or BRI since 2016) in 2013. Under the BRI, China planned to establish a multimodal connectivity route. The land-based BRI begins in Xi'an in Central China.[2] According to China's State Council Information Office white paper titled 'The Belt and Road Initiative: A Key Pillar of the Global Community of Shared Future' which was released in October 2023, the BRI framework comprising 'six corridors, six routes, and multiple countries and ports, a multitiered and multidimensional infrastructure network is taking shape'.[3] The whitepaper says that by June 2023, China had signed more than 200 BRI cooperation agreements with more than 150 countries and 30 international organisations across five continents. In maritime matters, the white paper informs that by the end of June 2023, the BRI connectivity network had reached to 117 ports in 43 countries. The maritime connectivity along with others have increased trade between China and its BRI partners.[4]

Unlike the benefactors of the BRI, the project is considered big challenge by the rival powers. The BRI is largely seen as a Chinese attempt to dominate the global geoeconomic and strategic connectivity routes. The projects under the BRI arrangement are invariably cited as a reason for growing debts on the many partner countries. Brahma Chellaney, on the basis of his analysis of China's BRI loan, describes the arrangement as a 'debt trap' diplomacy.[5] In a study, Ammar A.

---

[2] Port Economics, Management and Politics. The Belt and Road Initiative (BRI). https://porteconomicsmanagement.org/pemp/contents/part2/port-hinterlands-regionalization/belt-and-road-initiative-bri/.

[3] The State Council Information Office of the People's Republic of China. The Belt and Road initiative: A key pillar of the global community of shared future. http://www.scio.gov.cn/zfbps/zfbps_2279/202310/t20231010_773734.html.

[4] *Ibid.*

[5] Chellaney, B. (2017). China's debt-trap diplomacy. *Project Syndicate.* https://www.project-syndicate.org/commentary/china-one-belt-one-road-loans-debt-by-brahma-chellaney-2017-01.

Malik *et al.* finds that the average interest rate of a loan from an official sector in China is 4.2 %, while the average maturity length is 9.4 years and the average grace period is 1.8 years.[6] The interest rate on Chinese money is much higher than soft loans from the World Bank and the Asian Development Bank, which have a maximum interest rate of 1.3% and a longer repayment period.[7]

To tackle the Chinese challenges, India, Japan, the US, and Australia have joined hands to reinvigorate QUAD (Quadrilateral Security Dialogue). China termed QUAD a 'bloc' for confrontation with a 'Cold War mentality'.[8] On the line of QUAD, I2U2 (India, Israel, United Arab Emirates, and the USA), also termed by some scholars and commentators as 'new QUAD' or 'Second QUAD',[9] was initiated. Further, largely looked as an alternative to the BRI, India-Middle East-Europe Economic Corridor (IMEC) has been construed. The memorandum of understanding (MoU) to develop IMEC was signed on 9 September 2023, on the sidelines of the G-20 Summit at New Delhi.[10] The MoU on IMEC was signed by India, USA, Saudi Arabia, UAE, European Union, Italy,

---

[6] Malik, A. A., Parks, B., Russell, B., Lin, J. J., Walsh, K., Solomon, K., Zhang, S., Elston, T.-B. & Goodman, S. (2021). Banking on the Belt and Road: Insights from a new global dataset of 13,427 Chinese development projects. https://docs.aiddata.org/ad4/pdfs/Banking_on_the_Belt_and_Road__Insights_from_a_new_global_dataset_of_13427_Chinese_development_projects.pdf.

[7] Paudyal, P. (2023, September 11). China, Nepal and the BRI dilemma. *The Kathmandu Post.* https://kathmandupost.com/columns/2023/09/11/china-nepal-and-the-bri-dilemma.

[8] Patranobi, S. (2022, February 9). 'Cold War mentality': China says Quad is a 'bloc' for confrontation. *Hindustan Times.* https://www.hindustantimes.com/world-news/cold-war-mentality-china-says-quad-is-a-bloc-for-confrontation-101644405143190.html.

[9] Raja Mohan, C. (2021, October 20). India and the 'new' QUAD in West Asia. *The Indian Express.* https://indianexpress.com/article/opinion/columns/india-and-the-new-quad-in-west-asia-7578842/. Rajagopalan, R. P. (2023, June 1). A second quad in the making in the Middle East? *ORF.* https://www.orfonline.org/research/a-second-quad-in-the-making-in-the-middle-east/.

[10] Ministry of External Affairs, Government of India. (2023, September 9). Partnership for global infrastructure and investment (PGII) & India-Middle East-Europe economic corridor (IMEC). https://mea.gov.in/press-releases.htm?dtl/37091/Partnership+for+Global+Infrastructure+and+Investment+PGII++IndiaMiddle+EastEurope+Economic+Corridor+IMEC.

xviii   *Introduction*

France, and Germany.[11] It is believed that after completion, the IMEC will reduce trade time between India and Europe via the Middle East by 40%.[12]

This edited volume intends to answer the following questions:

- How have the regional chokepoints influenced foreign and strategic policies of the Middle East countries?
- Can the new ports, developed in the Gulf region, reduce vulnerabilities to oil trade from the Middle East to the other parts of the world?
- How have the USA, China, and India engaged with each other on port-related infrastructure strategy?

This book is divided into three parts with three chapters each. The first part is *Chokepoints and Strait of Hormuz*. The second part is *Ports of Duqm, Gwadar, and Chabahar*. The third part of this book is on *Regional and External Dynamics*.

The first part, titled *Chokepoints and Strait of Hormuz*, gives a theoretical framework to evaluate the issue of chokepoints as dealt in the rest of the book. Chapter 1, authored by Amit Ranjan, is titled 'Maritime Chokepoints and Ocean Infrastructures in Asia: strategic cooperation, geostrategic contests, and vulnerabilities.' The author begins by underlining the fact that Middle East is an important region for Asia and other parts of the world. It has a huge energy reserve on which a big part of the world's economy depends. For example, through the Strait of Hormuz, approximately 21 million barrels of oil per day passes per day. It is a primary maritime route for countries such as Bahrain, Iran, Iraq, Kuwait, Qatar, Saudi Arabia, and the United Arab Emirates to ship their oil to external markets. Only Iran and Saudi Arabia have an alternative route. Another important chokepoint in Asia is the Malacca Strait. More than about 15 million barrels of oil pass through it per day. Over 80% of China's oil imports (by sea) and around 60% of Japan's total oil imports pass through the strait. To circumvent the chokepoints and for strategic reasons, China, US, India, and other powers are developing infrastructures in ocean and carrying out connectivity projects in various parts of

---

[11] *Ibid.*

[12] Al Jazeera. (2023, September 9). G20 summit: Transport project to link India to Middle East, Europe unveiled. https://www.aljazeera.com/news/2023/9/9/g20-summit-transport-project-to-link-india-to-middle-east-europe-unveiled.

Asia. This chapter seeks to answer three questions: first, how and why chokepoints can be used as a geostrategic weapon against an adversary? Second, what measures are countries taking to avoid their chokepoint vulnerabilities? Finally, why have new port infrastructures triggered rivalry between the region's big powers and external actors?

Chapter 2 is authored by Asif Shuja and titled 'Comparative Strategies of the US, China and India on the Strait of Hormuz.' This chapter essentially deals with the comparative strategies of the US, China, and India on the Strait of Hormuz in particular and in the Persian Gulf region in general. The theoretical framework of this chapter is the twin factors of global US–China rivalry and China–India competition in the Middle East. The implications of this pair of competitions are assessed on the chokepoint politics in the Middle East, with a focus on the security of the Strait of Hormuz. In the past, when the US depended on the Gulf's oil for its energy security, there was great merit in its strategy to secure the Strait of Hormuz to keep the oil flowing. However, presently the US has become the largest producer of oil and is much less dependent on the Gulf's oil. This has brought new dynamics in the Middle East region, wherein the US is fast changing its 'oil-for-security' contract with the Gulf monarchies. This has implications on the US' strategy on the Strait of Hormuz. On the other hand, China's dependence on the Gulf's oil has now placed it in a situation wherein the Strait of Hormuz is much more important for China than the US. At the same time, freedom of navigation around this chokepoint is still important for both the US and China as far as their support to their respective regional friends are concerned. Under these backdrops, this chapter evaluates the respective strategies of the US, China, and India on the Strait of Hormuz. While looking at these perspectives, this chapter will also contextualise the three ports of Duqm, Gwadar, and Chabahar into the broader security calculus respectively of the US, China, and India.

Chapter 3 is co-authored by Nigel Li and Roger Kangas and is titled 'Russia in the Persian Gulf.' This chapter explores Russia's evolving geopolitical strategies and its growing influence in the Persian Gulf within the context of its broader global ambitions. It begins by contextualizing Russia's pursuit of a multipolar world order as a counter to the perceived US-dominated unipolar system, especially in the wake of the Russo–Ukrainian war. This conflict has disrupted the post-Cold War order and intensified interest in geopolitical dynamics. This chapter delves into the geopolitical implications of the Russo–Ukrainian war, examining its effects on Russia's interests in regions like Syria and the Niger, and the xx *Introduction*

burgeoning Russo–Iranian partnership, often viewed through the prism of autocratic convergence. The analysis critiques the tendency to oversimplify these complex relationships, emphasizing the need to consider the enduring nature of national interests and grand strategy. It argues that Russia's actions in the Persian Gulf are part of its grand strategy to establish a 'Greater Eurasia' and align with ideologically similar authoritarian regimes. This chapter highlights Russia's appeal in the Persian Gulf due to its non-Western identity, attractive to the region's leaders. It discusses strategic hedging by middle powers in the region and Russia's multifaceted involvement, from political engagement to infrastructure development in Iran, and its aspirations to be a major arms supplier. However, this chapter also points out the challenges Russia faces, including supply issues exacerbated by the Ukraine conflict, limited naval capabilities in the Persian Gulf, and underlying tensions with Iran. It concludes that for Russia to maximize its influence in the Persian Gulf, it must strategically prioritize its endeavours to avoid overextension.

The second part is *Ports of Duqm, Gwadar, and Chabahar* which essentially covers these three crucial ports which are central to this book's analysis. Chapter 4 is authored by Gürol Baba and is titled 'A Chokepoint of Asymmetric and Complex Rivalry: The Port of Duqm.' The author begins by stating that the great and regional powers' crisscrossing interactions on chokepoints exemplify how asymmetrical and complex rivalry patterns could coalesce. Relations between the US, China, Iran, and India on the port of Duqm is a mini-theatre of this coalescence in which the parties have unequal levels of power, but due to the complex nature of interactions, they still cannot dominate each other. Empirically, the port not only operates as a crucial channel for Arabian oil exports but also as an international and multipurpose commercial hub integrating the Gulf States with the rest of the region and the world. Theoretically, the asymmetry and complexities in these rivalries were a result of not only the global and regional power status of the above-mentioned parties but also the instruments and measures that they have been utilizing to increase their control on this chokepoint. This chapter first analyses the reasons for this complex asymmetry. By taking into consideration the dyadic accords between the US and India on the one hand and China and Iran on the other, this chapter applies this combined conceptual framework to their competition on Duqm.

Chapter 5 is authored by Atha Tahir and is titled 'Gwadar: Geopolitics, Development, and Social Change in a Strategic Port City.' This chapter provides an in-depth analysis of the geopolitical significance of Gwadar, a strategic port city located on the Balochistan coast in Pakistan. Emphasising Gwadar's proximity to the Strait of Hormuz, this chapter explores its physical characteristics, including topography, climate, and natural resources. A major focus is on the local grievances stemming from recent developmental projects, particularly how these grievances among local fisherfolk reveal the negative impacts of these economic initiatives. This chapter critiques the lack of consideration given to these local concerns in existing literature and emphasises their importance in policymaking processes. The analysis extends to the challenges and opportunities presented by bilateral megaprojects between China and Pakistan, especially under China's Belt and Road Initiative. Gwadar is highlighted as a critical asset for China, providing access to the Arabian Sea and the Strait of Hormuz, thus benefiting western China. This chapter argues that Gwadar's potential as a regional connectivity hub and growth engine for Pakistan is overshadowed by regional tensions and local discontent. The chapter asserts that Gwadar holds significant economic and strategic potential but also faces multifaceted challenges. The ability of Pakistan to address superpower competition and local political grievances effectively is crucial. This chapter concludes that the future of Gwadar as a geostrategic asset or liability hinges on Pakistan's approach to balancing these complex dynamics.

Chapter 6 is authored by Deepika Saraswat and is titled 'Chabahar: Geoeconomic Hopes and Geopolitical Games.' The author begins by stating that since 2016 when India, Iran, and then Islamic Republic of Afghanistan signed the 'Chabahar Agreement' committing India to develop Iran's Chabahar port, it has been projected as a 'gateway' port by officials and strategic communities of these countries. Iran sees the development of the port as crucial to enhance its transit potential, especially in the North-South transport Corridor linking Europe and Russia with South Asia and linking landlocked Central Asia to the Indian Ocean. For India, Chabahar is the pivot of its connectivity to Eurasia. The geoeconomic narrative around Chabahar as a 'gateway', a 'transshipment hub', and a driver for the development of the underdeveloped Makran coast has allowed Tehran to attract investment from India and at the same avoid dynamics of competition with China and its development of Gwadar as part of

xxii *Introduction*

the China–Pakistan Economic Corridor. As the Iran–China 25-year cooperation agreement came into force in January 2022, Iran opened a consulate in the port city of Bandar Abbas and a direct shipping line was established between China and Chabahar later in December. In geopolitical terms, Iran's development of Chabahar and a new energy export terminal at Jask port in the Gulf of Oman will allow Iran more freedom of action in the Persian Gulf and 'chokepoint' of the Strait of Hormuz. In recent years, as several security incidents in the Sea of Oman have raised maritime security concerns, inviting the presence of a variety of multilateral and extra-regional naval escort task forces, analysts have written about Iran revising its maritime posture with an intent to dominate its immediate sphere of influence in the Persian Gulf and the Sea of Oman. This chapter therefore analyses geoeconomic as well as geopolitical dimensions of Iran's development of Chabahar port.

The third part of this book is on *Regional and External Dynamics*, wherein it examines the role of regional and external powers and their strategies in dealing with the issue of chokepoint. Chapter 7 is co-authored by Alam Saleh and Zakiyeh Yazdanshenas and is titled 'The Strait of Hormuz and Iran's Active Deterrence Strategy.' The authors contend that the passage of around 30% of seaborne oil through the Strait of Hormuz has made it one of the key strategic chokepoints worldwide. Iran's geographic proximity to the shipping lane, coupled with its military capabilities, has provided Tehran geostrategic leverage to dominate the Strait. As such, Iran, as part of its active deterrence policy, has enlisted the Strait of Hormuz in its regional security strategy. Active deterrence is based on stalling adversaries by ascendingly making their collision with Iran costly and inefficient. With the new Middle East Security Architecture, introduced since the 2003 Iraq war, Iran, based upon its threat assessment, has employed different methods to deter external threats, mainly the United States. This chapter, accordingly, focuses on three critical tactics adopted by Tehran as follows: (a) prolongation of war (democracies are politically vulnerable and thus reluctant to enter long wars), (b) diversification of methods (frustrating the enemy by applying asymmetrical wars), and (c) widening the scope of possible collision (by expanding geographical entity of the war zone), to implement active deterrence. This chapter suggests that the Strait of Hormuz is a critical strategic chokepoint in applying these three tactics. While scrutinising the geopolitical importance of the Strait of Hormuz and Iran's constraints and opportunities in the Strait, this chapter investigates the position of the Strait in Iran's security doctrine and its active deterrence strategy.

Chapter 8 is authored by Eleonora Ardemagni and is titled 'Comparing UAE and Oman "Beyond Hormuz" Security Strategies.' This chapter analyses which kind of security strategies the member states of the Gulf Cooperation Council (GCC) have adopted to circumvent the Hormuz Strait, focusing on the United Arab Emirates (UAE) and Oman. Security strategies refer here both to defence and commercial dimensions, with maritime infrastructures playing a role in the interplay between civilian and military goals. With respect to Hormuz, the UAE and Oman stand in a different geographical and geostrategic position. While most of the Emirati territory is placed before or in the strait (with the notable exception of the Fujairah emirate), the Sultanate can directly access the Indian Ocean, also sharing with Iran the responsibility for Hormuz's viability (through the Musandam Peninsula inside the UAE territory). After a framework on the 'Hormuz issue' in GCC states' history and politics, this chapter addresses 'the state of the strait' in Gulf monarchies' contemporary security strategies outlining, for instance, Saudi Arabia's increased pivot to the Red Sea as alternative route for oil export. In a comparative way, this chapter's core focuses on the Emirati and Omani security strategies to secure their passage through Hormuz, as well as on building alternative routes. Efforts are analysed taking into account: threat perception and political strategy, post-hydrocarbon economic diversification, naval defence build-up, and bilateral and multilateral diplomacy (e.g. relations with Iran and implications of the Abraham Accords).

Chapter 9 is authored by Mohammed Al-Hajri and is titled 'The People's Republic of China Strategic Imperatives in Oman's Port of Duqm.' The author contends that Duqm has emerged as an attractive location for China's strategic interests in the western Indian Ocean region (IOR) and potentially serves as a critical node in the Maritime Silk Road Initiative (MSRI), introduced in 2013. Nevertheless, Chinese capital investments and strategic objectives in Duqm did not (yet) materialise as initially expected due to domestic and structural constraints. Compared to other Chinese port-park investments in the region such as in Gwadar, their presence in Duqm did not exceed more than just the establishment of a Sino–Omani Industrial Park, a provincial-level, group of private investments from the autonomous region of Ningxia, in western China. Thus, questioning the strategic imperative of such state versus private capital xxiv *Introduction*

and whether the latter is merely profit-driven and engages in a market basis. Similarly, in the Port of Duqm, China has made a marginal contribution through a concessional loan from the Asian Infrastructure Investment Bank (AIIB), which is often contested as to what extent the Chinese state has major control over the development bank. However, it is also important to study the implementation of the MSRI in Duqm from a 'localised' perspective, focusing on the imperatives of Oman to engage with China in developing its state capacity within the context of smaller states manoeuvring the space of the transition to a multipolar global order. Geostrategic competition in the western IOR and the emergence of a US–India–China strategic triangle matters, shaping both China and Oman level of economic and security cooperation in Duqm. Therefore, this chapter analyses the development of China's geostrategic imperatives in Duqm, arguing that the limited dual commercial and strategic interests of both Oman and China constrained the level of their engagement.

Part I

Chokepoints and Strait of Hormuz

© 2025 World Scientific Publishing Company
https://doi.org/10.1142/9789811294709_0001

Chapter 1

Maritime Chokepoints and Ocean Infrastructures in Asia: Strategic Cooperation, Geostrategic Contests, and Vulnerabilities

Amit Ranjan

Introduction

In his seminal essay 'Perpetual Peace: A Philosophic Essay', German philosopher Immanuel Kant writes, 'The spirit of commerce, here meant, cannot tolerate war and sooner or later take possession of every people. Because of all the powers of the state, the power of money is the most indispensable...'.[1] It is this power of money and the human spirit of trade and commerce that made human beings discover trade routes to carry commerce. Over the years, as the sea trade increased, a significant number of infrastructures have been developed to support it and keep Sea Lanes of Communications (SLOCs) secure. However, rivalries between the trade-carrying imperialist powers in colonial years had made them create hurdles and even attack the ship they found from the rival countries. Even the two World Wars (1914–1918 and 1939–1945) were fought between the imperialist powers to secure colonial assets and acquire more. During the Cold War (1948–1991)

---

[1] Kant, I. (Translated by B. F. Trueblood). (1897). *Perpetual Peace: A Philosophic Essay* (p. 29). The American Peace Society, 1795.

years, the Western and Eastern blocs continued to rival each other in the ocean region by maintaining close political ties with one or the other countries suitable for their political and strategic interests. In the post-Cold War years, as trade among the countries increased, rivalry to control SLOCs and ocean infrastructure has increased multiple times. The ocean infrastructures such as ports not only help carry out trade but also are considered chokepoints where ships passing from a rival or 'enemy' country can be choked. To deal with the chokepoints, the major powers are creating alternate infrastructures to avoid or make less use of the region they think can be choked.

China is one of the main major powers which, in recent years, has been spending huge money on territorial and maritime infrastructure projects in the different parts of the world. Soon after Chinese President Xi Jinping announced One Belt One Road (OBOR) in his speech at Nazarbayev University in Kazakhstan in September 2013, there has been an increase in rivalry over strategic connectivity and to attain greater influence over the road, rail, and sea routes. In that speech titled, 'Promote People-to-People Friendship and Create a Better Future' Xi Jinping proposed 'to join hands building a Silk Road economic belt with innovative cooperation mode and to make it a grand cause benefiting people in regional countries along the route'.[2] The official name of Xi Jinping's initiative was Silk Road Economic Belt and 21st Century Maritime Silk Road Development or OBOR. The English translation was officially changed to the Belt and Road Initiative (BRI) in 2016. In 2016, 193 members of the United Nations General Assembly passed a resolution unanimously agreeing to incorporate the BRI. In March 2017, the United Nations Security Council adopted Resolution 2344, calling for stronger regional economic cooperation through the BRI, among other initiatives.[3] In October 2023, in the 10th year of the BRI, representatives of more than 130 countries and many international organisations participated in the third

---

[2] Consulate-General of the People's Republic of China in Toronto, Canada. (2013, September 7). President Xi Jinping delivers important speech and proposes to build a Silk Road economic belt with Central Asian countries. http://toronto.china-consulate.gov.cn/eng/zgxw/201309/t20130913_7095490.htm.

[3] The State Council Information Office of the People's Republic of China (2023, October 10). The Belt and Road initiative: A key pillar of the global community of shared future. http://www.scio.gov.cn/zfbps/zfbps_2279/202310/t20231010_773734.html.

Maritime Chokepoints and Ocean Infrastructures in Asia 5

Belt and Road Forum for International Cooperation.[4] According to China's State Council Information Office white paper titled 'The Belt and Road Initiative: A Key Pillar of the Global Community of Shared Future' released in October 2023, the BRI framework comprises 'six corridors, six routes, and multiple countries and ports, a multitiered and multidimensional infrastructure network is taking shape'.[5] According to the white paper, by June 2023, China had signed more than 200 BRI cooperation agreements with more than 150 countries and 30 international organisations across 5 continents. In maritime matters, the white paper informs that by the end of June 2023, the BRI connectivity network had reached 117 ports in 43 countries. The maritime connectivity along with others have increased trade between China and its BRI partners. The white paper informs the following[6]:

> From 2013 to 2022 the cumulative value of imports and exports between China and BRI partner countries reached US$19.1 trillion, with an average annual growth rate of 6.4 percent. The cumulative two-way investment between China and partner countries reached US$380 billion, including US$240 billion from China. The value of newly signed construction contracts with partner countries reached US$2 trillion, and the actual turnover of Chinese contractors reached US$1.3 trillion. In 2022, the value of imports and exports between China and partner countries reached nearly US$2.9 trillion, accounting for 45.4 percent of China's total foreign trade over the same period, representing an increase of 6.2 percentage points compared with 2013; the total value of imports and exports of Chinese private enterprises to partner countries exceeded US$1.5 trillion, accounting for 53.7 percent of the trade between China and these countries over the same period.

The BRI is looked at by many countries as a part of the Chinese strategy to dominate the global geoeconomic and strategic routes. The BRI has made China to become more assertive in global political affairs, challenging the role of many other countries in world politics. To tackle the Chinese challenges, India, Japan, US, and Australia have joined hands to reinvigorate QUAD (Quadrilateral Security Dialogue). China termed

---

[4] The first meeting was held in May 2017 and second in 2019. See Belt and Road Portal. (2023, September 27). Belt and Road Forum for International Cooperation. http://2017.beltandroadforum.org/english/index.html. https://eng.yidaiyilu.gov.cn/p/0990413Q.html.
[5] The State Council Information Office of the People's Republic of China. *Op. cit.*
[6] *Ibid.*

QUAD a 'bloc' for confrontation with a 'Cold War mentality'.[7] Further, to provide an alternative to China's BRI, the US has also agreed on a corridor project from India to Europe via the Middle East. Earlier speaking on 10 August 2023, at Salt Lake City, Utah, US President Joseph (Joe) Biden pointed out his strategy to deal with China and the problems associated with the BRI. He said,[8]

> I don't want to hurt China. But in the meantime, I watched what China was doing. So I put together a thing called the Quad. We brought together as an alliance India, Japan, Australia, and the United States. We put ourselves in a position where now we have the Philippines and, soon, Vietnam and Cambodia wanting to be part of a relationship with us because they're — they don't want to — they don't want to have a defense alliance, but they want relationships because they want China to know that they're not alone... We — we got together literally billions of dollars in the G7 nations to provide for alternatives to China's — what they call Belt and Road Initiative, which is basically a debt and noose agreement that they have. There is not much going on. They're — they're — they're in real debt. They're going in trouble (*sic*).

On 9 September 2023, on the sidelines of the G-20 Summit in New Delhi, Indian Prime Minister Narendra Modi and Biden co-chaired a special event on the Partnership for Global Infrastructure and Investment (PGII) and India–Middle East–Europe Economic Corridor (IMEC). The objective was to unlock greater investment for infrastructure development and strengthen connectivity in various dimensions between India, the Middle East, and Europe.[9] The European Union, France, Germany, Italy, Mauritius, United Arab Emirates (UAE), Saudi Arabia, and the World

---

[7]Patranobi, S. (2022, February 9). 'Cold War mentality': China says Quad is a 'bloc' for confrontation. *Hindustan Times*. https://www.hindustantimes.com/world-news/cold-war-mentality-china-says-quad-is-a-bloc-for-confrontation-101644405143190.html.

[8]The White House. Remarks by President Biden at a campaign reception. https://www.whitehouse.gov/briefing-room/speeches-remarks/2023/08/10/remarks-by-president-biden-at-a-campaign-reception-salt-lake-city-ut/.

[9]Ministry of External Affairs, Government of India. (2023, September 9). Partnership for global infrastructure and investment (PGII) & India-Middle East-Europe economic corridor (IMEC). https://mea.gov.in/press-releases.htm?dtl/37091/Partnership+for+Global+Infrastructure+and+Investment+PGII++IndiaMiddle+EastEurope+Economic+Corridor+IMEC.

Bank participated in that event. PGII aims to develop infrastructure and accelerate progress on sustainable development goals in developing countries. The IMEC has two corridors: the Eastern Corridor connecting India to the Gulf region and the Northern Corridor connecting the Gulf region to Europe. The connectivity corridors will include a railway and ship-rail transit network and road transport routes. Subsequently, a Memorandum of Understanding (MoU) on IMEC was signed by India, USA, Saudi Arabia, UAE, European Union, Italy, France, and Germany.[10] After completion, the railway 'will provide a reliable and cost-effective cross-border ship-to-rail transit network to supplement existing maritime and road transport routes — enabling goods and services to transit to, from, and between India, the UAE, Saudi Arabia, Jordan, Israel, and Europe'.[11] The IMEC will also digitally connect the participants, and there will be a pipe for clean hydrogen export. The IMEC is expected to increase efficiencies, reduce costs, enhance economic unity, generate jobs, and lower greenhouse gas emissions.[12] It is believed that after completion, the IMEC will reduce trade time between India and Europe by 40%.[13] Although not officially declared, Michaël Tanchum's monograph for the Institute of South Asian Studies, National University of Singapore, and some media reports have configured the corridor's route.[14]

Haifa Port (Israel), which connects Asia with Europe via ship, presents an interesting political story of power rivalry. China developed the port under the BRI. In 2015, Shanghai International Port Group won a bid to operate the Haifa Bayport terminal for the next 25 years. The US was

---

[10] *Ibid.*

[11] The White House. (2023, September 9). Memorandum of understanding on the principles of an India — Middle East — Europe economic corridor. https://www.whitehouse.gov/briefing-room/statements-releases/2023/09/09/memorandum-of-understanding-on-the-principles-of-an-india-middle-east-europe-economic-corridor/.

[12] *Ibid.*

[13] Al Jazeera. (2023, September 9). G20 summit: Transport project to link India to Middle East, Europe unveiled. https://www.aljazeera.com/news/2023/9/9/g20-summit-transport-project-to-link-india-to-middle-east-europe-unveiled.

[14] Tanchum, M. (2021, August 27). India's Arab-Mediterranean corridor: A paradigm shift in strategic connectivity to Europe. *ISAS South Asia Scan, 7.* https://www.isas.nus.edu.sg/papers/indias-arab-mediterranean-corridor-a-paradigm-shift-in-strategic-connectivity-to-europe/. Singh, R. (2023, September 11). A corridor of immense promise. *The Hindu Businessline.* https://www.thehindubusinessline.com/opinion/a-corridor-of-immense-promise/article67296263.ece.

8 A. Ranjan

not happy with the Chinese company running Haifa. During his visit to Israel in May 2020, then US Secretary of State Mike Pompeo called on Israel to cease the infrastructure project deal with the Chinese. He said, 'We want the Chinese people to be successful, but we don't want the Chinese Communist Party to have access to Israeli infrastructure and to Israeli communication systems — all of the things that put Israeli citizens at risk — and in turn put the capacity for America to work alongside Israel on important projects at risk as well'.[15] A year after the Chinese began operations at Haifa port, tenders were opened for it. Dubai's DP World, Turkey, and China initially showed interest. US lobbied against Beijing acquiring Haifa, and DP World withdrew in December 2021. Finally, in July 2022, the contract was given to Adani Group from India.[16] Nevertheless, the Chinese cannot be entirely de-routed and ignored: Beijing has a presence at Haifa and Piraeus Port, the port of call in Europe under the IMEC. In 2021, operation rights of Haifa were handed over to China's state-run Shanghai International Port Group for 25 years. Likewise, China Ocean Shipping Company or COSCO, a Chinese shipping company, owns 51% of the Piraeus Port Authority in Greece.[17] Chinese investment in Piraeus Port is a part of the BRI. The Piraeus Port is a key entry point for Chinese goods into the European market.[18]

Rivalry with China and its projects is not limited to Asia; the competing parties have come out with an alternative to the BRI in different parts of the world. For instance, on the sidelines of the PGII event during the G-20 Summit in New Delhi, the US and European Union (EU) also welcomed the commitment made by Angola, Zambia, and the Democratic Republic of the Congo to develop Lobito Corridor connecting southern Democratic Republic of the Congo and northwestern Zambia to regional and global trade markets via the Port of Lobito in Angola. The US and EU

---

[15]Essa, A. (2023, March 10). Haifa Port, Gautam Adani and Israel's plan for the Middle East. *Middle East Eye*. https://www.middleeasteye.net/big-story/israel-india-haifa-port-adani-what-tells-middle-east-plans.

[16]*Ibid.*

[17]Rao, S. (2023). For IMEC to have any real impact, fix the finance first. Only then it can counter China's BRI. *The Print*. https://theprint.in/opinion/for-imec-to-have-any-real-impact-fix-the-finance-first-only-then-it-can-counter-chinas-bri/1794035/.

[18]Bloom, A. (2021, May 27). Greeks wage a court battle against Chinese-funded port that may poison the environment. *Global Voices*. https://globalvoices.org/2021/05/27/greeks-wage-a-court-battle-against-chinese-funded-port-that-may-poison-the-environment/.

plan to explore cooperation in three specific areas: (i) transport infrastructure investments; (ii) measures to facilitate trade, economic development, and transit; and (iii) support to related sectors to fuel inclusive and sustainable economic growth and capital investment in Angola, Zambia, and Congo in the longer term.[19] The Lobito Corridor is considered to be a part of US game to challenge the Chinese dominance in resourceful African region.

This chapter discusses the rivalry between the major powers over chokepoints. It analyses the strategic significance of chokepoints and how the countries are trying to develop or acquire new infrastructure to circumvent the difficult chokepoints. In this chapter, the author mainly argues that with the growing rivalry among the powerful Asian countries, chokepoints will attain significance. To have a strategic hand and counter their vulnerabilities, the powerful countries are building multimodal infrastructures circumventing the chokepoints. Second, this chapter argues that rivalry between major powers benefits the smaller countries. The rival powers assist the smaller powers to grow infrastructures; however, there is a political, strategic, and economic cost to such assistance. This chapter uses published primary documents, such as reports by government and international and regional organizations. This chapter uses critical secondary sources, such as journal papers and book chapters. It also uses opinion pieces and newspaper reports to gather factual information.

Major Chokepoints, Vulnerabilities, and Alternate Routes in Asia

The sea is an important source of power. Captain Alfred T. Mahan coined the term Sea Power. Talking about the sea, Mahan, in his book

---

[19]The White House. (2023, September 9). Joint statement from the United States and the European Union on support for Angola, Zambia and the Democratic Republic of the Congo's commitment to further develop the Lobito corridor and the U.S.-EU launch of a Greenfield rail line feasibility study. https://www.whitehouse.gov/briefing-room/statements-releases/2023/09/09/joint-statement-from-the-united-states-and-the-european-union-on-support-for-angola-zambia-and-the-democratic-republic-of-the-congos-commitment-to-further-develop-the-lobito-corridor-and-the/.

10   A. Ranjan

The Influence of Sea Power upon History, 1660–1783, writes the following:

> The first and most obvious light in which the sea presents itself from the political and social point of view is that of a great highway; or better, perhaps, of a wide common, over which men may pass in all directions, but on which some well-worn paths show that controlling reasons have led them to choose certain lines of travel rather than others. These lines of travel are called trade routes; and the reasons which have determined them are to be sought in the history of the world.[20]

Mahan observed that sea trade is safer than road routes as there is no danger from robbers; it is also quicker than land travel. When sea trade begins to pay larger profit, enough shipping interest will revive and there will also be revival of war fleets to protect the sea route and trade from hostile forces.[21] For Mahan, 'numerous and deep harbors are a source of strength and wealth, and doubly so if they are the outlets of navigable streams, which facilitate the concentration in them of a country's internal trade; but by their very accessibility they become a source of weakness in war, if not properly defended'.[22] He attributed British success during the colonial years to their strong naval power. Navies are guardians of the communication line and controlling factors of the war.[23]

Another great theorist on sea power and naval strategy during colonial years was Julian S. Corbett, who was trained in law but turned himself into a prominent British naval historian and strategist. Mahan preceded Corbet by about two decades. Unlike Mahan, Corbett was more interested in relative control and command of the sea and not only physical destruction or capture of enemy's warships. For Corbett, the objective of naval war must be to secure the command of the sea or to prevent the enemy from securing it.[24] He also talked about the importance of the naval blockade. Corbett writes 'A ripper and sounder view of war revealed that what

---

[20]Mahan, A. T. (1890). *The Influence of Sea Power upon History, 1660–1783* (p. 25). Boston: Little Brown and Company.

[21]*Ibid.*, p. 26

[22]*Ibid.*, p. 35.

[23]*Ibid.*, p. 529.

[24]Corbett, J. S. (1918). *Some Principles of Maritime Strategy* (p. 77). New York: Longmans, Green and Co.

may be called tactical commercial blockade — that is, the blockade of ports — could be extended to and supplemented by a strategic blockade of the great trade routes.'[25]

As trade volume increased over the years, chokepoints have become an important strategic point. A maritime chokepoint can be defined as a point of natural congestion along two broader and more critical navigable passages. It is a strategically located, naturally shaped shipping channel vital for global trade.[26] In the post-colonial years, the world has entered into a series of agreements and found many ways to circumvent chokepoints. Yet, they are perceived as strategically important points in the sea, giving benefits to the host over the countries that depend on the chokepoints for trade.

The Suez Canal is a 190.30 kilometres long waterway connecting the Mediterranean Sea to the Red Sea through the Isthmus of Suez and links Asia with Europe. Its construction began in 1859 and completed in 1869. The canal was operated by Egypt's Universal Company of the Suez Maritime Canal. In 1875, due to crisis, Egypt sold a big part of its share in the company to the British Government. After occupying Egypt in 1882, Britain also took control of the Suez Canal. In 1888, under the Convention of Constantinople, the canal was declared a neutral zone under the British. The convention came into effect in 1904. The canal's strategic significance increased during the First World War (1914–1918). The canal was closed for the non-allied partners of the war. In 1936, under the terms of the Anglo-Egyptian treaty, British troops stationed in Egypt were ordered to protect the Suez Canal area. During the Second World War (1939–1945), Suez Canal helped the Allied powers to shorten their sea movement between Europe and parts of Africa and Asia.[27]

After the end of the Second World War, in July 1956, Egyptian President Gamal Abdel Nasser announced the nationalisation of the Suez Canal Company, a British–French company operating the Canal since its operation in 1869. Naseer's decision created political tensions between

---

[25] *Ibid.*, p. 82.

[26] Maritime Insights. What are maritime chokepoints? https://www.marineinsight.com/marine-navigation/what-are-maritime-chokepoints/.

[27] Commonwealth War Graves Commission. (2023, March 17). Egypt in WW2-history, significance and commemoration. https://www.cwgc.org/our-work/blog/egypt-in-ww2-history-significance-and-commemoration/#:~:text=Part%20of%20Egypt's%20strategic%20value,the%20long%20trip%20around%20Africa.

Egypt, Britain, and France. In October 1956, with support and on-behalf of France and Britain, Israeli forces attacked Egypt's Sinai Peninsula, advancing to within 10 miles of the Suez Canal. Soon after, the possibility of the Soviet Union intervening on behalf of Egypt pressured Britain and France to accept the United Nations-backed ceasefire on 6th November.[28] In 1967, Egypt closed the Suez Canal during the Six-Day War (also called the Arab–Israel War). The canal opened after eight years in 1975. Since then a huge amount of global trade has taken place through the Suez Canal. In the first half of 2022, 11,101 ships transited through the Suez Canal, passing 656.6 million tons of goods.[29]

In the Arab–Asia region, two more prominent chokepoints are the Strait of Hormuz and the Bab-el-Mandeb Strait. They are in the Middle East. The Strait of Hormuz is about 96 miles long and only 21 miles wide at its narrowest point. It is bounded north by Iran and south by Oman and the UAE and connects the Gulf with the Arabian Sea.[30] In 2018, daily oil flow through the Strait of Hormuz averaged 21 million barrels or 21% of global petroleum liquids consumption.[31] Of the total flow, in 2018, the US Energy Information Administration estimates that 76% went to Asian markets. China, India, Japan, South Korea, and Singapore were the largest destinations for crude oil moving through the Hormuz.[32] In comparison with Hormuz, in 2018, an estimated 6.2 million barrels per day of crude oil condensate and refined petroleum products flowed through the Strait of Bab-el-Mandeb, located between Yemen, Djibouti, and Eritrea and connects the Red Sea with the Gulf of Aden and the Arabian Sea.[33] About 3.6 million barrels per day moved north towards Europe and 2.6 million

---

[28] Office of the Historian 'The Suez Crisis, 1956'. United States of America, Department of State, https://history.state.gov/milestones/1953-1960/suez.

[29] State Information Service. (2022, September 19). Suez Canal. https://www.sis.gov.eg/Story/171459/Suez-Canal?lang=en-us.

[30] BBC. (2019, July 29). Iran tanker seizure: What is the Strait of Hormuz? https://www.bbc.com/news/world-middle-east-49070882.

[31] U.S. Energy Information Administration. (2019, December 27). The Strait of Hormuz is the world's most important oil transit chokepoint. https://www.eia.gov/todayinenergy/detail.php?id=42338.

[32] Ibid.

[33] U.S. Energy Information Administration. (2017, July 25). World oil transit chokepoints. https://www.eia.gov/international/analysis/special-topics/World_Oil_Transit_Chokepoints.

barrels per day to Asian markets, such as Singapore, China, and India.[34] There is also the Turkish Straits. It includes the Bosporus and Dardanelles waterways that divide Asia from Europe.

As the Suez Canal, Strait of Hormuz, and Bab-el-Mandeb are important routes, any disturbance can create a ripple in the global economy. After the Second World War, in 1947, the US disestablished Fifth Fleet to draw dawn the presence of naval forces world wide. Afterwards, naval operations in the Persian Gulf region was directed by Commander, Middle Eastern Force (COMMIDEASTFOR). In 1995, the Fifth Fleet was reestablished. Its area of responsibility includes Persian Gulf, Red Sea, Arabian Sea, and parts of the Indian Ocean.[35] In February 2002, Combined Maritime Forces Command was established. At present, the command has a responsibility to look at about 2.5 million square miles of water area and includes the Arabian Gulf, Gulf of Oman, Gulf of Aden, Red Sea, and Arabian Sea. This includes three critical chokepoints at the Strait of Hormuz, the Suez Canal, and Bab-el-Mandeb.[36]

Countries have invested in alternate ports and routes to circumvent the chokepoints. The multipurpose deep-sea port of Duqm in Oman is a part of the Special Economic Zone at Duqm (SEZAD). China is an important investor in the industrial park in SEZAD.[37] The Indian Naval ships have access to the dry dock for repair and maintenance work at Duqm.[38] The second port is at Chabahar located in Sistan-Baluchestan Province in Iran. The Chabahar consists of two ports: Shahid Kalantari and Shahid

---

[34] U.S. Energy Information Administration. (2019, August 27). The Bab el-Mandeb Strait is a strategic route for oil and natural gas shipments. https://www.eia.gov/todayinenergy/detail.php?id=41073.

[35] Schneller Jr., Robert J. (2007). *Anchor of Resolve: A History of US Naval Forces Central Command/Fifth Fleet.* Naval Historical Center, Department of the Navy, Washington. https://www.history.navy.mil/content/dam/nhhc/browse-by-topic/War%20and%20Conflict/operation-praying-mantis/AnchorOfResolve.pdf, pp. 41–43.

[36] Naval Sea Systems Command: The Force Behind the Fleet. United States Government. https://www.navsea.navy.mil/Home/RMC/FDRMC/Bahrain/WhyBahrain/OurMission/5thFleet.aspx.

[37] Duqm: Special Economic Zone. (2022, November 7). Duqm materials market completes 70% of construction. https://www.duqm.gov.om/en/sezad/media/news/2022/duqm-materials-market-completes-70-of-construction.

[38] Chaudhury, D. R. (2023, June 29). NSA visits Oman's Duqm port where Indian Navy has strategic access. https://economictimes.indiatimes.com/news/defence/nsa-visits-omans-duqm-port-where-indian-navy-has-strategic-access/articleshow/101348083.cms?from=mdr.

Beheshti. Chabahar is about 353 nautical miles from Dubai, 456 nautical miles from Karachi, and 843 nautical miles from Mumbai. In 2016, India, Afghanistan and Iran signed an agreement on Chabahar port. Under the agreement, India is developing the first phase of Shahid Beheshti port at Chabahar. India agreed to invest US$85 million for procuring equipment for the port and provide a line of credit of approximately US$150 million for its development.[39] State-run India Ports Global Limited is involved in the development of the port. In 2022, India and Iran formed a joint technical committee for the functioning of the port. There were certain disagreements developed between India and Iran that have been cleared. First, the difference is in the amount of investment so far. As of 2022, India had supplied cranes and other equipment worth US$24 million out of the total US$85 million pledged. Second, Iran has been pushing India to speed up the development of its operations at Chabahar port, including the completion of the 700-kilometres Chabahar–Zahedan railway line.[40] Third, there was a difference in arbitration. In 2023, India and Iran agreed to not seek commercial foreign arbitration for disputes between users and operators at the deep sea Chabahar Port.[41] China is an equally important player in Iran. In 2021, Iran and China signed a 25-year comprehensive cooperation agreement. Under the deal, China agreed to invest US$400 billion in Iran in the next 25 years in exchange for a steady oil supply.[42] Two years later, in March 2023, China brokered an agreement between Iran and Saudi Arabia to restore diplomatic ties which was severed in 2016. In 2023, China also established a direct shipping line to Chabahar. Earlier, Chinese ships had to be unloaded in Bandar Abbas, the capital city of Iran's

---

[39] Embassy of India, Tehran. India-Iran relations (p. 3). https://mea.gov.in/Portal/Foreign Relation/India-Iran__Aug_2020_.pdf.

[40] Laskar, R. H. (2022, September 10). India, Iran close to finalising long-term agreement on Chabahar port. *Hindustan Times*. https://www.hindustantimes.com/india-news/india-iran-close-to-finalising-long-term-agreement-on-chabahar-port-101662801370797.html.

[41] Tansim News Agency. (2023, August 28). India, Iran agree on legal terms for deep sea port deal: Report. https://www.tasnimnews.com/en/news/2023/08/28/2948303/india-iran-agree-on-legal-terms-for-deep-sea-port-dealreport#:~:text=TEHRAN%20(Tasnim)%20%E2%80%93%20India%20and,media%20outlet%20reported%20on%20Monday.

[42] Fassihi, F. & Myers, S. L. (2021, March 27). China, with $400 billion Iran deal, could deepen influence in mideast. *The New York Times*. https://www.nytimes.com/2021/03/27/world/middleeast/china-iran-deal.html.

southern province of Hormozgan, and then transferred to Chabahar via smaller ships.[43]

Another option to circumvent the chokepoints in Middle East Asia is making supply via pipelines. Saudi Arabia and the UAE have pipelines to supply crude oil outside the Persian Gulf and additional pipeline capacity to circumvent the chokepoint at the Strait of Hormuz. In 2016, the total available crude oil throughput pipeline capacity from the two countries combined was estimated at 6.6 million barrels per day, while their unused bypass capacity was roughly 3.9 million barrels per day.[44] Saudi Arabia has the 746-mile Petroline, also known as the East-West Pipeline. It runs across Saudi Arabia from its Abqaiq complex to the Red Sea. The 48-inch pipeline had been previously operating as a natural gas pipeline, but Saudi Arabia converted it to an oil pipeline. Saudi Arabia also operates the Abqaiq-Yanbu natural gas liquids pipeline. The UAE operates the Abu Dhabi Crude Oil Pipeline that runs from Habshan (a collection point for Abu Dhabi's onshore oil fields) to the port of Fujairah on the Gulf of Oman.[45]

Saudi Arabia has two additional pipelines that run parallel to the Petroline system, but neither can transport additional oil volumes if the Strait of Hormuz is closed. Iraqi Pipeline in Saudi Arabia (IPSA) runs parallel to the Petroline from pump station #3 (11 pumping stations run along the Petroline) to the port of Mu'ajjiz, just south of Yanbu, Saudi Arabia. It was built in 1989 to carry crude oil from Iraq to the Red Sea. The pipeline closed indefinitely following the August 1990 Iraqi invasion of Kuwait. In June 2001, Saudi Arabia seized ownership of IPSA as compensation for debts Iraq owed and converted it to transport natural gas to power plants. The Trans-Arabian Pipeline (TAPLINE) running from Qaisumah in Saudi Arabia to Sidon in Lebanon and a strategic oil pipeline between Iraq and Turkey are other strategic pipelines. A smaller quantity, several hundred thousand barrels per day at most, could also be transported by truck if the Strait of Hormuz were closed.[46] In the Suez Canal region, a 200-mile-long SUMED or Suez-Mediterranean Pipeline

---

[43] Hellenic Shipping News Worldwide. (2023, January 3). China launches direct shipping line to Iran's Chabahar port. https://www.hellenicshippingnews.com/china-launches-direct-shipping-line-to-irans-chabahar-port/.

[44] U.S. Energy Information Administration. (2017). *Op. cit.*

[45] *Ibid.*

[46] *Ibid.*

transports crude oil through Egypt from the Red Sea to the Mediterranean Sea. It is owned by the Arab Petroleum Pipeline Company, a joint venture between the Egyptian General Petroleum Corporation (50%), Saudi Aramco (15%), Abu Dhabi's International Petroleum Investment Company (15%), multiple Kuwaiti companies (15%), and Qatar Petroleum (5%).[47]

Another chokepoint in Asia is the Strait of Malacca, which is around 800 kilometres long and stretches between the Malay Peninsula and the Indonesian island of Sumatra. Malacca connects the Andaman Sea in the Indian Ocean with the South China Sea. It is estimated that, every year, approximately 90,000 ships pass through the Malacca Strait. Indonesia, Malaysia, Singapore, and Thailand cooperatively police the strait.[48] About 20% of global maritime trade and 60% of China's total trade moves through the Malacca Strait and South China Sea.[49] Due to its high dependence on Malacca Strait for trade and transit, in November 2003, former Chinese President Hu Jintao underscored the need to adopt new strategies to mitigate the perceived vulnerabilities, as some major world powers desired to control the Malacca Strait. The Chinese and global media picked up from Jintao's speech and paid considerable attention to China's 'Malacca Dilemma'.[50] Nine years later, at the 18th Party Congress, Jintao underlined the significance of the ocean for China saying, 'We should enhance our capacity for exploiting marine resources, develop the marine economy, protect the marine ecological environment, resolutely safeguard China's maritime rights and interests, and build China into a maritime power'.[51]

Gwadar Port is one of such projects which China is developing in Pakistan's Balochistan province under the China-Pakistan Economic Corridor (CPEC). In their study, Alam, Li and Baig (2019) found that once the CPEC routes come into full operation, the transport cost for a 40-foot container between Kashgar (a city in China's Xinjiang Uyghur

---

[47] Ibid.

[48] Ough, T. (2023, January 18). Malacca Strait: How one volcano could trigger world chaos. BBC. https://www.bbc.com/future/article/20230117-malacca-strait-the-sea-lane-that-could-trigger-world-chaos.

[49] Paszak, P. (2021, February 28). China and the 'Malacca Dilemma'. China Monitor. https://warsawinstitute.org/china-malacca-dilemma/.

[50] Storey, I. (2006, April 12). China's 'Malacca Dilemma'. China Brief, 6(8). https://jamestown.org/program/chinas-malacca-dilemma/.

[51] Full Text of Hu Jintao's Report at 18th Party Congress. (2012). http://in.china-embassy.gov.cn/eng/xwfw/xxfb/201211/t20121118_2373709.htm.

Autonomous Region) and destination ports in the Middle East is likely to be decreased by about US$1,450, and for destination ports in Europe, it is expected to decrease by about US$1,350. Transportation time will be cut short by 21–24 days for destination ports in the Middle East and 21 days for destination ports in Europe. Also, the total travel distance from Kashgar to destination ports in the Middle East and Europe is likely to be shorten by 11,000–13,000 kilometers.[52] It has also been argued that China's primary objective with CPEC is to hedge against India by establishing a physical 'basing' presence in the Indian Ocean region.[53] However, the overland connection from Gwadar to Xinjiang is arguably beset with various difficulties because of geographical, economic, and security problems.[54] Interestingly, amidst the plunge in Pakistan's economic situation, undecided dates for upcoming parliamentary elections, and escalating Sino–US tensions, the US ambassador to Pakistan, Donald Blome, visited Gwadar, Balochistan on 12 September 2023. The press release says that the visit was 'to underscore the United States' commitment to the people of Balochistan, a partnership that remains steadfast and robust. The visit explored opportunities to enrich development, trade, and commercial ties, building on the successful outcomes that underpin the robust US — Pakistan bilateral relationship.'[55] Blome met Gwadar Port Authority Chairman Pasand Khan Buledi and also had a meeting with Pakistan Naval West Command. It is well known that US is working on to challenge China's quest for military bases, logistical facilities, and access to civilians across the Indo-Pacific. In this regard, the visit of Blome to Gwadar demonstrates the US' interest in access to the Gwadar port for multiple purposes.[56]

---

[52] Alam, K. M., Li, X., & Baig, S. M. (2019). Impact of transport cost and travel time on trade under China-Pakistan economic corridor (CPEC). *Journal of Advanced Transportation, 2019*(2), 1–16.

[53] Garlick, J. (2018). Deconstructing the China–Pakistan economic corridor: Pipe dreams versus geopolitical realities. *Journal of Contemporary China, 27*(112), 519–533.

[54] Krishnan, A. (2020). *India's China Challenge: A Journey through China's Rise and What It Means for India*. Noida: Harper Collins. Garlick (2018). *Op. cit.*

[55] US Embassy & Consulates in Pakistan. Readout of US Ambassador Donald Blome's visit to Gwadar. https://pk.usembassy.gov/readout-of-u-s-ambassador-donald-blomes-visit-to-gwadar/.

[56] Raja Mohan, C. (2023, September 19). The United States in Gwadar: Testing China's dominance in Pakistan. *ISAS Briefs*. https://www.isas.nus.edu.sg/papers/the-united-states-in-gwadar-testing-chinas-dominance-in-pakistan/.

18   *A. Ranjan*

Like CPEC, in 2018, the China-Myanmar Economic Corridor (CMEC) was signed. One of the important projects under CMEC is the Kyaukphyu Special Economic Zone with a port. The Kyaukphyu port will grant easy direct access to China to the Indian Ocean and allow its oil imports to bypass the Strait of Malacca.[57]

Infrastructures beyond Chokepoints

The end of the Cold War in 1991 only transformed international politics — the international system remains the same. The disintegration of the Soviet Union has reconfigured the international structure[58] where a new challenger — China — emerged. A large part of post-Cold War international politics is devoted to the rise of China and its tussle with the US and other countries from Asia and the Western world. Theoretically, as proponents and supporters of the Regional Security Complexes (RSCs) find, in the post-Cold War years, a more decentralised pattern of international security is in operation[59] where regional powers are actively deciding the region's fate. However, with an escalation of regional contests which may have global impact, there is a direct presence of outside powers in different regions. Such presence influences regional and global security architectures. For instance, the US has about 750 bases spread across 80 countries worldwide. The actual number may be higher as the names of many bases are kept secret by the Pentagon. There are 120 active US bases in Japan, 119 in Germany and South Korea has 73. Around 439 or 60% are Large Bases or 'Bases'.[60] Large Bases have military installations larger than 4 hectares (10 acres) or worth more than US$10 million and have more than 200 US military personnel. Small Bases or 'Lily Pads' are smaller than 4 hectares (10 acres) or have a value of less than US$10 million. Around 173,000

---

[57]Lwin, N. (2020, January 18). Myanmar, China sign dozens of deals on BRI projects, cooperation during Xi's visit. https://www.irrawaddy.com/news/burma/myanmar-china-sign-dozens-deals-bri-projects-cooperation-xis-visit.html.

[58]Waltz, K. (2000). Structural realism after the cold war. *International Security, 25*(1) (Summer) 5–41, 39.

[59]Buzan, B. (2003). Regional security complex theory in the post-Cold War world. In Söderbaum, F. & Shaw, T. M. (Eds.), *Theories of New Regionalism: A Palgrave Reader* (pp. 150–159, p. 145).

[60]Hussein, M. & Haddad, M. (2021, September 10). Infographic: US military presence around the world. *Al Jazeera.* https://www.aljazeera.com/news/2021/9/10/infographic-us-military-presence-around-the-world-interactive.

US soldiers have been deployed in 159 countries as of 2020. The largest US military installation in the Middle East is the Al Udeid Air Base, located west of Doha, Qatar. It was established in 1996. It hosts around 11,000 American and coalition service members and is spread over 24 hectares.[61] The US has maintained most of its bases since the Cold War years.

After the end of the Cold War, the nature has changed, but the rivalry continues. The US now has maintained bases, mainly in Asia, focusing on China. One of the important regions in Asia is the South China Sea (SCS) where the US and its friends try to check the Chinese assertion. In April 2023, the Philippines identified the locations of four new military bases the US will gain access to, as part of an expanded defence agreement which is aimed at China. The four bases identified are Balabac Island in Palawan; Camilo Osias Naval Base in Santa Ana, Cagayan province; Lal-lo Airport in Cagayan; and Camp Melchor F. dela Cruz in Gamu, Isabela.[62] The new locations opened under the 2014 Enhanced Defense Cooperation Arrangement (EDCA). It allows the US to rotate troops to nine bases throughout the Philippines, including on Balabac Island close to Chinese installations in the SCS. The US Marine Corps also opened a new base on Guam island, Camp Blaz, in the US sovereign territory in the western Pacific Ocean. It is east of the Philippines. Washington and Manila are bound by a mutual defence treaty signed in 1951 that remains in force. The treaty makes the Philippines the oldest bilateral treaty alliance partner of the US in the SCS region.[63] In its 501-page verdict, in July 2016, the arbitral tribunal adjudicating the Philippines' case against China in the SCS favoured Manila.[64] China termed the verdict 'null and void.'[65]

---

[61] *Ibid.*

[62] Lendon, B. (2023, April 4). US gains military access to Philippine bases close to Taiwan and South China Sea. *CNN.* https://edition.cnn.com/2023/04/04/asia/us-philippines-military-base-access-intl-hnk-ml/index.html.

[63] *Ibid.*

[64] PCA Case No. 2013-19. (2016, July 12). In the matter of the South China Sea Arbitration-before-an Arbitral Tribunal Constituted Under Annex VII to the 1982 United Nations Conventions on the Law of the Sea-between The Republic of the Philippines -and-The People's Republic of China. https://docs.pca-cpa.org/2016/07/PH-CN-20160712-Award.pdf. Accessed Date is 09 November 2024.

[65] U.S. China Economic and Security Review Commission. (2016, July 12). South China Sea arbitration ruling: What happened and what's next. https://www.uscc.gov/research/south-china-sea-arbitration-ruling-what-happened-and-whats-next#:~:text=On%20July%2012%2C%202016%2C%20the,other%20activities%20in%20Philippine%20waters%E2%80%94.

Seven years after the verdict, in June 2023, India upgraded its position and called for the parties to abide by the award.[66] In a joint statement, India and the Philippines '...underlined that both countries have a shared interest in a free, open and inclusive Indo-Pacific region. They underlined the need for peaceful settlement of disputes and for adherence to international law, especially the UNCLOS and the 2016 Arbitral Award on the South China Sea in this regard'.[67] India had also offered for 'concessional Line of Credit to meet Philippines' defense requirements, acquisition of naval assets, and expansion of training and joint exercises on maritime security and disaster response, among others'.[68]

The two countries had also called for early operationalisation of the Standard Operating Procedure for the White Shipping Agreement between the Indian Navy and the Philippines Coast Guard and the signing of the MoU on Enhanced Maritime Cooperation between Indian and the Philippines Coast Guard.[69]

Vietnam is also a party to the SCS dispute. The Indo-Pacific Command of the US oversees the Indo-Pacific region's developments, including SCS. In June 2023, nuclear-powered USS Ronald Reagan arrived in Danang in central Vietnam, after Hanoi protested about Chinese vessels sailing in its waters.[70] In September 2023, US President Joseph Biden visited Hanoi after attending the G-20 Summit in New Delhi. During Biden's visit, the US and Vietnam elevated their relations to a Comprehensive Strategic Partnership from a Comprehensive Partnership established in 2013. The US announced new programmes and equipment donations worth US$8.9 million to build Vietnam's capacity to improve its security. The two countries also agreed on collaboration between Seattle-based port operator SSA Marine and Vietnamese private company

---

[66]Mitra, D. (2023, June 29). For the first time, India calls for abiding by the 2016 arbitral award on South China Sea. *The Wire*. https://thewire.in/diplomacy/for-the-first-time-india-calls-for-abiding-by-the-2016-arbitral-award-on-south-china-sea.

[67]Ministry of External Affairs, Government of India. (2023, June 29). Joint statement on the 5th India-Philippines joint commission on bilateral cooperation. https://www.mea.gov.in/bilateral-documents.htm?dtl/36743/Joint_Statement_on_the_5th_IndiaPhilippines_Joint_Commission_on_Bilateral_Cooperation.

[68]*Ibid.*

[69]*Ibid.*

[70]Al Jazeera. (2023, June 25). US's Ronald Reagan aircraft carrier arrives in Vietnam's Danang. https://www.aljazeera.com/news/2023/6/25/uss-ronald-reagan-aircraft-carrier-arrives-in-vietnams-danang.

Maritime Chokepoints and Ocean Infrastructures in Asia   21

Gemadept on strategic port projects in southern Vietnam, including developing the proposed US$6.7 billion Cai Mep Logistics Centre.[71] In September 2023, Chinese satellite ground stations were installed on the disputed SCS reefs. The two stations are connected to China's land-based ship automatic identification system and are installed at lighthouses located on North Reef and Bombay Reef in the Paracel Islands, which Vietnam and Taipei also claim.[72]

More than 5,000 kilometers away from the SCS is Diego Garcia which is exclusively a military installation located on an atoll in the Chagos Archipelago. The Chagos island was under the UK. In October 2024, following negotiations with Mauritian government, UK announced that it is giving up its sovereignty over Chagos. Diego Garcia is the largest among the 58 small isles that make up the Chagos Archipelago. Along with Guam, Chagos is an important anchor of the US strategy in the Indo-Pacific region.[73] Near Diego Gracia, the US entered a defence deal with the Maldives to gain more strategic depth. In 2013, the US and the Maldives agreed on a Status of Forces Agreement (SOFA) draft, but it was not signed then. In 2020, the US and Maldives finally signed a defence deal; in 2023, Washington sent its first resident commissioner Hugo Yue-Ho Yon to Malé.

China has also sped up its investments in ocean infrastructures to protect its interests in Asia and counter the growing strategic spread of the US. China began spreading its wings in the Indian Ocean and beyond mainly since the 1980s. In January 2005, the US Department of Defence report termed the Chinese plan to challenge the US in the Indo-Pacific region as China's 'string of pearls' strategy. This strategy features a three-pronged approach. First, China is building a series of naval bases along

---

[71] The White House. (2023, September 10). FACT SHEET: President Joseph R. Biden and General Secretary Nguyen Phu Trong announce the U.S.-Vietnam comprehensive strategic partnership. https://www.whitehouse.gov/briefing-room/statements-releases/2023/09/10/fact-sheet-president-joseph-r-biden-and-general-secretary-nguyen-phu-trong-announce-the-u-s-vietnam-comprehensive-strategic-partnership/.

[72] Zhen, L. (2023, September 20). Chinese satellite ground stations installed on disputed South China Sea reefs. *South China Morning Post.* https://www.scmp.com/news/china/diplomacy/article/3235147/chinese-satellite-ground-stations-installed-disputed-south-china-sea-reefs?utm_source=whatsapp&utm_campaign=3235147&utm_medium=share_widget.

[73] Harris, P. (2023, February 6). U.S. should accept that its Indian Ocean base belongs to Africa. *Nikki Asia.* https://asia.nikkei.com/Opinion/U.S.-should-accept-that-its-Indian-Ocean-base-belongs-to-Africa.

the sea lanes to Middle East Asia. Second, China is strengthening diplomatic ties with countries in the region. Third, the Chinese are rapidly building a blue-water navy, developing advanced missile technology, deploying new submarines, and stockpiling undersea mines to counter US Navy capabilities and protect their energy security.[74] Since then, the US has been trying to check Chinese spread and secure its power influence in the region. However, the Chinese have been able to develop, built, in process, and planned many significant infrastructures. China completed CSP Terminal Khalifa Port in UAE, working on Gwadar in Pakistan, completed Karachi Deepwater Terminal in Pakistan, completed Hambantota Port, completed Colombo International Container Terminal in Colombo, is working on Chittagong Port in Bangladesh, and is working on Kyaukphyu port in Myanmar. China is also modernising Myanmar's Coco Islands in the Bay of Bengal. It is close to the Strait of Malacca and around 55 kilometres from India's Andaman and Nicobar Islands. It is reported that military construction in the Coco Islands increased after the Myanmar military coup in 2021. There are also reports about Chinese assistance in building a surveillance post on the Coco Islands. China has dismissed such claims.[75]

In 2021, a consortium including Thailand's Gulf Energy Development, Thai state-owned oil and gas company PTT, and China's state-owned Harbour Engineering signed a US$922 million deal to expand a central port in Thailand. They have formed a GPC International Terminal consortium and will build two container terminals in Thailand's largest port, Laem Chabang. Gulf Energy has a 40% stake in GPC, with PTT and CHEC each holding 30%.[76] China is also working on the Thai Canal

---

[74] Spinetta, L. (2006). Cutting China's 'String of Pearls'. Vol. 132/10/1,244 https://www.usni.org/magazines/proceedings/2006/october/cutting-chinas-string-pearls.

[75] Ratcliffe, R. (2023, May 1). Military construction on Myanmar's Great Coco island prompts fears of Chinese involvement. *The Guardian.* https://www.theguardian.com/world/2023/may/01/military-construction-on-myanmars-great-coco-island-prompts-fears-of-chinese-involvement.

[76] Muramatsu, Y. (2021, November 27). Thai port to be expanded with Chinese Belt and Road builder. *Nikkei Asia.* https://asia.nikkei.com/Business/Construction/Thai-port-to-be-expanded-with-Chinese-Belt-and-Road-builder. Li, M. (2021, November 30). Thai-Chinese consortium to build Laem Chabang Phase III container terminals. *The Loadstar.* https://theloadstar.com/thai-chinese-consortium-to-build-laem-chabang-phase-iii-container-terminals/.

(earlier known as Kra Canal), a proposed 135-kilometre-long canal in southern Thailand connecting the Gulf of Thailand with the Andaman Sea. Its estimated construction cost is around US$28 billion plus another US$30 billion for related infrastructure. Once it comes into operation, the canal will likely shorten the travelling distance to China by up to 1,200 kilometres. By diverting them through the canal, Beijing hopes to save around 80% of the current cost of shipping energy imports through the Strait of Malacca. China has been pushing for the construction of the Thai Canal.[77] In May 2023, China Harbour Engineering Company Limited secured a contract from a Cambodian firm to construct a multipurpose seaport in southwestern Cambodia's Kampot province.[78] Another important port in Cambodia is the state-owned Sihanoukville Autonomous Port, or PAS in its French acronym. The Japanese government has largely financed it for almost two decades, symbolising the rivalry between Tokyo and Beijing.[79] In Malaysia, a US$10.5 million deal on the port at Melaka was cancelled due to differences and opposition. In 2022, China agreed to invest US$7.2 billion to redevelop a deep-sea port in Malacca.[80] China has heavily invested in infrastructure in Indonesia. However, since 2008, only one major new port has been developed, Patimban (to the east of Tanjung Priok), with the support of funding from the government of Japan.[81]

---

[77] Naing, Y. (2022, March 8). Regional effort needed to resist China's renewed push for Thai Canal. *The Irrawaddy*. https://www.irrawaddy.com/opinion/guest-column/regional-effort-needed-to-resist-chinas-renewed-push-for-thai-canal.html.

[78] Xinhua. (2023, May 5). Chinese firm wins deal to build 3rd largest port in Cambodia. https://english.news.cn/20230505/ae08342b973e482ab790899d5e7391ef/c.html#:~:text=The%20600%2Dhectare%20Kampot%20Logistics,been%20divided%20into%20three%20phases.

[79] Kawase, K. (2018, August 3). Cambodia's biggest port sees China coveting Japan's dominant role. *Nikkei Asia*. https://asia.nikkei.com/Business/Company-in-focus/Cambodia-s-biggest-port-sees-China-coveting-Japan-s-dominant-role.

[80] Yin, K. Y. (2022, December 21). China wants this Malaysian port to rival Singapore. *Investor*. https://klse.i3investor.com/web/blog/detail/koonyewyinblog/2022-12-21-story-h-302907727-China_wants_this_Malaysian_port_to_rival_Singapore_Koon_Yew_Yin.

[81] G20, Indonesia. Howard Dick, Ninan Biju Oomen, Jakob Sorensen, Daniel van Tuijll, Erik Wehl, David Wignall. (2022). Maintaining and encouraging private sector port investment through sustainable PPP arrangements: A case study of Indonesia. Policy Brief Task Force 8 Inclusive, Resilient, and Greener Infrastructure Investment and Financing. https://www.global-solutions-initiative.org/policy_brief/maintaining-and-encouraging-private-sector-port-investment-through-sustainable-ppp-arrangements-a-case-study-of-indonesia/.

Besides the US and China, India is also involved in developing ocean infrastructures in its neighbourhood. In 2021, an agreement was signed between India and the Maldives to develop, support, and maintain a Maldives National Defence Force Coast Guard Harbour at Sifvaru (Uthuru Thilafalhu).[82] India's Adani Group is constructing Colombo Port's Western Container Terminal (WCT) in Sri Lanka. The group will have the majority stake in the WCT Joint Venture (JV) valued at US$700 million. The build-operate-transfer (BOT) agreement is valid for 35 years. Earlier, a memorandum of understanding signed with India and Japan on developing the Eastern Container Terminal in 2019 was withdrawn following the protest by Sri Lankan trade unions and some political parties. In March 2021, the Sri Lankan Cabinet approved the WCT's development through a public–private partnership in collaboration with the SLPA and investors nominated by the Indian and Japanese governments. The WCT is likely to be completed by 2024.[83] In Myanmar, India-backed Sittwe port opened in May 2023. It is the main component of the US$484 million Kaladan Multi-Modal Transit Transport Project. Sittwe port is connected to Kolkata in India via sea lane. The Multi-Modal Transit Transport Project traverses an inland route through Myanmar via the Kaladan River and a highway, crossing into northeastern India.[84] In collaboration with Japan, India is developing *the Matarbari port* in Bangladesh. Dhaka has also given India access to Chattogram and Mongla ports for transit and trans-shipment of cargo vessels. India is also developing a deep-sea port in Indonesia's Sabang, close to the Andaman and Nicobar Islands. This port is being developed in partnership with Indonesia.[85]

---

[82] Ministry of External Affairs, Government of India. (2021, February 21). Joint press statement on official visit of External Affairs Minister of India to the Maldives. https://www.mea.gov.in/bilateral-documents.htm?dtl/33556/Joint_Press_Statement_on_Official_Visit_of_External_Affairs_Minister_of_India_to_the_Maldives.

[83] Business Standard. (2022, November 9). Adani Group enters Sri Lanka's port industry as the first Indian operator. https://www.business-standard.com/article/companies/adani-group-enters-sri-lanka-s-port-industry-as-the-first-indian-operator-122110900477_1.html.

[84] Nikkei Asia. (2023, May 11). Indian-backed port opens in Myanmar in answer to China's corridor project. https://asia.nikkei.com/Spotlight/Myanmar-Crisis/Indian-backed-port-opens-in-Myanmar-in-answer-to-China-s-corridor-project.

[85] Chaudhury, D. R. (2019, March 20). Eyeing Southeast Asia, India builds port in Indonesia. *The Economic Times.* https://economictimes.indiatimes.com/news/defence/

India promotes SAGAR (meaning sea) which stands for Security and Growth for All in the Region. The term was first used by Indian Prime Minister Narendra Modi in his remarks at the Commissioning of Offshore Patrol Vessel Barracuda in 2015 at Port Louis, Mauritius. Explaining India's vision of the Indian Ocean region, Modi said[86]:

(1) We will do everything to safeguard our mainland and islands and defend our interests. Equally, we will work to ensure a safe, secure and stable Indian Ocean region that delivers us all to the shores of prosperity.

(2) We will deepen our economic and security cooperation with our friends in the region especially our maritime neighbours and island states. We will also continue to build their maritime security capacities and their economic strength.

(3) Collective action and cooperation will best advance peace and security in our maritime region. It will also prepare us better to respond to emergencies.

(4) We also seek a more integrated and cooperative future in the region that enhances the prospects for sustainable development for all.

(5) Those who live in this region have the primary responsibility for peace, stability, and prosperity in the Indian Ocean. But, we recognize that there are other nations around the world, with strong interests and stakes in the region. India is deeply engaged with them. We do this through dialogue, visits, exercises, capacity building and economic partnership.

Modi added: 'We seek a future for Indian Ocean that lives up to the name of SAGAR — Security and Growth for All in the Region. We should be inspired by Monsoon, which nurtures and connects us all in region. We will strive to unite our region in partnership, as we were once in

---

eyeing-southeast-asia-india-builds-port-in-indonesia/articleshow/68490478.cms?from=mdr.

[86]Ministry of External Affairs, Government of India. (2015, March 12). Prime Minister's remarks at the commissioning of offshore patrol vessel (OPV) Barracuda in Mauritius. https://www.mea.gov.in/Speeches-Statements.htm?dtl/24912/prime+ministers+remarks+at+the+commissioning+of+offshore+patrol+vessel+opv+barracuda+in+mauritius+march+12+2015.

geography. An ocean that connects our world should become the pathway of peace and prosperity for all.'[87]

India also launched Project Mausam in June 2014 at the 38th World Heritage Session in Doha, Qatar. This project focuses on monsoon patterns, cultural routes, and maritime landscapes. Its objectives are (1) to re-connect and re-establish communications between countries of the Indian Ocean world, which would lead to an enhanced understanding of cultural values and concerns, and (2) to understand national cultures in their regional maritime milieu.[88] The project has not been performing in the way it was projected initially. Instead of the Mausam Initiative, it has remained a project to re-connect with maritime neighbours and revive the Indian Ocean culture.[89]

Conclusion

As discussed in this chapter, in the Middle East and Asia, ports at Duqm and Gwadar are considered important infrastructures to circumvent traditional chokepoints at the Strait of Hormuz, Suez Canal, and Strait of Bab-el-Mandeb. The alternatives have created a strategic rivalry in the region. China is trying to spread its influence through various means, while the US is witnessing some antagonism because of its interference in regional affairs and carrying out war against Iraq, Syria, and Afghanistan. The US has also imposed long-term sanctions on Iran. However, the US has a strong military presence in the region.

The growing rivalry on developing ocean infrastructure in Asia has escalated tension among Asian powers. As the theatre of the global contest has shifted to Asia, many external actors such as the US and Western European countries have also joined in the race to develop strategic infrastructures in Asia. One of the major infrastructure projects announced is IMEC. C. Raja Mohan writes that completing the project could transform India's geopolitics in several ways[90]: (1) The IMEC would help reinforce

---

[87] *Ibid.*

[88] Ministry of Culture, Government of India. Project Mausam. https://www.indiaculture.gov.in/project-mausam.

[89] Bhalla, M. (2020, July 20). India should revive the Mausam initiative – but not as it stands now. *The Wire*. https://thewire.in/diplomacy/mausam-initiative-indian-ocean-world.

[90] Raja Mohan, C. (2023, September 11). Connecting India, Arabia and Europa. *ISAS Briefs*. https://www.isas.nus.edu.sg/papers/connecting-india-arabia-and-europa/.

India's partnership with the US in the Middle East. (2) It could help India to connect with west and north-west Asia, undermining Pakistan's veto. (3) It would allow India to explore commercial opportunities through its overland connectivity. (4) It will deepen India's strategic engagement with the Arabian Peninsula. (5) It will help lower regional tensions in the Arabian Peninsula by promoting intra-regional connectivity. (6) IMEC will mobilise the EU into infrastructure development and turn it into a major stakeholder in integrating India with the Middle East and Europe. (7) IMEC is considered by many as an alternative to the BRI but its expansion scale has to be seen. The IMEC, unlike BRI, is a collaborative effort indulging private capital.[91] Before comparing the IMEC with BRI, one has to wait how China reacts to the project. The future of IMEC hinges on how Saudi Arabia, UAE, and Jordan deal with the Israel–Hamas war that began in October 2023. The global powers are divided over the war. The US and Western world have extended support to Israel while China and Russia's position is considered to be soft on Hamas. India has taken a middle path. New Delhi has criticised Hamas and sympathised with Israeli victims but also sent relief materials for Palestinians and reiterated its position to create two states to resolve the matter permanently.

Unlike many in the US, Western world, and India, the Middle East countries do not see the IMEC as an 'anti-China project' or through the lens of power rivalry. The IMEC is part of their diversification push plan for Saudi Arabia and the UAE.[92] There are also reports that Saudi Arabia may enter into a peace agreement with Israel. In 2020, brokered by the USA, Israel signed an agreement normalising its ties with the UAE and Bahrain. The deal is popularly called the Abraham Accords. Peace between Israel and the Middle East Arab world will strengthen the bonding over the IMEC. However, the Israel–Hamas war has put on hold the deal to normalise ties between Tel Aviv and Riyadh.

Due to their economic capacity and political position, major powers easily attract the relatively weak smaller countries with offers to develop infrastructures and assist them to meet economic challenges. The smaller countries feel that they would become a part of the global economic chain

---

[91] Rao (2023). *Op. cit.*

[92] Hussain, T. (2023, September 23). Why India's new US-backed trade corridor to Europe is no 'anti-China project' for the Middle East. *South China Morning Post.* https://www. scmp.com/week-asia/economics/article/3235497/why-indias-new-us-backed-trade-corridor-europe-no-anti-china-project-middle-east?module=spotlight&pgtype=homepage.

beneficial to their economy with increased connectivity. However, many of them are now facing a serious debt problem and some of them are even pushed into what Brahma Chellaney calls the 'debt trap'. For him, 'debt-trap' is a form of diplomacy to knuckle under the smaller countries under debt.[93] Looking at the Chinese activities under the BRI, in a study, Ammar A Malik *et al.* find that the average interest rate of a loan from an official sector in China is 4.2 %, while the average maturity length is 9.4 years and the average grace period is 1.8 years.[94] Chinese money is available at a much higher interest rate than soft loans from the World Bank and the Asian Development Bank, which have a maximum interest rate of 1.3% and a longer repayment period.[95] The debt issue remains a concern to many developing countries who have signed a memorandum of under-standing on the BRI, notwithstanding what China says in the third white paper on foreign aid published in 2021. The white paper talks about increasing aid to developing countries within the BRI framework.[96]

Not only Chinese loans but also money from other countries has forced the weaker countries in a serious debt problem. For instance, due to debt pressure and default in interest payment, Sri Lanka had to give Hambantota Port on lease to China. A 70% stake in the port was leased to China Merchants Port Holdings Company Limited (CM Port) for 99 years for US$1.12 billion. The money earned was used to cover the balance of payment because of soaring debt. Contrary to the widely prevalent belief, the deal was not in exchange for growing Chinese debt in Colombo.[97] In 2022, Sri Lanka failed to pay interest on foreign borrowing, leading to an

---

[93] Chellaney, B. (2017). China's debt-trap diplomacy. *Project Syndicate.* https://www.project-syndicate.org/commentary/china-one-belt-one-road-loans-debt-by-brahma-chellaney-2017-01.

[94] Malik, A. A., Parks, B., Russell, B., Lin, J. J., Walsh, K., Solomon, K., Zhang, S., Elston, T.-B., & Goodman, S. (2021). *Banking on the Belt and Road: Insights from a new global dataset of 13,427 Chinese development projects.* https://docs.aiddata.org/ad4/pdfs/Banking_on_the_Belt_and_Road__Insights_from_a_new_global_dataset_of_13427_Chinese_development_projects.pdf.

[95] Paudyal, P. (2023, September 11). China, Nepal and the BRI dilemma. *The Kathmandu Post,* https://kathmandupost.com/columns/2023/09/11/china-nepal-and-the-bri-dilemma.

[96] The State Council, The People's Republic of China. (2021, January). China's international development cooperation in the new era. https://english.www.gov.cn/archive/whitepaper/202101/10/content_WS5ffa6bbbc6d0f72576943922.html.

[97] Mohamed-Ali, U. (2020, January 1). The Hambantota port deal: Myths and realities. *Diplomat.* https://thediplomat.com/2020/01/the-hambantota-port-deal-myths-and-realities/.

economic crisis followed by massive protests against President Gothabaya Rajapaksa's government. At that time, Sri Lanka owed US$7 billion to China and US$1 billion to India.[98]

Besides a real or perceived or constructed threat of sinking under debt pressure, the smaller countries are also acting or asked to act as soldiers in big powers rivalry. As rivalry between big powers intensifies, some or many smaller countries may be asked to take a side to reap further economic and political benefits. For instance, in 2021, China's Ambassador to Bangladesh Li Liming said Dhaka's ties with Beijing will 'substantially be damaged' if it joins the QUAD.[99] Until now, the smaller countries are trying hard to evade such a situation, maintaining 'equidistance' and 'balancing' their ties with rival powers. However, this may not be very effective in case of middle powers or resourceful countries such as Saudi Arabia, which can effectively deal with the rival powers because of its economic significance and strategic location.

---

[98] Perera, A. (2022, March 29). Sri Lanka: Why is the country in an economic crisis? *BBC*. https://www.bbc.com/news/world-61028138.

[99] The Daily Star. Relations with China will be damaged if Bangladesh joins US-led 'Quad': Envoy. https://www.thedailystar.net/bangladesh/news/relations-china-will-be-damaged-if-bangladesh-joins-us-led-quad-envoy-2091345.

© 2025 World Scientific Publishing Company
https://doi.org/10.1142/9789811294709_0002

Chapter 2

Comparative Strategies of the US, China, and India on the Strait of Hormuz

Asif Shuja

Introduction

While the economic rivalry between the US and China is the most important strategic issue of the current era, India–China competition in the Middle East is equally important. Since the end of the Cold War, the global supremacy that the US had enjoyed now stands threatened due to China's economic rise. The trade war between these two global powers has multiple dimensions, transcending into the strategic domain. Control of global supply chains and ensuring energy security are two important facets of this rivalry. Similarly, political tension is witnessed between China and the US in different parts or the world and the Strait of Hormuz is one of them. A direct corollary of this strategic issue is the ensuing India–China competition in the Middle East. This comes from the fact that an important strategy of the US to check China is by lessening its security burden in the Middle East and focussing more on China's backyard, viz., in the Asia-Pacific. And India appears to be the most likely contender apart from China to potentially fill the security void in the Middle East.

While the significance of the Strait of Hormuz as a crucial waterway to the global energy supply chain remains the same for much of history, the nature of strategic significance of this chokepoint has changed over the years for the US and China. To understand this, one needs to first look at the US' journey towards energy self-sufficiency and how that has impacted its calculations towards the Strait of Hormuz. During the period preceding the Cold War, the US sourced the bulk of its energy supply from the Gulf, a region which was mired by the Cold War rivalry. Therefore, the US espoused the Carter Doctrine, declaring that it would intervene militarily in the Gulf region if its national interests were threatened. The primary national interest of the US at that time was securing energy supply. However, by 2020, the US has not just become the largest producer of oil but has also become a net oil exporter. Thus, generally speaking, the US no longer needs to be involved in this region purely for its energy security. Nevertheless, the Strait of Hormuz is crucial for the US due to the security of the interests of its Gulf allies, which stand threatened by the increasing power of Iran, which has often threatened to close the Strait of Hormuz.

It is notable that in terms of energy, the position in which the US was found before the Cold War, now China is seen in the same position. For instance, China is now the world's largest importer of oil, and bulk of its oil is sourced from the Gulf, most of them passing through the Strait of Hormuz. Thus, securing the freedom of navigation around the Strait of Hormuz is as crucial for China now as it used to be for the US earlier. In this situation, it is widely believed that China would also be inclined to come up with something equivalent to the US' version of Carter Doctrine. However, China has not come up with any such overarching security and military doctrine. The reason for the difference in approach between the US and China in ensuring the safety of this waterway is due to the nature of the respective relationships of the US and China with other Gulf countries, prominently with Iran.

During the Cold War, the primary rival of the US was the former Union of Soviet Socialist Republics (USSR). However, due to the Islamic Revolution in Iran in 1979, just before the end of the Cold War, and the sudden change in relationship between Iran and the US, Iran became a threat for the US and its allies from the Gulf region. Thus, despite less dependence on Gulf energy, the US has maintained a massive military presence in the region. On the other hand, China shares a friendly relationship with Iran and its threat perception in the Gulf region is not the same as that perceived by the US. Nevertheless, the strategic angle of this waterway for China is not missed, and a crucial reason for that is China's global economic ambition, especially via its Belt and Road Initiative (BRI), which pits it directly against the US' global economic interests. Thus, it is perceived that the US has been watching every step of China in the Gulf region, especially its involvement in the port development and similar partnerships with the countries of the region. These are prominently reflected in China's interests in Pakistan's Gwadar port, Oman's Duqm port, and Iran's Chabahar port. The fact that India has already invested heavily in Iran's Chabahar Port makes this dynamic complex.

Iran's Threat to Close the Strait of Hormuz

Although the Iranian strategy of asymmetric warfare against a highly advanced US military deployment in the region stands little chance of success in the long term,[1] Iran's strategy to close the strategic Strait of Hormuz is considered as a potential threat to the global energy supply. In the wake of the western economic sanctions, crippling its oil exports, Iran has time and again expressed its threat to close the Strait of Hormuz, a threat that was particularly accentuated after the US unilaterally withdrew from the Joint Comprehensive Plan of Action (JCPOA). This strategy is a complex mix of Iran's military posturing and geopolitical calculations, which is a result of Iran's standoff with the US, especially due to its continued nuclear programme. To keep alive its threat of closure of the Strait of Hormuz, Iran has regularly conducted military exercises in that region, the most important of them being a 10-day military exercise in December 2011 and six-day war games, codenamed 'Velayat 91', on December 28, 2012. The intensity of this threat can be gauged by the fact that a bill to close the Strait of Hormuz was backed by more than half of Iranian Members of Parliament in July 2012.[2]

---

[1] Shuja, A. (2013, January 10). Iran's threat to close the Strait of Hormuz. *Indian Council of World Affairs*. https://icwa.in/showfile.php?lang=1&level=3&ls_id=747&lid=687.
[2] *Ibid.*

34   A. Shuja

The US Office of Naval Intelligence gives a comprehensive account[3] of the Iranian naval prowess posing a threat to the Strait of Hormuz:

> Iran's defense strategists recognize the growing importance of the maritime environment and are shaping its naval forces to secure Tehran's interests accordingly. The Islamic Revolutionary Guard Corps Navy (IRGCN) emphasizes an asymmetric doctrine to ensure national security in the Persian Gulf against regional neighbors and foreign presence. The Islamic Republic of Iran Navy (IRIN), dubbed by the Supreme Leader as a strategic force, employs a more conventional doctrine and focuses on forward presence and naval diplomacy. Its mission areas include the Caspian Sea, the Gulf of Oman and out-of-area operations. Both navies have considerable equities and are well positioned to influence and leverage the Strait of Hormuz; a vital chokepoint for the flow of resources and international commerce.[4]

Notably,[5] the reorganisation of Iran's two navies, the Islamic Republic of Iran Navy (IRIN) and the Islamic Revolutionary Guard Corps Navy (IRGCN), has significant implications for Gulf regional security. Both navies have undergone leadership and structural changes to enhance command and control. The IRIN, in particular, requires further changes to accommodate its larger ships along the Makran coast. Since 2007, both navies have actively upgraded their fleets. The IRGCN focuses on smaller, faster vessels with advanced weaponry, aligning with its asymmetric warfare approach. The IRIN has modernised its surface fleet and expanding its submarine capabilities. Iran's naval capabilities are bolstered by acquisitions from other military branches, including air-launched cruise missiles and anti-ship ballistic missiles, underscoring the strategic importance Iran places on maritime control. Iran's navy has demonstrated its capability through exercises simulating attacks on US military assets, support for Houthi rebels in Yemen, and the interception of commercial vessels in the Strait of Hormuz. These actions highlight Iran's capacity to influence regional maritime security. The assessment of US Naval Intelligence stresses that reorganisation and modernisation of Iran's navy, along with

---

[3] United States Government, Office of Naval Intelligence. (2017). *Iranian Naval Forces: A Tale of Two Navies* (p. 5). Washington DC: U.S. Government Publishing Office.
[4] *Ibid.*
[5] *Ibid.*

its offensive actions, present growing challenges to the stability and security of the Persian Gulf region.[6]

The US' Interests in the Persian Gulf

The US' strategy in the Strait of Hormuz is a direct corollary of its broader policy in the Persian Gulf and therefore it is pertinent to first understand how the US sees its national and security interests in this region. A report[7] published by the United States State Department gives a comprehensive account of these national interests of the US as seen in July 1987. This was a time when the Cold War as well as the Iran–Iraq war were ongoing and the trigger for this report was the tragic attack on the U.S.S. Stark in May 1987 in which scores of US military personnel were killed and some wounded. This incident focused the US' national attention on its interests and policies in the Gulf region. Based exclusively on this report, a summary of the US interests in the Gulf is given as follows.

Strategic Interests: Due to the Gulf's position as 'an important crossroad of vital economic and political importance to the free world',[8] the United States considered it in its strategic interests to prevent its control from any other power which was hostile to either the US, its Western allies, or its Gulf partners. Two such hostile powers identified at that time were the Soviet Union and the Islamic Republic of Iran. So, the US policy towards maintaining regional stability was to prevent the two powers from taking control of the Gulf.[9]

Economic Interests: The US has a vital economic interest in the Gulf, primarily due to its substantial oil reserves:

> The United States, and particularly our allies, remain substantially dependent on oil imports, a good portion of which currently come from the gulf. The gulf countries supply 25% of all oil moving in world trade today; they possess 63% of the world's known petroleum reserves. In 1986, about 30% of Western Europe's oil imports came from the gulf; the comparable figure for Japan was about 60%. This Western dependency

---

[6]*Ibid.*

[7]Schloesser, J. (1987, July). U.S. Policy in the Persian Gulf. Special Report No. 166, United States Department of State.

[8]*Ibid.*

[9]*Ibid.*, p. 1.

36 A. Shuja

will sharply increase in the future, as the free world's oil reserves are depleted. Whereas only about 5% of U.S. oil consumption (15% of imports) originated in the gulf in 1986, this level is certain to rise significantly in the future as our own reserves decline, our supplies from other nongulf sources are depleted, and our need for oil imports rises. (The March 17, 1987, energy security study of the Department of Energy shows that total U.S. imports could double to 8–10 million barrels per day by the mid-1990s.) Finally, the vast majority (about 70%) of the world's excess oil production capability is located in the gulf, and this share will increase in the future.[10]

The two oil crises of 1973–1974 and 1978–1979 had proved to be economic disasters for the US and its allies. These oil shocks showed a small disruption — of less than 5% — can trigger a sharp escalation in oil prices. In the first oil crisis, the cost of oil quadrupled; in the second, it more than doubled. Thus, they anticipated similar crises in future and espoused a policy to pre-empt the following:

The oil market will react almost as sharply to expectations of a supply cutback as to a real drop in production, at least in the short run. A large oil price increase would cause major damage to the U.S. economy and the economies of our allies in the West; it would be especially devastating to the developing countries. Thus, we have a vital and unquestionable economic stake in ensuring that oil flows unimpeded from the gulf to the free world, both now and in the future.[11]

Political Interests: The US' relations with the moderate Arab states were central to its political interests in the Gulf. The report enumerated this in the following words:

The United States has longstanding, friendly relations and shares mutual interests with the moderate Arab states, which, because of their great wealth and oil reserves, are influential both within and beyond the region. Our policies have long been aimed at promoting regional security and stability while assisting our friends in their resistance to increased Soviet influence and presence. Our political concerns also are

---

[10] *Ibid.*, p. 2.
[11] *Ibid.*

certainly directed at Iran, because of its size and strength and because of its location beside the Soviet Union and Soviet-occupied Afghanistan. Although we look to an eventual improvement in U.S.-Iranian relations, today our interests remain directly threatened by the Iranian Government's pursuit of its bellicose, expansionist, subversive, and terrorist policies — directed against the United States as well as a number of friendly states, and including its deep involvement in the the the holding of hostages and attacks upon Israeli forces by the pro-Iranian Hezbollah movement in Lebanon as well as actions against Kuwait and other gulf states.[12]

Over a period, the US interests in the Persian Gulf have dramatically changed. Still, its military presence in the region has not decreased. Some markers of this changing trend could be identified: the end of the Cold War, the Iranian nuclear controversy and related concern of nuclear proliferation, 9/11 and the US' efforts of democratisation of the Gulf, and finally the Arab Spring. Accordingly, in the present times, four US interests could be identified: preserving oil security, stopping proliferation, fighting terrorism, and supporting democracy.[13]

The US Strategy in the Strait of Hormuz

The permanent military positioning of the US in the Persian Gulf began in 1949 when the US Navy founded the Middle East Force (MEF) and continued to increase its naval presence in the region in the next two decades. This military posture was further cemented through the establishment of a military base in Bahrain by the MEF in 1971. In 1983, four years after the Islamic Revolution in Iran, a major military restructuring resulted in the formation of the US Naval Forces Central Command (NAVCENT) out of the US Central Command. The next major landmark was 1995, when the US 5th Fleet (5th Fleet) was created and NAVCENT and 5th Fleet were consolidated under a unified command and the base was officially named Naval Support Activity Bahrain. In 2002, a year

---

[12] *Ibid.*

[13] Byman, D. (2016). Assessing current US policies and goals in the Persian Gulf. In Glaser, C. L. & Kelanic, R. A. (Eds.), *Crude Strategy: Rethinking the US Military Commitment to Defend Persian Gulf Oil* (pp. 49–78, p. 49). Washington DC: Georgetown University Press.

after the 9/11 incident, this unified command was also charged with the newly formed Combined Maritime Forces (CMF), an international coalition for maritime security against non-state actors, which today consists of 34 nations and supports three task forces focussing on counter-terrorism, counter-piracy, and maritime security. 'NAVCENT/5th Fleet consists of eight task forces focused on strike, contingency response, mine warfare, surface, expeditionary combat, unmanned systems, and logistics to support naval operations that ensure maritime stability and security in the Central Region, which connects the Mediterranean and Pacific through the western Indian Ocean and three strategic choke points.'[14]

Essentially, 'with the creation of the MEF in 1949, the Navy assumed the role as the first line of defense for America's interests in the region. The founding of the MEF also marked the transition of the Navy's presence in the Gulf from periodic to permanent.'[15] Similarly, the Carter Doctrine has become the bedrock of the use of the US military force in the Gulf region. Carter Doctrine is essentially the following excerpt from President Carter's State of the Union Address, on 23 January 1980:

> Let our position be absolutely clear: An attempt by any outside force to gain control of the Persian Gulf region will be regarded as an assault on the vital interests of the United States of America. and such an assault will be repelled by any means necessary, including military force.[16]

Just as the changing trend in the US interests in the Persian Gulf, the strategic approach of the US has also seen some changes. Some markers of these changes include the following: US' rebalancing from the Middle East to Asia Pacific and transitioning into 'collective security' in the Middle East; involving other countries to create a maritime coalition in the wake of US' maximum pressure in 2019 and the Iranian threat to close the Strait of Hormuz; and the Houthi's attack in Abqaiq and Khurais in Saudi Arabia and the US' reluctance to respond militarily.

---

[14] U.S. Naval Forces Central Command. History: U.S. Naval Forces Central Command. https://www.cusnc.navy.mil/Subs-and-Squadrons/.

[15] U.S. Naval Forces Central Command. Growing American Interests (p. 4). https://www.cusnc.navy.mil/Portals/17/New%20Arrivals/2007_History_of_Fifth_Fleet.pdf?ver=2016-02-11-155439-760.

[16] Schloesser (1987). *Op. cit.*, p. 8.

The concept of 'Collective Security' in the Middle East as outlined by the US is centred on integrated deterrence, partnership, and multilateral coalition building. Colin Kahl, in his remarks[17] at the IISS Manama Dialogue in November 2022, emphasised the United States' commitment to reinforcing and upgrading partnerships in the Middle East. This approach is rooted in the National Defense Strategy, which advocates for synchronised investments in advanced military capabilities across various domains, including land, air, sea, cyberspace, and outer space. Key to this strategy is the enhancement of interoperability and secure communications across defence sectors, complemented by regular exercises and training. This approach aims to test and improve collective action capabilities. The US strategy focuses on leveraging its network of partners to form effective coalitions that address common security objectives. This is evident in the US Central Command's leadership in experimentation, innovation, exercises, and training.[18]

The US commitment to the Middle East is also demonstrated in forums like the Global Coalition to Defeat ISIS and the US–GCC Defense Working Groups. Additionally, the US is actively working towards regional integration by building political, economic, and security connections among its Middle Eastern partners, while respecting their sovereignty. The strategy also encompasses a strong stance against threats to regional stability, such as Iran's activities, and aims to promote human rights and uphold international law principles. The US seeks to deter and disrupt Iran's Unmanned Aerial Vehicle programme and strengthen regional air defences. This reflects a broader approach to security that transcends traditional military presence and focuses on rapid response, information sharing, and interoperability among allies and partners. In short, the US concept of collective security in the Middle East is a multi-faceted strategy that combines advanced military capabilities, diplomatic efforts, and coalition building to promote stability, deter aggression, and advance shared security interests in the region.[19]

---

[17]U.S. Department of Defense, Remarks by Under Secretary of Defense for Policy Dr. Colin Kahl at the IISS Manama Dialogue (As Delivered). November 18, 2022. https://www.defense.gov/News/Speeches/Speech/Article/3223837/remarks-by-under-secretary-of-defense-for-policy-dr-colin-kahl-at-the-iiss-mana/.

[18]*Ibid.*

[19]*Ibid.*

China's Interests in the Persian Gulf

In January 2016, the Chinese government issued the first China's Arab Policy Paper[20] which gives crucial glimpses of China's perceived interests in the Gulf region and how it wishes to achieve them. According to this paper, China's engagement in the Gulf region primarily revolves around securing energy resources, given the region's position as the largest supplier of crude oil. Additionally, China also focuses on deepening trade and economic ties with the Arab countries, which has made them China's 7th largest trading partner. This policy paper particularly mentioned the following: 'China's proposed initiatives of jointly building the "Silk Road Economic Belt" and the "21st Century Maritime Silk Road", establishing a "1+2+3" cooperation pattern (to take energy cooperation as the core, infrastructure construction and trade and investment facilitation as the two wings, and three high and new tech fields of nuclear energy, space satellite and new energy as the three breakthroughs), and industrial capacity cooperation, are well received by Arab countries.'[21]

China's primary interest in the Middle East in general and the Gulf region in particular can be summarised[22] as geared towards maintaining stability to secure its economic interests to ensure the energy supplies and safety of shipping routes. Beijing seeks to attain these objectives through intense economic activities combined with diplomatic caution and limited military and political prowess. Except for its modest military presence in the Gulf of Aden, China lacks any significant naval or air power projection capabilities in the Middle East. This contrasts starkly with the massive military presence of the US in the region. China attempts to compensate for its limited military might with diplomatic outreach, a good example of which is the mediation in Iran–Saudi rapprochement in 2023. In fact, an important strategy of China is to maintain good relations with almost all players in the region so that it can advance its economic interests without much risk of being involved in regional conflicts. This

---

[20]The State Council, The People's Republic of China. (2016, January 13). China's Arab Policy Paper. https://english.www.gov.cn/archive/publications/2016/01/13/content_281475271412746.htm.

[21]*Ibid.*

[22]Scobell, A. (2023, November 1). What China wants in the Middle East. United States Institute of Peace. https://www.usip.org/publications/2023/11/what-china-wants-middle-east.

risk aversion is also due to the Chinese Communist Party's efforts to ensure a pleasant sight in the eyes of the domestic audience that China is respected everywhere.[23]

The BRI, a major foreign policy and economic strategy of China, has multiple dimensions, including those that could be linked to China's military presence in the Middle East. Notably, Chinese officials have downplayed the security dimensions of the BRI, but internal analyses extensively discuss the strategic benefits and security challenges. 'The main strategic benefits of the BRI include bolstering regional stability, improving China's energy security, and amassing influence in Eurasia.'[24] The central theme of this project is the six economic corridors linking China to the rest of the world. 'Perhaps the most well-known is the China-Pakistan Economic Corridor (CPEC), involving $46 billion in Chinese investments, mainly in the energy sector; other corridors link China with Central, South, and Southeast Asia, the Middle East, and ultimately Europe.'[25] Chinese strategic planners recognise that as China's overseas interests, notably under the BRI, expand beyond its immediate neighbourhood, military support must follow. Despite official denials of BRI's military or geostrategic motives, its prioritisation has accelerated China's overseas activities, necessitating state and military protection.[26] The growing apprehension in the United States centres on the belief that China's military aims to create supply bases and gain global footholds through BRI, thereby broadening its influence worldwide.[27]

---

[23] *Ibid.*

[24] Wuthnow, J. (2017, September 27). *Chinese Perspectives on the Belt and Road Initiative: Strategic Rationales, Risks, and Implications* (p. 4). U.S. National Defense University Press. https://ndupress.ndu.edu/Media/News/Article/1326867/chinese-perspectives-on-the-belt-and-road-initiative-strategic-rationales-risks/.

[25] *Ibid.*

[26] Rolland, N. (2019, September 3). *Securing the Belt and Road: Prospects for Chinese Military Engagement Along the Silk Roads*. The National Bureau of Asian Research. https://www.nbr.org/publication/securing-the-belt-and-road-prospects-for-chinese-military-engagement-along-the-silk-roads/.

[27] Makita, K. & Oki, S. (2022, August 10). China expands military presence under Belt and Road initiative. *Asia News Network*. https://asianews.network/china-expands-military-presence-under-belt-and-road-initiative/

China's Strategy in the Strait of Hormuz

China's Arab Policy Paper[28] also outlined China's approach to achieve its objectives in the Arab world, which is essentially a multifaceted strategy to deepen its ties with all players of the Middle East. The chosen diplomatic tools include establishing comprehensive strategic partnerships and dialogue mechanisms, notably with the Gulf Cooperation Council. This strategy also underpins the principles of mutual respect, equality, and non-interference in internal affairs. China's 'Silk Road Economic Belt' and the '21st Century Maritime Silk Road' were considered as an important vehicle to achieve its multiple objectives in the region.[29]

China is intensifying its presence in the Middle East, particularly near the Strait of Hormuz, to fulfil its extensive energy demands. This key oil transit route has seen significant investments by Chinese firms in ports and energy infrastructure. The People's Liberation Army (PLA) is also focusing on this strategic waterway, possibly mirroring tactics used in Djibouti, where commercial ventures preceded military and intelligence expansions.[30]

In 2017, China established its first overseas military base in Djibouti, strategically located near the Bab-al-Mandab Strait, a vital passage for Europe–Asia trade. Prior to this, China invested heavily in Djibouti's infrastructure, including ports, railways, and a free-trade zone, gaining substantial political influence. This 'first civilian, then military' approach allowed China to convert these commercial investments to support military objectives.[31]

Chinese military experts consider the Djibouti base a 'strategic strongpoint' for safeguarding crucial trade routes. As China's interests in the Middle East grow, it may seek to establish a similar strategic point near the Strait of Hormuz. This strait, through which a significant portion of the world's seaborne crude oil passes, is already identified by the US Department of Defense as a key area of interest for Chinese military planners.[32]

---

[28] The State Council, The People's Republic of China (2016). *Op. cit.*

[29] *Ibid.*

[30] Funaiole, M. P. *et al.* (2023, February 3). *Dire Straits: China's Push to Secure Its Energy Interests in the Middle East.* Centre for Strategic and International Studies. https://features. csis.org/hiddenreach/china-middle-east-military-facility/.

[31] *Ibid.*

[32] *Ibid.*

Indeed, the PLA is most interested in military access along the Sea Lanes of Communications [SLOCs] from China to the Strait of Hormuz, Africa, and the Pacific Islands. This was an observation of the US Department of Defense in its annual 'China Military Power Report'[33] released on 29 November 2022. This congressionally mandated document provides a comprehensive assessment of China's military and security developments, highlighting the department's pacing challenge and outlining the current trajectory of China's military and security strategy.

India's Interests in the Persian Gulf

The fact that India and the Persian Gulf countries are separated only by the Arabian Sea makes the two regions practically 'immediate' neighbours of each other, making it imperative for India to be mindful of the developments happening within the eight countries surrounding the Persian Gulf. Consequently, the political stability and economic prosperity of Iran, Iraq, and the six Gulf Cooperation Council states are of paramount importance in India's security calculus, especially under the framework of its status as an emerging global power. The same is true of the geopolitical position of the Gulf including the Strait of Hormuz, which serves as an important waterway connecting India with the region. Iran's position is especially important in the India–Gulf dynamics as Iran shared its border with India until India's partition in 1947. In the near term and considering the core national interests of India, the Gulf's position as a rich source of hydrocarbon and India's position as an energy-deficient country underlines their interdependence. After the removal of Saddam Hussein in 2003, India–Iraq trade had slowed down, but in recent years, Iraq has become India's largest source of oil, a position which was traditionally enjoyed by Iran. Interestingly, the US has now become India's second largest[34] source of oil, displacing Saudi Arabia to the third position. Another factor tying the two regions together is the presence of a significant Indian Diaspora in the

---

[33] U.S. Department of Defense. (2022). *Military and Security Developments Involving the People's Republic of China* (p. 145). Annual Report to Congress. https://media.defense. gov/2022/Nov/29/2003122279/-1/-1/1/2022-MILITARY-AND-SECURITY-DEVELOPMENTS-INVOLVING-THE-PEOPLES-REPUBLIC-OF-CHINA.PDF.

[34] The Hindu Business Line. (2021, March 15). US becomes India's second biggest oil supplier. https://www.thehindubusinessline.com/markets/commodities/us-becomes-indias-second-biggest-oil-supplier/article34072376.ece.

Gulf region, numbering approximately 6 million, which sends huge chunks of remittances back home.

Notably, India is the world's topmost[35] recipient of remittances with US\$69 billion of remittances received in 2017 from Indian migrants working abroad. Out of this total, 82% of the remittances were received by India originating from seven countries, viz., the United Arab Emirates (UAE), the United States (US), Saudi Arabia, Qatar, Kuwait, the United Kingdom (UK), and Oman. About 90% of overseas Indians work in the Gulf and Southeast Asian regions. Notwithstanding a sharp decline in oil prices and fiscal tightening in these countries, the GCC countries accounted for more than 50% of the total remittances received in 2016–2017. 'For India, the flow of inward remittances has been pivotal in financing the trade deficit (43 per cent in 2017–2018).'[36]

India–GCC relations got into 'high gear' after Prime Minister Narendra Modi's second visit to the United Arab Emirates in 2020. India–GCC relation is marked by India's energy import from the region reciprocated in the realm of food security. Notably, 'most of the investments by GCC countries in India are in the agricultural sector. Crops bound for the Gulf, and the logistical infrastructure that underpins shipments, form the bulk of such investments.'[37]

India's Strategy in the Strait of Hormuz

Much like China, India has traditionally been averse to playing any security role in the Gulf, focussing primarily on the economic aspects. Notwithstanding this, India's geostrategic outreach to Iran stands out, which is a result of India's focus on Afghanistan and is compelled by the dynamics of India–Pakistan relations. India's efforts to forge a strategic partnership with Iran including its readiness to participate in the development of the Chabahar port project and related investments are the result of such dynamics. These overtures are geared towards getting

---

[35] Reserve Bank of India. (2018, November 14). Globalising people: India's inward remittances. https://m.rbi.org.in//scripts/BS_ViewBulletin.aspx?Id=17882.

[36] *Ibid.*

[37] Event Report, The Arab Gulf's pivot to Asia: From transactional to strategic partnerships, held on March 17, 2021, organized by the Arab Gulf States Institute in Washington (AGSIW).

access to Afghanistan, a crucial security interest for India, and Central Asia, a potential source of riches. Barring this exception, which has also been recognized by the United States in terms of exempting Chabahar from the US' Iran sanctions, India has strived to balance its relations not just with all major players of the Gulf but also with other Middle East actors such as Israel, with which it has deep security partnership. Chabahar's significance is crucial to understand India's potential role in the Persian Gulf:

> While Chabahar is extremely significant economically and from the point of view of trade between India and Iran, it's primary signifi-cance lies in its political and strategic value for India. It is notable that China could achieve strategic gains by building the Gwadar port in Pakistan. Building the Chabahar port by India in Iran would act as a counter weight against China's gain. Effectively, the significance of Chabahar has to be seen and appreciated in the context of Gwadar port.[38]

In recent years, especially under the intensified Iran–US standoff and India–US closeness, the Indian strategic community has debated on the merit of India's closeness with Iran and the involved costs. Nevertheless, such debates are often pacified due to the imperatives of China's BRI and consequent Gulf outreach, which is likely to adversely impact India's overtures in that region, especially in the long run. Notwithstanding such realisations and regardless of US' attempts to bring India into its fold in its mission to counter China, especially through the Quadrilateral Security Dialogue — Quad, which is a group consisting of the United States, Japan, Australia, and India — it appears unlikely either India can, or will, throw much weight in the ring. India's decision to opt out[39] of the Regional Comprehensive Economic Partnership (RCEP) is indic-ative of its intention to focus inwardly for the time being.

---

[38] Shuja, A. (2017). *India-Iran Relations under the Shadow of the Iranian Nuclear Issue: Challenges for India's Diplomacy* (p. 171). New Delhi: Knowledge World.

[39] The Indian Express. (2020, November 26). Explained: The economic implications of India opting out of RCEP. https://indianexpress.com/article/explained/india-out-of-rcep-china-economy-trade-angle-7053877/.

Conclusion

In the final analysis, it is amply clear that despite its independence in oil, the US' other interests in the Middle East, is keeping it engaged in the region. In the same vein, this can also be said that despite its increasingly augmented military presence in the region, the modality of military engagement has also changed in the current times. Thus, the US prefers a cooperative approach rather than the previously adopted unilateral approach. So far as China is concerned, it prefers to trade in the Middle East very carefully due to its risk-averse nature. Thus, its primary tool is diplomacy rather than military approach. Regardless of this current approach, it cannot be completely ruled out that China may become more and more active militarily in the region, as evidenced by its carefully crafted overseas civil infrastructure, which can be quickly converted into military assets. On the other hand, India is yet to be involved fully across the Middle East's security spectrum. However, due to its own energy requirements and increased competition with China in the Middle East, India is also likely to increase its military footprint in the region.

© 2025 World Scientific Publishing Company
https://doi.org/10.1142/9789811294709_0003

Chapter 3

Russia in the Persian Gulf

Nigel Li and Roger Kangas

The Russian is not only a European, but also an Asiatic. Not only that; in our coming destiny, perhaps it is precisely Asia that represents our main way out. In Europe we were hangers-on, whereas to Asia we shall go as masters. In Europe we were Asiatics, whereas in Asia we, too, are Europeans. Our civilizing mission in Asia will bribe our spirit and drive us thither.

— Fyodor Dostoevsky[1]

Introduction

Russia is a country with global ambitions. Moscow has over the years increasingly expressed its vision for a multipolar world order that would replace what it perceives as a unipolar order dominated by the United States. The war in Ukraine has unleashed a wave of violence and tragedies unspeakable upon a part of the world which has enjoyed the post-1945 'long peace' upending not only the European security architecture but the very logic of the post-Cold War order. In the midst of great power competition, discussions on geopolitics have become *en vogue* at best as a protean term and at worst as a mere buzzword. Noticeably growing is the

---

[1]Dostoevsky, F. (1881, January). *The Diary of a Writer*, p. 1044. https://archive.org/details/the-diary-of-a-writer/The-Diary-Of-A-Writer/page/n16/mode/1up.

general interest in the ways states interact with each other and how they find a compromise between the infinite possibilities of their grand strategies and the limitations of their geography. Much research has been spent on the geopolitics of the current Russo–Ukrainian war that has been occasionally supplemented with its impact on Moscow's interests in countries like Syria or the Niger. Attention has been given to the growing Russo–Iranian partnership but often through the lens of 'autocratic convergence' and the formation of a new geopolitical 'axis'.[2] Such analysis can sometimes be short-sighted or fall into the trap of ideological thinking, disregarding the permanence of national interests and grand strategy.

The Persian Gulf is a strategically significant region. Since the discovery of oil and its utilisation in machines of war to the everyday automobile, great powers have sought to dominate and influence this region in the interests of their own national security. From the British Empire, the United States, and now, observably, China, the Persian Gulf is a global geopolitical focal point and neither does Russia neglect it. This chapter provides an analysis of Russia's geostrategic interests in the Persian Gulf, recalling its historic interactions in the region and highlighting the evolving contemporary developments there. This chapter identifies Moscow's short-, medium-, and long-term interests while differentiating primary and persistent goals throughout these timeframes.

Western response to diplomatically and economically isolate Russia after its invasion of Ukraine has prompted Moscow to seek alternative partners in an effort to evade sanctions. This has prompted further investment and interest in the development of the International North-South Trade Corridor (INSTC) connecting India to Russia, via Iran, and bypassing the Suez Canal. The 'geopolitical shock' of the war has also triggered an acceleration of — even if partially — Sino–Russian alignment and the long-term goal to consolidate Eurasia as a geopolitical entity, which can be evidenced by Iran's accession to the Shanghai Cooperation Organization (SCO), complemented by the Beijing-brokered Iranian-Saudi *detente*. These time-dependent goals stand apart from Moscow's persistent goals in the Persian Gulf which are (1) to be a 'non-Western' alternative for the states of the region, (2) to maintain and increase its share of the regional arms market, (3) to become an economic partner to the Gulf states, and (4) to strengthen regional energy partnerships.

---

[2] Esfandiary, D. (2023, February 17). Axis of convenience. *Foreign Affairs*. https://www.foreignaffairs.com/russian-federation/axis-convenience.

The mistake geopolitical analysts should not make is to swiftly dismiss Russia's global geopolitical ambitions as an unreachable dream, the likes of a world-wide proletarian conflagration that the Soviets had hoped for. Our current geopolitical tumult is *in fact* a product of Russian attempts to challenge the post-Cold War order which became increasingly visible after the 2008 invasion of Georgia, the annexation of Crimea in 2014, and the invasion of Ukraine in 2022. For as long as Russia remains a nuclear-armed geopolitical entity capable of projecting its power globally — no matter how limited — it will continue to play an important role in international politics. Russia is first and foremost a land power. Unlike the United States, it is geographically tied to the states of the Persian Gulf by dry land. For Russia, interaction with the region is not a choice.

Russia: The Middle East's Latent Power

Up until its intervention in the Syrian Civil War in 2015, contemporary Russia has been a relatively distant power to the Middle East. Moscow's primary focus since 1991 has been — and remains — the consolidation of the post-Soviet space and, up until the invasion of Ukraine in February 2022, trying to figure out its relationship with the West which has now turned into confrontation. In the times of the Russian Empire, St Petersburg was limited in its ability to project power into the Middle East with the Ottoman Empire, supported by Great Britain, acting as a 'bulwark' against Russian expansionism. In Persia and Central Asia, the British and Russians vied for influence in what has been coined by Arthur Conolly and immortalised by Rudyard Kipling as 'The Great Game', ending in 1907 with the Anglo-Russian Convention dividing Persia into respective spheres of influence.

Russian expansionism into the Persian Gulf was arguably guided by two main geostrategic motivations: access to warm water ports in Southern Persia and securing a gateway towards India which Peter the Great coveted in order for Russia to be a Great Power. Soviet actions in the region demonstrated a continuity of these interests especially when it conducted its joint invasion of Iran with the British in 1941, ostensibly to secure the country's oil fields and thus deny Nazi Germany access, but to also ensure a stable route for Allied lend-lease to the Soviet Union. At the war's end, Stalin was reluctant to withdraw, exploiting the Azeri national question in Iran's north-western provinces seeking to integrate them into the

Azerbaijan Soviet Socialist Republic. In exchange for withdrawal, Stalin demanded oil concessions. Under duress, Tehran concluded the Soviet–Iranian oil agreement handing Moscow 51% ownership and *de facto* control. This was later rejected by the *Majles* (Iran's legislature) 102 to 2 after diplomatic support from the US. The Soviets withdrew empty-handed but would return to the region in 1979 when it intervened in Afghanistan. The Kremlin followed the Brezhnev Doctrine, named after the then leader of the Soviet Union Leonid Brezhnev, of socialist interventionism to protect 'fraternal' socialist regimes. There were also fears in the politburo that the situation in Afghanistan would be exploited by the CIA to create a 'new Great Ottoman Empire' which would encompass the Soviet Union's southern republics and prevent a 'domino effect' of Iran's Islamic Revolution into Afghanistan and Soviet Central Asia.[3] The Soviets would fail to achieve their objectives, withdrawing from Afghanistan in 1989. What can be observed of Russian behaviour in the region is its never-ending process of expansion and contraction. As a land power, Russia's frontiers are its land borders. Unlike the British or the Americans with the sea defining their nations' core boundaries, Russia's ever-changing borders have resulted in geopolitical insecurities spanning kilometres and centuries.

Contemporary Russia and Its Interests in the Persian Gulf

The dissolution of the Soviet Union in 1991 marked a new era for Russia and its foreign policy. No longer constrained by communism as an ideological guide, the 1990s was a period of intense debate over Russia's place in the world with two major schools of thought dominating the discourse: the Liberals, seeking to democratise Russia and align Westward, and the Statists, who adopt a realist worldview and maximise Russia's power. Ultimately, the tumultuous 90s, from the wars in Chechnya, to the rise of oligarchic capitalism, and the 1998 Ruble Crisis disenchanted the Russian populace from the country's liberal pursuits. For this reason, the rise in popularity of Vladimir Putin and the resurgence of Russia stand in stark contrast to the country he had inherited. As someone who served in the

---

[3]Lyakhovsky, A. (1995). *The Tragedy and Valor of the Afghani* (pp. 109–112). Moscow: GPI Iskon.

State Security Committee (KGB), Putin's worldview is calculated, cold, and based on power. For the past two decades, a plethora of works have been published assessing what is 'going on in his mind' and drawing conclusions on Russia's foreign policy based on that. Putin and his circle represent the *Siloviki* who consist of individuals from the various ministries and agencies responsible for Russia's security with the interest of preserving the Russian state. Undoubtedly, the beginning of the Ukrainian Crisis in 2014 was a demonstration of Russia's re-assertiveness in international relations as a 'great power'. This assertiveness was not limited to the post-Soviet space, however. As the regime of Bashar Al-Assad was nearing defeat by rebel forces, Russia moved into Syria to intervene on the regime's side. Moscow's intentions were to prevent regime change and signal to the West, particularly the United States, that it could challenge their geopolitical ambitions.

The Persian Gulf: A Building Block for Greater Eurasia

A year into its 'Special Military Operation' in Ukraine, Russia released an updated version of its 'Foreign Policy Concept', a fundamental document articulating the country's national interests, strategic goals, and priorities.[4] Not only does the document denounce Western hegemony and anti-Russian policies pursued by the so-called 'Collective West', but it also recognises that the international system *should be* multipolar based on the principles of sovereignty, cooperation, non-interference, indivisible security, abandoning double standards in the international rule of law, and rejection of hegemony. More significantly, it identifies Russia as a unique 'country-civilization' that is both a Eurasian and Euro-Pacific power.[5] In this vein, the focus on Russia's place in Eurasia is stressed throughout the document with calls for the realisation of 'Greater Eurasia' through the region's various multilateral institutions (e.g., Eurasian Economic Union (EAEU), SCO, and BRICS). The Greater Eurasian Partnership (GEP) was introduced by Russian President Vladimir Putin in 2015 to consolidate the continent, described by the British geographer Halford Mackinder as the

---

[4] Its previous version was released in 2016.

[5] The Concept of the Foreign Policy of the Russian Federation. (2023, March 31). https://mid.ru/en/foreign_policy/fundamental_documents/1860586/.

'World Island'. The unification of Eurasia has been achieved arguably only twice in history: once by force by the Mongols and the second by trade with the Silk Road. The GEP sets forth the vision that establishing the foundations of Eurasian integration can only be achieved first through a strong economic architecture bolstered by and not competing with regional integration projects like the SCO, EAEU, RCEP, Association of Southeast Asian Nations (ASEAN), and to an extent BRICS.[6] The 2023 Russian Foreign Policy Concept dedicates a section to the Islamic world which Moscow views as a partner in the GEP. This can only be achieved if a solid security architecture is established in the Middle East, one where the normalisation of relations between belligerent regional states has been achieved. Therefore, Russia's grand Eurasian ambitions are contingent upon a stabilised Persian Gulf.

Moscow had expressed its vision for the Persian Gulf in its 2019 document 'Russia's Collective Security Concept for the Persian Gulf', which is referred to in the latest Foreign Policy Concept. It recognises the existing tensions between states of the region and their challenges to find common understanding. Despite this, Russia noted that it was prepared to develop traditional friendly relations with all countries of the region and called for an inclusive peace and security architecture in the Gulf. It has since been amended and in 2021 the latest version of the document provides further specifics such as establishing mechanisms for dispute settlement and conflict resolution, concluding arms control agreements, and integrating development of energy and transport infrastructure. Russia considers the most pressing issues of the region to be the freedom of navigation in the Strait of Hormuz, nuclear non-proliferation, and combating international terrorism.[7]

Russia's Southern Gateway to the World

Moscow's Eurasian ambitions long preceded the worsening of the Ukrainian crisis considering that the EAEU succeeded the Eurasian Customs Union (2010) and the Eurasian Economic Community (2000). Arguably, this was a result of Russia's evolving foreign policy goals as it

---

[6]Kortunov, A. (2020, September 28). Eight principles of the 'Greater Eurasian Partnership'. *Russian International Affairs Council*. https://russiancouncil.ru/en/analytics-and-comments/analytics/eight-principles-of-the-greater-eurasian-partnership/.
[7]https://mid.ru/en/foreign_policy/international_safety/1466420/.

moved from the consolidation of the post-Soviet space towards the East when relations with the West began to decline especially after Russia's invasion of Georgia in 2008. The worsening of relations between the US and Russia, particularly, warranted what was known as the 'Russian reset' during President Barack Obama's administration. This was famously marked when US Secretary of State Hillary Clinton and Russian Foreign Minister Sergey Lavrov pushed a red button with the English word 'reset' and the poorly translated Russian '*peregruzka*' which meant 'overload'. The correct translation for 'reset' would have been '*perezagruzka*'. This and subsequent attempts to warm relations failed to convince Russia about its perceived concerns about NATO expansionism. Russia's response to the 2014 Maidan Revolution with the annexation of Crimea and the support of separatist forces in Eastern Ukraine only worsened Russia's relations with the US and much of the West.

The war in Ukraine has severely tested the current international system, but it has also presented new opportunities. Western pressure resulted in Russia becoming the most sanctioned nation in the world. Almost half of the country's US$600 billion Central Bank assets were frozen, and the ruble rose as high as 134 to the dollar when it never exceeded 80 to the dollar during the COVID-19 pandemic. However, despite the overwhelming global support and sympathy for Ukraine, this has hardly translated into policy as the countries and territories that have sanctioned Russia represent only 16% of the world's population.[8] Due to their neutral position on the war in Ukraine, not a single Middle Eastern country has sanctioned Russia or has been declared 'unfriendly' by the Kremlin. At the United Nations Security Council on 27 February 2022, when voting for the eleventh emergency special session of the General Assembly to resolve the situation in Ukraine, the United Arab Emirates (UAE) surprised its traditional Western partners when it abstained from voting on the resolution, alongside India and China. This was a significant gesture by the Emiratis considering its military cooperation with the US. The UAE remained open to Russians and over a million of them, a 60% increase from 2021, visited the country after the war began. The UAE is also ranked within the top five places for Russians interested in establishing an overseas franchise. Seeking alternative trade partners

---

[8] https://www.wilsoncenter.org/blog-post/countries-have-sanctioned-russia.

after intense Western sanctions, Russian bilateral trade with the UAE grew by 68%.[9]

The case of the UAE is one of many opportunities for Russia in the Persian Gulf as it seeks non-Western alternatives. However, where this is most evident is in the intensifying Russo–Iranian partnership. In the summer after Russia's invasion of Ukraine, President Putin visited Tehran and was warmly received by Supreme Leader Ali Khamenei with the two leaders moving to further deepen the relationship between their two countries, such as removing the US dollar from bilateral trade and signing a memorandum of understanding for Russia to invest US$40 in Iran's gas industry. The two countries saw their trade turnover increase by 20% with a value of US$4.9 billion. Before 2022, agricultural products made up approximately 80% of Russo–Iran trade, however, this has begun to change. There was an increase in Iranian exports of industrial goods to Russia by 30% of products including polystyrene, machine tools, and auto components, indicating that not only is mutual trade growing but so is its complexity. There has also been further financial integration between Moscow and Tehran. Blocked from the SWIFT banking network, Russia has been connecting its own Financial Messaging System of the Bank of Russia (SPFS) with Iran's SEPAM national financial messaging service allowing Russia to bypass Western financial restrictions.[10]

Beyond strengthening its bilateral partnership with Tehran, Moscow recognises the broader implications of its increased interaction with its southern neighbours. Fitting into Moscow's 'Greater Eurasian' vision, Iran plays a vital role as a conduit in the ambitious International North South Transport Corridor (INSTC). The INSTC is a 7,200 kilometres long network of naval, rail, and road routes connecting India, Iran, Azerbaijan, Russia, Central Asia, and Europe. The objective of the project has been to identify bottlenecks in existing transport corridors and find methods to reduce costs in time and money. It is worth highlighting that plans for the INSTC predate the worsening of Russo–Western relations and the war in Ukraine. Russia, Iran, and India signed an agreement for the project in May 2002 which then involved more member states over the years.

---

[9]Smagin, N. (2023, April 13). Is the blossoming relationship between Russia and the UAE doomed? *Carnegie Politika*. https://carnegieendowment.org/politika/89531.

[10]Avdaliani, E. (2023, April 13). Russia and Iran — 2023 bilateral trade and investment dynamic. *Russia Briefing*. https://www.russia-briefing.com/news/russia-and-iran-2023-bilateral-trade-and-investment-dynamic.html/.

Shipping cargo through the standard route from Mumbai to St. Petersburg via the Suez Canal would take 30–45 days, whereas the new route shortens this to 15–24 days and reduces the cost of transporting goods from India to Russia by one-fifth.[11] Currently, Iran's southern Chabahar deep sea port is operational and handles the bulk of shipments from India as part of the first leg of the INSTC. The journey through Iran remains a bottleneck as its infrastructure cannot yet handle the scale expected of the project. As Moscow is increasingly cut off from access to the West and Turkey's openness to Russia is checked by Ankara's NATO commitments, the INSTC will become a lifeline for Russia to access warm water ports and much more so if Moscow were to remain isolated from Europe. Unfortunately, of all the INSTC member states, only Russia is the only country able, albeit limited, and willing to foot the bill. In March 2023, Moscow issued a loan valued at $1.3 billion Euros for Tehran to develop the Rasht-Astara railway between Iran and Azerbaijan. The plan was already in place since 2005 and had made little progress. Current estimates are that the 162 kilometres railway will only be operational in 2027. Iranian debts in other areas are also racking up as well. In 2021 alone, Russia provided a total of US$5 billion loans in infrastructure loans to Iran on top of the $500 million Euro debt incurred by Iran for the construction of the Bushehr power plant.[12] Yet, counting the cost may seem unproductive as mutual dependency between Russia and Iran continues to grow and neither country has many other options in the region apart from themselves.

Shifting Landscape of Energy Politics in the Persian Gulf

Oil and gas are Russia's major exports. Western sanctions and the European Union weaning off of Russian gas will present challenges to Russia's energy sector which is now being forced to sell its products at discounted prices. Yet, Russia's participation in OPEC+ enabled it to influence global energy prices. In July 2023, Saudi Arabia and Russia

---

[11] Vinokurov, E. (2022, February 21). Russia and Middle East need international North-South transport corridor. *Valdai Discussion Club.* https://valdaiclub.com/a/highlights/russia-and-middle-east-need-international/.

[12] Smagin (2023). *Op. cit.*

made further oil cuts that increased prices at a time of global inflationary pressures.[13] Shortly after the beginning of the war in Ukraine, the US fought rising oil prices both to ease inflation at home and prevent opportunities for Moscow to enrich its war chest. Both the Saudi and Emirati leadership declined calls from the White House, signalling that the Gulf states were not only exercising their agency but raising the question as to whether Washington's global influence was waning. Both serve Moscow's interests as these developments embolden its vision for a multipolar world order which has to come at the expense of American unipolarity. Saudi Arabia has already significantly increased imports of discounted Russian oil to fuel its power plants enabling it to export more of its own crude products. Shipping data also indicated that more Russian crude is arriving in UAE refineries.[14]

In the arena of energy politics, Moscow will still have to balance its relations between Iran and the rest of the Gulf states as there have been episodes of tensions within this 'Energy Triangle'. In October 2018, Moscow and Riyadh separately agreed to increase production in an effort to drive prices down. Tehran accused the two of breaking, at the time, OPEC's agreement on output cuts. Then, in March 2020, Russia and Saudi Arabia found themselves in an oil price war. As a result of the COVID-19 pandemic, oil prices fell dramatically, to which OPEC+ responded by proposing cutting oil production. Russia rejected the proposal. Saudi Arabia then moved to provide price discounts of US$6–US$8 per barrel to purchasers in Europe, Asia, and the US, triggering a 30% fall in Brent crude prices with the Russian ruble slumping 7% to the US dollar. The oil price war, even if observed as a response to the shock of the pandemic, in fact, worsened the global economic situation resulting in the crash of global stock markets. Moscow and Riyadh would later agree to oil production cuts in April and June 2020, but the 2020 oil price war demonstrated to the two that cooperation and coordination in energy politics might serve to be mutually beneficial.

---

[13]El Dahan, M. (2023, July 3). Saudi Arabia, Russia deepen oil cuts, sending prices higher. *Reuters*. https://www.reuters.com/business/energy/saudi-arabia-will-extend-voluntary-cut-1-million-bpd-august-spa-2023-07-03/.

[14]Lawler, A. (2023, March 6). Russian crude oil heads to UAE as sanctions divert flows. *Reuters*. https://www.reuters.com/business/energy/russian-crude-oil-heads-uae-sanctions-divert-flows-2023-03-06/.

Despite the appearance that Russia and Iran are heading towards a partnership the likes of an alliance, divergent energy interests drive a wedge between Moscow and Tehran.[15] Both heavily sanctioned, Russia and Iran are energy producers in a restricted market with the former's discounted oil prices coming at the cost of the latter's competitiveness. Increased Russian oil exports to China have also been noted to be 'a huge potential threat [to Iran]' by Hamid Hosseini, Chairman of the Iranian Oil, Gas and Petrochemical Products Exporters' Union.[16] However, it has been observed that in order to alleviate the negative aspects of the Russo–Iranian price competition, Russia is investing in developing Iran's energy sector. In July 2022, Gazprom signed a memorandum with the National Iranian Oil Company (NIOC) worth approximately US$40 billion to develop Iran's energy infrastructure from oil and gas fields to the construction of pipelines.[17] Similar to Moscow's INSTC dilemma, despite the shared interests of participant states, only Russia is willing and able to finance these efforts.

Certainly, the buyers list of Russian oil has shrunk tremendously leaving Moscow little alternative, yet, the current geopolitical situation has guaranteed the Kremlin customers like India and China. This has also made cooperation with OPEC+ members even more important if pressure from the West is not eased. The inclusion of Iran into the SCO as a member state while the UAE and Saudi Arabia become dialogue partners may help facilitate more resilient energy partnerships, but this means Moscow will have to pay closer attention to the Persian Gulf states and show why Russia would be a worthwhile alternative.

Russia: The Non-Ideological, Non-Western Alternative?

Russian foreign policy since the fall of the Soviet Union has experienced phases of evolution and self-re-evaluation, a process that is arguably still ongoing. Three intellectual traditions have influenced Russian foreign

---

[15] Vogel, A. (2023). Russo-Iranian energy relations: Navigating the tension between competition and cooperation. *International Business* (Международный бизнес), № 1 (3). Moscow: МГИМО МИД России, 2023. https://ibj.mgimo.ru/jour/article/view/22/39.

[16] *Ibid.*

[17] *Ibid.*, p. 93.

policy throughout its history: Westernism, statism, and civilisationism.[18] Westernisers saw Russia as essentially part of Europe and, during the Tsarist era, the 'West' served as an ideal to aspire towards and rid Russia of its perceived backwardness after enduring subjugation of the Mongols referred to as the 'Tatar yoke' (*tatarskoye igo*). During the Soviet period, Westernism had a major influence on the political and economic reforms of Mikhail Gorbachev. The initial leadership of the post-Soviet period identified a natural affinity towards the West and sought to build Western liberal institutions and instil liberal values in Russian society.

The Statists consider the highest priority of Russia is to protect its sovereignty, maintain the state's ability to govern, and preserve the social and political order. For the Statists, the premise for the country's foreign policy is assessing the national interest (*raison d'être*) and pursuing these goals in a calculated and pragmatic manner. Statists are neither inherently pro-Western nor anti-Western but adopt whichever approach is necessary given the circumstances of the Russian state. Russia during the Presidencies of Vladimir Putin and Dmitry Medvedev exhibited Statist approaches, for example, Putin's early years were marked by generally warm relations with the West during the global 'War on Terror' and Medvedev oversaw Russia's accession to the World Trade Organization in 2012.

The Civilisationists view the world through cultural oppositions, supposing that Russian civilisation is distinct from Western civilisation. More ardent Civilisationists advocate spreading Russian values abroad and fighting to defend the 'Russian World' (*Russkiy Mir*). It finds its intellectual and metaphysical roots from a period when Russia was emerging from Mongol subjugation and considering Moscow as the 'Third Rome'. Arguably, there are degrees of continuity of the Civilisationist thought during the Soviet era as the Communists saw themselves on the right side of history as opposed to the 'decadent' Western capitalist world. Since the invasion of Ukraine, Kremlin propaganda has echoed much of Civilisationist thinking recalling concepts like the 'Russian World'. On 21 February 2023, Putin gave a lengthy national address where he decried Western degradation of faith and values while calling for Russia to protect its children from this perceived road to destruction.[19]

---

[18]Tsygankov, A. P. (2023). Three traditions in Russian IR theory. In Lagutina, M. (Ed.), *The Routledge Handbook of Russian International Relations Studies*. London: Routledge.
[19]Putin, V. (2023, February 21). Address to the Federal Assembly. http://kremlin.ru/events/president/news/70565.

The question that many may have is as follows: 'Which intellectual tradition now dominates Russian foreign policy decision-making?' It is clear that the Westernisers have lost the influence and authority they had during the initial decade of post-Soviet Russia, but it would be too bold to claim that Russia purely adopts Civilisationist thinking. Policymakers in the Kremlin do not sit down at the table and follow these traditions strictly. It may be more prudent to argue that Statist philosophy still grounds Russia's pursuit of its interests that has, leading up to and since February 2022, become more heavily influenced by Civilisationist and nationalist thinking. It is more likely that Kremlin decision-makers are in fact using Civilisationist approaches instrumentally to pursue Statist goals (such is the logic of Statist thinking and political realism). However, it may be still too early to give a conclusive assessment and any further investigation would divert from the purpose of this chapter.

This discussion on the intellectual roots of Russian foreign policy is important in an analysis of Russia's relations with states of the Persian Gulf and the Middle East as a whole. Authoritarian states of the region have been keen to cooperate with Russia as they view Moscow as a 'non-ideological' partner as compared to the United States, which conditions its cooperation with democratisation and other reforms unsavoury to authoritarian rulers. Russia's intervention in the Syrian Civil War served as a demonstration that Moscow sought to put an end to Western-led regime change interventions in the Middle East.[20] The regime of Bashar al-Assad has survived, and after 12 years of war, Syria has been readmitted to the Arab League. With this in mind, Russia has succeeded in accomplishing its strategic goals set out when it entered the fray in 2015. It also showed the region Russia's interest in maintaining the status quo and thus regional stability for like-minded authoritarian leaders.

The challenge for Russia is to discern how much of its non-ideological approach to the region translates into substantial positive returns for Moscow as opposed to superficial nods and handshakes. The Russo–Iranian convergence is grounded by joint strategic interests to face the American geopolitical challenge, but as Russia continues down the path of tapping into Civilisationist thinking, it may find itself closer in form to a state like Iran. Whereas Iran considers itself the defender of Shia Islam and the successor of Persian civilisation, Russia is now increasingly

---

[20] Charap, S. (2019). Understanding Russia's intervention in Syria (p. 6). Rand Corporation. https://www.rand.org/pubs/research_reports/RR3180.html.

embracing its Orthodox traditions and galvanising the concept of the 'Russian World'. Perhaps superficially, we can expect growing mutual affinities between Russia and the civilisational centres of the Middle East, but we will observe in a later section highlighting Moscow's limitations in the region that convergence may not be as sanguine. Still, Russia has made attempts throughout 2023 calling for further normalisation of relations between Iran and Saudi Arabia.[21] With both Riyadh and Tehran viewing Moscow as a partner they can cooperate with, Russia will remain an alternative, despite its immediate challenges, for many other Middle Eastern states in the years to come.

Praise the Kremlin and Pass the Ammunition?

Russia is the second largest arms exporter in the world and the third largest arms provider in the Middle East. It is however outshined by the United States which accounts for 54% of the region's arms imports followed by France (12%) and Russia (8.6%).[22] Iran remains the largest consumer of Russian weaponry since the 1990s, making various purchases ranging from vehicles, anti-tank missiles, surface-to-air missile systems (Tor-M1 and S-300PMU2 Favorit), and Su-25 ground attack aircraft for the Islamic Revolutionary Guard Corps. In 2022, an agreement was made to purchase 24 Su-35S fighter jets which were initially designated for Egypt until Cairo cancelled the deal in 2021.[23] In August 2022, Russia launched an Iranian satellite from the Baikonur Cosmodrome in southern Kazakhstan.[24] This has raised concerns that Moscow is providing Tehran with assistance to improve its intelligence capabilities. The war in Ukraine has also witnessed Russia's use of Iranian Shahed-136 drones, damaging critical infrastructure and striking untold terror on Ukrainian civilians. The sale of Iranian drones to Russia also points to the growing

---

[21] TASS. (2023, July 11). Lavrov announces Russia's interests in the normalization of the situation in the Persian Gulf. https://tass.ru/politika/18245199.

[22] Wezeman, P. D. (2022). Trends in international arms transfers, 2022. SIPRI. https://www.sipri.org/publications/2023/sipri-fact-sheets/trends-international-arms-transfers-2022.

[23] SIPRI Arms Transfers Database. https://www.sipri.org/databases/armstransfers.

[24] Reuters. (2022, August 9). Russia puts Iranian satellite into orbit. https://www.reuters.com/world/russia-launches-iranian-satellite-into-space-under-shadow-western-concerns-2022-08-09/.

partnership between the two countries but also 'equalising' the relationship as both see their interests converging. Russia seeks cheap options to fuel its war effort and achieve its battlefield objectives (the single-use drones cost US$20,000 while Russia's Kalibr cruise missiles cost US$1 million per piece) while Iran is able to participate in 'upending the U.S.-led world order'.[25] It is estimated that Moscow has ordered 1,700 of such drones. In the summer of 2023, the White House reported that a plant set to produce Iranian drones in the Alabuga special economic zone in the Russian region of the Republic of Tatarstan was in construction.[26]

Viewed broadly, the arms market in the Persian Gulf remains dominated by the United States and its allies, making it difficult for Russia to compete. However, Moscow's non-ideological approach towards its relations with Middle Eastern states in particular remains a comparative advantage despite attempts to diplomatically isolate it. Rosoboronexport, Russia's state arms exporter, participated in the International Defense Exhibition (IDEX) hosted by the UAE in February 2023.[27] With states of the Gulf remaining neutral in the Russo–Ukrainian war, the region will remain strategically important for Russia as an outlet for its military–industrial complex. This, however, will be subject to a number of factors: fulfilling arms demands for its war in Ukraine, overcoming (circumventing) sanctions, and hoping that potential buyers will not be swayed by US pressure.[28]

Russia's Limitations in the Persian Gulf

Grand strategies inevitably have their limits. Historian John Lewis Gaddis once defined grand strategy as the alignment of potentially unlimited

---

[25] Feldstein, S. (2022, October 26). The larger geopolitical shift behind Iran's drone sales to Russia. Carnegie Endowment For International Peace. https://carnegieendowment. org/2022/10/26/larger-geopolitical-shift-behind-iran-s-drone-sales-to-russia-pub-88268.

[26] Madhani, A. (2023, June 9). White House says Iran is helping Russia build a drone factory east of Moscow for the war in Ukraine. *AP News*. https://apnews.com/article/ russia-iran-drone-factory-ukraine-war-dfdfb4602fecb0fe65935cb24c82421a.

[27] VOA. (2023, February 20). Sanction-hit Russia displays Combat-tested arms at UAE fair. https://www.voanews.com/a/sanction-hit-russia-displays-combat-tested-arms-at-uae-fair-/6971356.html.

[28] Sladden, J. (2017). Russian strategy in the Middle East. Rand Corporation. https://www. rand.org/pubs/perspectives/PE236.html.

aspirations with necessarily limited capabilities. Throughout its history, Russia has demonstrated a character of limitless visions which, during the Soviet Union, took on a global ambition. Unfortunately for Russian grand strategists throughout the generations, internal and external forces have ebbed and flowed, curtailing the pursuit of Russia's greater dreams. 21st-century Russia is not immune to this. The war in Ukraine has already severely limited Moscow's ability to project power in the post-Soviet space, what the Kremlin considers its own 'sphere of influence'. For example, in 2023, both Armenia and Azerbaijan criticised Moscow for its inability to ensure the implementation of security measures in the contested region of Nagorno-Karabakh. Meanwhile in 2022, border clashes broke out between Kyrgyzstan and Tajikistan and Moscow did little to intervene. Considering these developments in the regions of traditionally strategic interests to Moscow, one is prompted to wonder whether Russia will be able to be a capable player in geopolitical arenas elsewhere like the Persian Gulf.

Russia had before demonstrated its reluctance to increase its security presence in the Gulf when Iran allegedly fired upon two oil tankers in 2019.[29] One argument at the time to explain this was that Russia had alternative routes to export its hydrocarbon, namely through Europe, which since 2022 is no longer an option. Yet, even if Russia *does* move to increase its naval presence in the Gulf, it simply does not have the means to at the moment. However, Moscow seems to be making up for its military limitations by employing diplomatic options, in partnership or in parallel with Beijing, to stabilise the Persian Gulf through its engagement with states of the region. It explains the widening of the SCO with the inclusion of Iran as a member and Saudi Arabia and the UAE as dialogue partners. But even Moscow's recent diplomatic engagements have met challenges. In the summer of 2023, participants of the 6th Russia-Gulf Cooperation Council (GCC) issued a joint statement which included a paragraph supporting the UAE's endeavours to peacefully resolve the disputed islands of Greater Tunb, Lesser Tunb, and Abu Musa, which are administered by Iran. Iran considers the islands part of its southern

---

[29]Bainazarov, E. (2019, June 17). Na net i sudov net: Rossiya ne budet usilivat' okhranu v ormuzskom prolive. Izvestiya. https://iz.ru/889516/elnar-bainazarov/na-net-i-sudov-net-rossiia-ne-budet-usilivat-okhranu-v-ormuzskom-prolive.

Hormozgan province, but they are claimed by Abu Dhabi.[30] Tehran expressed its protest of Russia's endorsement of the UAE's position. There seemed to be a brief cooling of relations during the incident, but expert analysis has qualified that more pressing matters would continue to ensure strong relations between Russia and Iran.[31] This brief diplomatic spat, however, does serve as a reminder that Russia will have to cautiously navigate its relations with both Iran and the Arab countries of the Gulf. Even though there may be signs of Arab-Iranian detente, differences over identity, religion, and land — the most potent source for division — could still flare up if left completely unresolved.

Despite the growing cooperation between Moscow and Tehran, Iranians hold onto historical memories of Russian imperialism. In the first days of the war in Ukraine, Iranian social media was flooded with pictures of Soviet tanks in Tabriz, recalling the Soviet's attempts to annex Iran's north-western provinces into the Azerbaijan SSR.[32] Additionally, although the Civilisational argument was mentioned initially in this chapter as a stage upon which Moscow and Tehran may find commonalities for cooperation, one counterargument to this view is that the Civilisational approach in international relations, in fact, accentuates differences and only accelerates the process of identifying civilisational 'other-ness'.[33] Moreover, divergences between Russia and other civilisational centres of the Persian Gulf have occurred before as evidenced by the 2020 oil price war and unresolved dispute of the Persian Gulf islands between Iran and Saudi Arabia (Table 1).

One remaining challenge for Russia to contend with is the extent to which the Gulf states will continue their cooperative relations with Moscow. Though the Gulf states are now asserting themselves as middle powers, prompting the United States to reassess its relations with them,

---

[30] Ministry of Foreign Affairs of the Russian Federation. (2023, July 10). Joint statement of the 6th Russia — GCC joint ministerial meeting for strategic dialogue. https://mid.ru/en/foreign_policy/rso/1896567/.

[31] Laginova, K. (2023, July 15). Prava na ostrova: Iran i Rossiya edva ne possorilis' iz-za territorii v Persidskom zalive. Izvestiya. https://iz.ru/1544349/kseniia-loginova/prava-na-ostrova-iran-i-rossiia-edva-ne-possorilis-iz-za-territorii-v-persidskom-zalive.

[32] Smagin, N. (2022, December 5). Nesvoevremennaya bliznost'. Pochemu v druzhestvennom Irane rastut antirossiiskie nastroenniya. *Carnegie Politika*. https://carnegieendowment.org/politika/88558.

[33] Interview with Iranian international relations researcher, July 28, 2023.

Table 1. Russian interests in the Persian Gulf.

Duration	Short term	Medium term	Long term
Primary	• Sanctions Evasion	• SCO Integration • Regional infrastructure development	• Formation of a 'Greater Eurasia' • Streamline the INSTC
Persistent	• Be a 'non-Western' alternative • Maintain and increase share in the arms market • Become an economic partner to states of the Gulf • Strengthen energy partnerships within the region		

many of them are still dependent on America for security. Pressure from Washington or, more likely, renegotiations on the nature of US–Gulf relations may prompt the Gulf states to 'close the tap' for Russia. Such dynamism and frequency in relational re-balancing should be expected in our emerging age of great power competition.

Conclusion

This study of Russia in the Persian Gulf in the context of Moscow's geostrategic interests will certainly not be the last. There is greater interest in the study of geopolitics and the ever-changing state of the international system. In its grand plan, the Persian Gulf is a building block to the creation of a 'Greater Eurasia' and the consolidation of ideologically similar authoritarian regimes across the Eurasian landmass. Russia's advantage, and it will remain to be the case for as long as the current regime survives, is its non-Western branding most palatable to leaders of the Persian Gulf. Middle powers will continue to strategically hedge their partnerships, and states of the region in question are no exception to this new norm. With all that has been said about Russia, its current position in the Persian Gulf can be illustrated by the phrase 'jack of all trades, master of none'. Moscow wants to be, and is already, involved in various aspects of cooperation with the region. Its political engagement will certainly continue to grow in light of limited trade access elsewhere and it has little choice but to bankroll infrastructure development in Iran to streamline the INSTC. It hopes to be a reliable arms provider to the region, but the war in Ukraine will continue to sap supply, and neither does Moscow have the resources to deploy naval assets to the Persian Gulf, especially after the collapse of the Black Sea Grain Initiative. Furthermore, beneath the facade of friendship and cooperation, animosities and contradictions exist between Russia and Iran which are rooted in historic memories and unresolved territorial disputes in the Persian Gulf. To avoid spreading itself thin, Moscow needs to decide where it can best be a master of its endeavours in the Persian Gulf.

Part II

Ports of Duqm, Gwadar and Chabahar

© 2025 World Scientific Publishing Company
https://doi.org/10.1142/9789811294709_0004

Chapter 4

A Chokepoint of Asymmetric and Complex Rivalry: The Port of Duqm

Gürol Baba

Introduction

Around 90% of global trade is performed via sea routes,[1] and chokepoints act as vital organs of this global supply chain. Chokepoints are narrow shipping lanes and because of their strategic location, they constantly experience high maritime traffic, including energy sources, essential cargo, and naval force elements. Due to this vitality and narrowness, and their 'absolute or relative exclusivity of access',[2] they not only offer control over global sea lanes of communication but also are targets of international terrorism or other international security threats, such as accidents, piracy, or war. Chokepoints are quite vulnerable to blockages. When they are blocked due to any of these reasons, they directly affect food security and energy prices which could indirectly cause political and social chaos, especially in fragile regimes. A good example was the

---

[1] OECD. Ocean shipping and shipbuilding. World Economic Forum (2024, 15 February) "These are the world's most vital waterways for global trade" https://www.weforum.org/stories/2024/02/worlds-busiest-ocean-shipping-routes-trade/#:~:text=Supply%20chain%20disruptions%20at%20key,these%20waterways%20flowing%20is%20crucial.
[2] Guzansky, Y., Lindenstrauss, G., & Schachter, J. (2011, July). Power, pirates, and petroleum: Maritime choke points in the Middle East. *Strategic Assessment, 14*(2), 85–98, 85.

blockage of the Suez Canal by Evergreen in March 2021, which caused US$16 billion of revenue loss per day.[3]

Several primary chokepoints link the major global trade routes: the Turkish Straits links the Black Sea and the Mediterranean, the Bab-el-Mandeb Strait links the Middle East and the Horn of Africa, the Strait of Malacca links the Persian Gulf to several Asian destinations, the Panama Canal links the West to Asia, and the Strait of Hormuz links the Persian Gulf to the Gulf of Oman. There are also secondary, or non-traditional, but almost equally important chokepoints, such as the Strait of Dover, the Taiwan Strait, the Strait of Magellan, and the Duqm.[4]

What makes Duqm a noteworthy element of chokepoint research is not only the fact that it has been relatively overlooked by the literature, but also, more importantly, it provides a clear case for the asymmetrical rivalry between China and India, and the US and Iran separately, and also the complex rivalry between China–Iran and US–India as dyads.[5] On the other hand, the literature on the rivalry between the US and China, China and India, and the US and Iran do not specifically merge asymmetrical and complex rivalry patterns, especially regarding the Middle East. This chapter argues that these two types of rivalries between the above-stated great and regional powers and their dyads are not separate but entangled and operate in an eclectic way in Duqm.

Besides the introduction and conclusion, this chapter is organised into three parts. The first part discusses the asymmetrical and complex rivalry concepts regarding their applications between China, Iran, US, and India. The second part explains Duqm's specifics and strategic value as an international, integrated commercial facility and as a chokepoint. The third

---

[3] Safi, M., Smith, H., & Farrer, M. (2021). Suez Canal: Ever given container ship freed after a week. *The Guardian*, March 29. https://www.theguardian.com/world/2021/mar/29/suez-canal-attempt-re-float-ever-given-delay-salvage-tugboats.

[4] This chapter uses Duqm to refer to the Port of Duqm, the seaport and road terminal at Duqm in the Al Wusta governorate of Oman. The Port is a joint venture between Consortium Antwerp Port and ASYAD Port and is integrated in the Special Economic Zone at Duqm (SEZAD).

[5] The dominating rivalry in these two seemingly separate dyads has been between the US and China. Yet, this study aims to focus on the coalescence of asymmetric and complex rivalries in Duqm. Therefore, the details of the US–China global rivalry, which is more symmetrical, are deliberately kept outside of the analysis.

part brings up the links between the theory and the case, it analyses the amalgamation of asymmetrical and complex rivalry on Duqm. Through this amalgamated theoretical framework and its applications to the empirical case of Duqm, this chapter aims to unfold the relations between China, US, India, and Iran, both as individual actors and dyads. The asymmetrical rivalry is a result of the imbalanced power status and capabilities between the great and regional powers as individual actors, i.e., China and the US *vis-à-vis* India and Iran. The complex rivalry, on the other hand, is the result of the complicated relations and contests between the great and regional powers against their corresponding rivals as dyads. What makes this dyadic contest complex is that neither India–US nor China–Iran dyads are effectively clutched. They were formed due to regional powers', i.e., India and Iran's, need for great power protection or support, i.e., the US and China, respectively, and great powers' need for a regional partner to amplify their presence and achieve an additional economic or strategic advantage. This chapter argues that Duqm as a chokepoint, although not a traditional one, is a very important theatre to examine the operations of these two patterns of rivalries.

Asymmetrical and Complex Rivalry Between China and India *Vis-à-Vis* the United States and Iran

The asymmetrical rivalry comes from business and biology studies that the competition between two entities which could not utilise the same type or size of material capabilities and resources to achieve a higher position.[6] In international relations, it is obvious that political units, i.e., states or international organisations, have unequal power status. Yet, this power inequality does not prevent these units from performing a rivalry-based relationship.[7] What makes this relationship particularly asymmetrical is that some parts of these units' capabilities do not correspond or match 'to one another in shape, size, or arrangement'.[8] This naturally creates

---

[6]For details, see Womack, B. (2015). *Asymmetry and International Relationships.* Cambridge: Cambridge University Press.

[7]For details, see Diehl, P. F. & Goertz, G. (2001). *War and Peace in International Rivalry.* Michigan: The University of Michigan Press.

[8]Brown, L. (Ed.). (1993). *The new shorter Oxford English Dictionary.* Oxford: Oxford University Press, p. 200.

specific advantages or disadvantages for these units.[9] However, what is interesting regarding the behaviours of states is that[10] the advantages of asymmetrical rivalry do not put the more powerful one in an automatically dominating position, but it pushes the less powerful one to look for and utilise asymmetrical measures and instruments to deal with the disadvantages.

The concept of asymmetrical rivalry fits into the main parameters of China–India competition[11] which due to the 'material power gap' between these two countries led China to understate India at least in official terms. This does not necessarily mean that it is a one-sided rivalry.[12] China does not always see India as a rival because the extent of threat perception of each side towards the other has been imbalanced. This imbalance relies on three major elements: the material power asymmetries which favour China,[13] the asymmetries of threat perceptions that India perceives as a more serious threat from China,[14] and their international power status that China is a well-established great power, but India is between a regional and a great power.[15] Another important reason for this asymmetry is China has been under a more significant US threat in both East Asia and to an extent in the Middle East regarding its recently growing posture. In other words, the US is a more significant threat to China than India.

Out of all these four main reasons for asymmetry, the material power gap has been the clearest and seemingly the most significant one. Looking into the material facts of this gap, the economic criteria show that India's

---

[9] Womack, B. (2016). Asymmetric parity: US-China relations in a multinodal world. *International Affairs, 92*(6), 1463–1480, 1463.

[10] See Mazarr, M. J., *et al.* (2018). *Understanding the Emerging Era of International Competition: Theoretical and Historical Perspectives.* Santa Monica, CA: RAND Corporation.

[11] Garver, J. (2002). Asymmetrical Indian and Chinese threat perceptions. *Journal of Strategic Studies, 25*(4), 109–134.

[12] Shirk, S. (2004). One-Sided Rivalry: China's perceptions and policies toward India. In F. R. Frankel & H. Harding (Eds.), *India–China Relationship: What the United States Needs to Know* (pp. 75–100). New York: Columbia University Press.

[13] See Paul, T. V. (Ed.). (2018). *The China-India Rivalry in the Globalization Era.* Washington, DC: Georgetown University Press.

[14] Garver, 'Asymmetrical Indian', 109–134; see also, Fang, T.-S. (2013). *Asymmetrical Threat Perceptions in India-China Relations.* Delhi: Oxford University Press.

[15] Pu, X. (2017). Ambivalent accommodation: Status signaling of a rising India and China's response. *International Affairs, 93*(1), 147–163.

A Chokepoint of Asymmetric and Complex Rivalry: The Port of Duqm   73

current economic position is like China's in 2007. Moody's research shows that India's economy has recently surpassed US$3.5 trillion and is expected to exceed US$3.7 trillion at the end of 2023, similar to China's economic size in 2007. In terms of per capita income, China had US$2,694 in 2007, while the International Monetary Fund (IMF) projects India's per capita as US$2,601 in 2023.[16] Wall Street's leading sell-side research and brokerage firm Bernstein's research report echoes this gap by claiming that India's nominal GDP and per capita income are 15 years behind China's.[17] In military-strategic terms, a similar gap is also visible. China's 2023 Budget shows that the defence spending rose roughly to US$225 billion. This rise of 7.2% was higher than not only the 2022 Budget but also the eighth consecutive year of China's military spending. India's defence budget in 2023–2024 is US$72.6 billion. Accordingly, China's defence budget has been over three times higher than that of India.[18]

This asymmetry is much clearer in the US–Iran rivalry. Iran is no match for the US in either economic or military capabilities. For example, in 2022, Iran's military expenditure was US$24.6 billion,[19] and in 2023, the US defence budget was US$816.7 billion.[20] In economic terms, the gap is even more significant. Iran's GDP in 2022 was

---

[16] Drishti The Vision. (2023, July 4). Comparing India and China's economic growth. https://www.drishtiias.com/daily-updates/daily-news-editorials/comparing-india-and-china-s-economic-growth.

[17] Business Standard. (2023, September 4). India's economy 16.5 years behind China's, says Bernstein research report. https://www.business-standard.com/economy/news/overall-india-is-at-a-median-16-5-years-behind-china-economically-123090300495_1.html.

[18] *The Economic Times*. (2023, March 8). India vs China: A tale of two defence budgets. https://economictimes.indiatimes.com/news/defence/india-vs-china-a-tale-of-two-defence-budgets/articleshow/98498491.cms?utm_source=contentofinterest&utm_medium=text&utm_campaign=cppst.

[19] *Iran International*. (2022, April 26). Iran boosts military budget to stand among top 15. https://www.iranintl.com/en/202204261827.

[20] US Department of Defense. (2022, December 23). Biden signs national defense authorization act into law. https://www.defense.gov/News/News-Stories/Article/Article/3252968/biden-signs-national-defense-authorization-act-into-law/.

US\$352.21 billion[21] and the US' US\$25,461.3 billion. To address this materially asymmetric rivalry, Iran has been utilising its regional allies such as Hezbollah, the militant group operating as a network of proxy forces, to maintain its strike capability to its enemies at range to deter direct attacks. Its missile programme is another deterrent to any prospective conventional attack. Although politically Iran cannot dominate the region, particularly *vis-à-vis* the US and American allies, it still demands a role in affecting regional power balance.[22] Due to its strong threat perceptions towards the West, particularly the US, Iran aims to shape the regional power balance[23] to prevent these perceived threats from being transformed into actual threats. This threat perception-oriented aim has been augmented by a mixture of Shia ideology and Iranian nationalism which pushes Tehran to have a stronger political role in the region and reject any regional order that excludes Iran. On the other hand, its political capabilities and means are not powerful enough to develop an Iran-centered regional order. Therefore, it rather utilises its military potential and presence in the region to shape regional political outcomes.[24]

In other words, this asymmetrical rivalry has ideological and instrumental aspects such as the parameters of the parties' respective regional order and methods of expanding their influence.[25] The 1979 revolution oriented Iran's presumption of regional order to a Shia Islamic rule which has been tried to be expanded via Iran-supported non-state elements in the Middle East. The US traditionally aims to maintain a liberal regional order in the Middle East with the most beneficial scheme for its energy inflow and arms sales with a particular priority of protecting and supporting its regional allies and their official ideologies, i.e., Israel and Saudi Arabia.

---

[21]*Statista.* (2023, August 8). Iran: Gross domestic product (GDP) from 2018 to 2028. https://www.statista.com/statistics/294233/iran-gross-domestic-product-gdp/.

[22]Barnes-Dacey, J., Geranmayeh, E., & Lovatt, H. (2018, May). The Middle East's new battle lines.

[23]*Ibid.*

[24]Zarif, J. (2017). Iranian foreign minister: Arab affairs are Iran's business. *Atlantic*, October 9. https://www.theatlantic.com/international/archive/2017/10/iran-persian-gulf-jcpoa/542421.

[25]Meraji, E. (2022, August 11). Iran and the US face obstacles in their goals in the Middle East. https://www.atlanticcouncil.org/blogs/iransource/iran-and-the-us-face-obstacles-in-their-goals-in-the-middle-east/.

A Chokepoint of Asymmetric and Complex Rivalry: The Port of Duqm   75

This ideological and strategic rivalry between Iran and the US in the Middle East has been due to Washington's threat perception towards Tehran that Iran is a threat to US interests in the region regarding the proliferation of nuclear weapons, security of Israel, and terrorism. One of the clearest examples of this perception was the US National Security Strategy in 2017 which stated that 'the Islamic Republic of Iran' is 'determined to destabilize' the region and 'threaten Americans and [their] allies and brutalize their own people'. The 'Iranian regime sponsors terrorism around the world'. Iran 'is developing more capable ballistic missiles and has the potential to resume its work on nuclear weapons that could threaten the United States and our partners'.[26] In addition to the US reaction to Iran's position on these tangible security and strategic elements, there is also a normative element, including democratic values and human rights. Iran is seen as a threat to these values as well. That is the reason why the US is sympathetic and even supportive of campaigns against the Iranian regime. For example, the US Institute of Peace labelled the persistent campaign of imprisoned Iranian scientist, journalist and human rights activist, Narges Mohammadi as the spearhead of the first counterrevolution in history led and sustained by women.[27] US President Joe Biden gave a special statement on Mohammadi's winning of the 2023 Nobel Peace Prize. Biden's words underlined US support for protesters against the Iranian regime. Biden congratulated that 'Mohammadi's commitment to building the future that women and all people in Iran deserve is an inspiration to people everywhere who are fighting for human rights and basic human dignity'. Biden added that 'the people of Iran refuse to be silenced or intimidated as they fight for a free and democratic future for their nation, and their peaceful movement — 'Woman, Life, Freedom' — demanding respect for their human rights has brought hope to people (around) the world'. He also clarified the US reaction to the above-stated normative threat by stating that the US 'will continue working to support Iranians' ability to advocate for their own future, for freedom of

---

[26] The White House. (2017, December). National security strategy of the United States of America. p. 2. https://trumpwhitehouse.archives.gov/wp-content/uploads/2017/12/NSS-Final-12-18-2017-0905.pdf.

[27] United States Institute of Peace (2023, October 6). Iranian human rights activist wins Nobel peace prize. https://www.usip.org/publications/2023/10/iranian-human-rights-activist-wins-nobel-peace-prize.

expression, for gender equality, and to end gender-based violence against women and girls'.[28]

In this asymmetrical rivalry, the US uses political and economic instruments, and Iran, to an extent, utilises a threat of use of coercive power. President Biden's Joint Comprehensive Plan of Action on Iran's nuclear deal and continuing sanctions on trade with Iran had a severe impact, which enabled the hardliners in Tehran to win the presidential elections in June 2021. Accordingly, the stop-and-start negotiations in Vienna did not bring any tangible results for the parties to return to the nuclear deal.[29] More importantly, Iran exposed a new ballistic missile and seized two tankers in April and May 2023.[30] In reply, the US sent F-16s and an aircraft carrier through the Suez Canal.[31] These show that the tension in this rivalry would not ease in the short term.

But what if these two separate rivalries are combined, i.e., China and Iran versus India and the US? The changes in the geopolitical needs of the

---

[28] The White House. (2023, October 6). Statement from President Joe Biden on Iranian activist Narges Mohammadi winning the Nobel peace prize. https://www.whitehouse.gov/briefing-room/statements-releases/2023/10/06/statement-from-president-joe-biden-on-iranian-activist-narges-mohammadi-winning-the-nobel-peace-prize/#:~:text=October%2006%2C%202023-,Statement%20from%20President%20Joe%20Biden%20on%20Iranian%20Activist,Winning%20the%20Nobel%20Peace%20Prize&text=I%20join%20with%20people%20around,in%20celebrating%20her%20unshakable%20courage.

[29] Liechtenstein, S. (2022, September 13). Iran nuclear talks head into deep freeze ahead of midterms. https://www.politico.com/news/2022/09/13/iran-nuclear-talks-midterms-00056312.

[30] Fattahi, M. & Gambrell, J. (2023, May 26). Iran unveils latest version of ballistic missile amid wider tensions over nuclear program. https://apnews.com/article/iran-khorramshahr-ballistic-missile-nuclear-tensions-017382e19220700c618eeb51d0bd8b94; The Associated Press. (2023, July 5). Iran tried to seize 2 oil tankers near Strait of Hormuz and fired shots at one of them, US Navy says. https://apnews.com/article/gulf-iran-us-tensions-shipping-oil-127f8b77aa7e41dcd8266b6fbe5800dc.

[31] Al Jazeera (2023, July 15). US to send F-16 fighter jets to Gulf amid Iran shipping tensions. https://www.aljazeera.com/news/2023/7/15/us-to-send-f-16-fighter-jets-to-gulf-amid-iran-shipping-tensions; Al-Monitor. (2023, August 7). Why is US sending 3,000 Navy, Marines force to Persian Gulf? https://www.al-monitor.com/originals/2023/08/why-us-sending-3000-navy-marines-force-persian-gulf#ixzz8EuSJajok.

A Chokepoint of Asymmetric and Complex Rivalry: The Port of Duqm   77

US and China, which have been one of the most fashionable discussions of international relations recently, form a complex rivalry.[32] Complex rivalries are not merely dyadic. They are influenced by two additional factors: 'interactions with the belligerents' other rivals as well [as] interactions with the belligerents' other partners'.[33] Yet, the complex rivalry between and among China, Iran, the US, and India requires a clearer and more *haute couture* definition. This particular complex rivalry is the result of three different types of interactions: (1) the dyadic interactions between rivals, e.g., China–Iran vs. US–India; (2) individual interactions on a more symmetrical basis, e.g., China vs. the US; (3) interactions between the parties which are rivals in dyads but partners on an individual basis, e.g., India and Iran.

The US actions in this composite geopolitical equation are presumably the most significant since they aim to 'strategically encircle'[34] China from Afghanistan to Japan in Asia and limit its slowly growing influence in the Middle East, especially in terms of its traditional partners, i.e., Saudi Arabia, Türkiye, and Israel. The US alliance would empower India *vis-à-vis* China at least within the military realm.[35] In 2023's terms, it is difficult to talk about a full-fledged alliance between the US and India. It is more of an intensifying strategic partnership, in other words, a 'non-aligned alliance'.[36] This includes cooperation on artificial intelligence, computer chips, telecommunications, higher education, access to shipping lanes in the Indo-Pacific, climate change, and a developing defence partnership.[37] In addition to this factual deepening of relations between

---

[32] For details on the complex rivalry concept, see Thompson, W. R. (2015). Trends in the analysis of interstate rivalries. In R. A. Scott & S. M. Kosslyn (Eds.), *Emerging Trends in the Social and Behavioral Sciences* (pp. 7–9). New York: Wiley.

[33] Pardesi, M. S. (2021). Explaining the asymmetry in the Sino-Indian strategic rivalry. *Australian Journal of International Affairs, 75*(3), 341–365, 355.

[34] Wang, J. (2013). Changing global order. In A. J. Tellis & S. Mirski (Eds.), *Crux of Asia: China, India, and the Emerging Global Order* (45–52). Washington, DC: Carnegie Endowment for International Peace.

[35] Wu, X. (2018). New phase of the United States' China policy under the Trump administration. *China International Studies*, (4), 5–24.

[36] Tharoor, S. (2023, July 5). The US and India's non-aligned alliance. https://www.project-syndicate.org/commentary/us-india-relations-remarkable-transformation-by-shashi-tharoor-2023-07?barrier=accesspaylog.

[37] The White House. (2023, June 22). Joint statement from the United States and India. https://www.whitehouse.gov/briefing-room/statements-releases/2023/06/22/joint-statement-from-the-united-states-and-india/.

New Delhi and Washington DC, which would strengthen India's position *vis-à-vis* China in South Asia, East Asia, and the Western Pacific, there were also some ideological messages implicitly delivered against China's dominance in the region. US President Biden stated that 'it is in America's DNA, and I believe in India's DNA that both of us would maintain our democracies'. This 'makes us appealing partners and enables us to expand democratic institutions across the world'.[38] Beijing, as being concerned by the slow development of this implicit 'anti-China bloc', gave some early warnings. In 2020, Chinese officials 'have warned U.S. officials to not interfere with [China]'s relationship with India'.[39] China's concerns about the anti-China bloc have not been baseless in practice. A good example of such a bloc is the I2U2 Group bringing India, Israel, the United Arab Emirates, and the United States with an undercover aim of working as a diplomatic instrument to strengthen Washington's efforts to counter the Chinese influence in West Asia and the Middle East.[40]

On the other hand, China's developing relations with Iran have been concerning the US. This goes back to July 2020 when Iran announced an incoming agreement, which was formulated in March 2021[41] with China making the two countries strategic partners in expanding the Chinese presence in Iranian in 'banking, telecommunications, ports, railways and dozens of other projects'. China in exchange 'would receive a regular — and, according to an Iranian official and an oil trader, heavily discounted — supply of Iranian oil over the next 25 years'. In addition, the agreement

---

[38] Collinson, S. (2023, June 23). China was the ghost at the US-India feast. https://edition.cnn.com/2023/06/23/politics/china-us-india-state-visit/index.html.

[39] US Department of Defense (2022). Military and security developments involving the People Republic of China. p. 117. https://media.defense.gov/2022/Nov/29/2003122279/-1/-1/1/2022-MILITARY-AND-SECURITY-DEVELOPMENTS-INVOLVING-THE-PEOPLES-REPUBLIC-OF-CHINA.PDF.

[40] US Department of State. I2U2 India, Israel, United Arab Emirates, United States. https://www.state.gov/i2u2/; Calabrese, J. (2022, September 27). The US and the I2U2: Cross-bracing partnerships across the Indo-Pacific. Middle East Institute. https://www.mei.edu/publications/us-and-i2u2-cross-bracing-partnerships-across-indo-pacific.

[41] *Reuters* (2021, March 27). Iran and China sign 25-year cooperation agreement. https://www.reuters.com/article/us-iran-china/iran-china-sign-25-year-cooperation-agreement-idUSKBN2BJ0AD?il=0.

A Chokepoint of Asymmetric and Complex Rivalry: The Port of Duqm   79

aims to deepen mutual military cooperation.[42] The US was particularly disturbed by the agreement due to its anti-American nature. Iran was in need of China to confront the West.[43] With the help of China, Iran increases its potential to limit or at least deter US actions or power projection in the Middle East. The US concern was bolstered by the China-brokered Iran–Saudi rapprochement in March 2023.[44] Although the US Secretary of State Antony Blinken,[45] the National Security Advisor Jake Sullivan,[46] and State Department Spokesperson Ned Price repeatedly stated that such a rapprochement would deescalate the tensions in the Middle East, Price underlined that these advantages are only in the theoretical sense but, 'in a very real and practical sense', they would only happen 'if Iran takes the steps that it has pledged to take'.[47] The US statements stress the fragility of the rapprochement due to their lack of confidence in Iran's future actions. More importantly, this China-brokered development would increase Beijing's influence in the region and particularly in one of the US' traditional and closest allies. Although China currently does not have a military presence compared to the US in the region, Washington's detachment from the Middle East slowly moves its allies closer to China.

The Middle East is the area to elaborate on this asymmetrical and complex rivalry and illustrate how these two rivalries operate together.

---

[42]Fassihi, F. & Myers, S. L. (2020). Defying U.S., China and Iran near trade and military partnership. *New York Times*, July 11.

[43]Saleh, A. & Yazdanshenas, Z. (2023). China-Iran strategic partnership and the future of US hegemony in the Persian Gulf Region. *British Journal of Middle Eastern Studies*, 1–24.

[44]The Iran Primer. (2023, March 15). U.S. on Iran-Saudi rapprochement & China. https://iranprimer.usip.org/blog/2023/mar/15/us-iran-saudi-rapprochement-china.

[45]Blinken, A. J. (2023, March 15). Remarks. US Department of State. https://www.state.gov/secretary-antony-j-blinken-at-a-press-availability-31/.

[46]The White House. (2023, March 13). Press Gaggle by Press Secretary Karine Jean-Pierre and National Security Advisor Jake Sullivan En Route San Diego, CA. https://www.whitehouse.gov/briefing-room/press-briefings/2023/03/13/press-gaggle-by-press-secretary-karine-jean-pierre-and-national-security-advisor-jake-sullivan-en-route-san-diego-ca/.

[47]Price, N. (2023, March 13). Department press briefing. US Department of State. https://www.state.gov/briefings/department-press-briefing-march-13-2023/.

Both the lesser actors of this combination, i.e., Iran and India, naturally looked for great power allies to cover their pressure points. Yet, this dyadic alliance does not necessarily increase India and Iran's position due to the strategic and economic capabilities and priorities of China and the US, respectively. Duqm, as a chokepoint, gives an illustration of this continuing complex asymmetry.

The Specifics and Strategic Value of Duqm

The Duqm port is on the southeastern part of Oman and the northwestern tip of the Indian Ocean. It lies along the Arabian Sea, Indian Ocean, Strait of Hormuz, and Gulf of Oman. Via its location, the port provides access both to East Africa and the Red Sea. It is situated in the locale of the international trade routes between Europe and Asia. It is a part of the Special Economic Zone (SEZ) project of the Sultanate of Oman, thus becoming a hub of economic activity in the region.[48] It covers 2,000 square kilometres with 90 kilometres of coastline, which makes it the largest SEZ in the Middle East and North Africa. It has a multipurpose port, a dry dock for ship repairs, a fishing port, a regional airport, and logistical and industrial areas.[49] Its Asyad drydock, which is the biggest in the Middle East and North Africa, 'can handle vessels up to 600,000 DWT efficiently'.[50] It has a 2,800-metre pier, covering industrial workshops and 453,000 square metres of workspace. The complex also has a multipurpose fisheries port to serve for investments in marina-related activities, livestock, fish processing, and general food industries.[51]

Duqm connects Gulf States and Indian Ocean Rim countries. It serves both the Western and Eastern corridors as it is located in the middle of the Indian Ocean. It is located just away from the Strait of Hormuz and is very close to Asian and European international trade routes. It is also quite accessible to the shipping lines to both African and Indian markets.

---

[48] Strategic port of the future. https://portofduqm.om/.

[49] Inside SEZAD. https://www.duqm.gov.om/en/sezad/inside-sezad/profile.

[50] ASYAD. (2023). About. https://asyad.om/maritime/drydock.

[51] Inside Recent. (2022, February 6). Oman's Duqm port draws US$9.36b in investments. https://www.insiderecent.com/omans-duqm-port-draws-us9-36b-in-investments-51237.html.

Although Duqm is not traditionally known as a chokepoint like some other maritime locations, e.g., the Strait of Hormuz or the Malacca Strait, the development and utilisation of the port influence shipping routes and trade dynamics in the Middle East. Its growth and effective operation of the above-stated SEZ impacts the flow of goods and vessels, altering existing trade patterns and potentially diversifying options for global shipping.

Another important feature of Duqm as a 'non-traditional' chokepoint is related to the Strait of Hormuz, which is situated between Oman and Iran, connecting the Persian Gulf to the Gulf of Oman and the Arabian Sea. The Port of Duqm, while not directly on the Strait of Hormuz, is in proximity to it, and developments in Duqm influence trade dynamics and transportation routes in the region. The significance of Duqm lies in its potential to offer an alternative route for trade, bypassing the Strait of Hormuz, which is well known for its 'geopolitical sensitivity'.[52] With its strategic location and ongoing development, Duqm began to act as a key player in regional trade and maritime activities, offering an alternative or supplementary route for goods moving through the region.

Oman with Duqm, in addition to Sohar and Salalah Ports, aims to receive more investment in its national shipping industry. This investment could enhance overseas trade and promote coastal shipping between Omani ports.[53] Duqm's attractiveness has been fulfilling the investment expectations that in 2022 it has already drawn US$9.36 billion. Investment opportunities in Duqm although mainly in industrial projects also include logistics, tourism, storage, real estate development, and fish and food industries.[54]

Via these projects and investments, Oman envisages a series of strategic roles for Duqm in several regional and global domains. One obvious role is in trade and the economy. Duqm is a key element of Oman's attempts to diversify its economy due to its location and strategic position which makes it a transshipment hub along major international shipping

---

[52]Nadim, F., Bagtzoglou, A. C., & Iranmahboob, J. (2008). Coastal management in the Persian Gulf region within the framework of the ROPME programme of action. *Ocean & Coastal Management, 51*(7), 556–565.

[53]For details, see Aljabri, K. S. S. (2012). Oman's maritime doctrine. PhD diss., University of Exeter.

[54]Inside Recent (2022, February 6). Oman's Duqm port draws US$9.36b in investments. https://www.insiderecent.com/omans-duqm-port-draws-us9-36b-in-investments-51237. html.

lanes.[55] The port has already attracted quite a significant level of foreign investment and has been contributing to Oman's economic growth by facilitating trade between East and West.[56] The other domain is logistics, in which Duqm serves as a crucial logistics hub both for Oman and the region by offering facilities for heavy industries and manufacturing services.[57] Duqm also plays a significant military and security role as a base for naval operations and provides logistics, strategic, and tactical support to security initiatives in the region.[58] This role directly enhances Oman's strategic value for the great and regional power politics in the Middle East. Duqm also plays an important role in Oman's aims to develop its energy sector, particularly in terms of becoming a clean energy export hub.[59] In addition, the port's SEZ contributes to Oman's energy security and trade by its special focus on the oil refinery and petrochemical industries.[60] Another very crucial domain in which Duqm could play a significant role is geopolitics. The port strengthens Oman's geopolitical position by providing an alternative to congested and potentially vulnerable chokepoints in the region, such as the Strait of Hormuz.

All these features turn Duqm into a focal point of rivalry for all relevant great and regional powers to increase their sphere of influence in the

---

[55] Oman Observer (2020, August 10). Port of Duqm seeks to evolve into transshipment hub. https://www.omanobserver.om/article/11459/Business/port-of-duqm-seeks-to-evolve-into-transhipment-hub.

[56] Asian Infrastructure and Investment Bank (2020). Oman: Connecting commerce and future-proofing the economy. https://www.aiib.org/en/news-events/annual-report/2020/our-investments/detail/oman2/index.html.

[57] Logistics Middle East (2021, January 28). Duqm: A port to watch. https://www.logisticsmiddleeast.com/comment/36500-duqm-a-port-to-watch.

[58] Brewster, D. (2018, February 15). Indian Ocean base race: India responds. https://www.lowyinstitute.org/the-interpreter/indian-ocean-base-race-india-responds.

[59] Yousuf, K. (2023). Duqm to become clean energy export hub. *Oman Observer*, August 11. https://www.omanobserver.om/article/1141329/business/economy/duqm-to-become-clean-energy-export-hub.

[60] *Oman Observer* (2022, December 28). OQ, SABIC and KPI sign pact to set up world-scale petrochemical complex in Duqm. https://www.omanobserver.om/article/1130434/business/energy/oq-sabic-and-kpi-sign-pact-to-set-up-world-scale-petrochemical-complex-in-duqm.

A Chokepoint of Asymmetric and Complex Rivalry: The Port of Duqm   83

port to achieve a strategic advantage over their rivals. The significance of Duqm, as a chokepoint, could be more clearly seen through the asymmetrical and complex rivalry between China–Iran and the US–India.

The Asymmetrical and Complex Rivalry on Duqm

The rivalry on Duqm is an extension, if not a mini-display, of the asymmetrical and complex rivalry amalgam between China, Iran, US, and India in the Middle East. In other words, the competition over the port of Duqm serves as a smaller representation or an extension of the broader geopolitical tensions among China, Iran, the United States, and India in the Middle East. Therefore, this eclectic rivalry's main parameters determine the rivalry on Duqm.

For India, the Middle East, which has been mostly labelled as West Asia,[61] has been important not only due to its industrial investments but also due to its huge diaspora in the region. Oman has a peculiar significance in both aspects, which transformed its relations with India to a strategic partnership level as early as November 2008.[62] According to the records of the Indian Embassy in Muscat in February 2021, approximately 624,000 Indians were living in Oman, almost 485,000 of whom are professionals and workers.[63] Such humanitarian links were bolstered by increasing Indian investments in Oman in sectors, such as engineering, construction, logistics, waste management, manufacturing, capital, software solutions, communications, and oil and gas.[64] Duqm is a particular

---

[61] The term 'Middle East' has gained traction with the India–Middle East–Europe Economic Corridor initiative which aims to give India a more prominent role in the Middle East. For details, see Ministry of External Affairs, Government of India (2023, November 3). Interviews of external affairs minister, Dr. S. Jaishankar during his Portugal visit (2023, November 2). https://www.mea.gov.in/interviews.htm?dtl/37226.

[62] Ministry of External Affairs, Government of India (2023, August 12). India-Oman bilateral brief. https://www.mea.gov.in/Portal/ForeignRelation/India-Oman_2023.pdf.

[63] Embassy of India, Muscat. India and Oman bilateral relations. https://eoi.gov.in/eoisearch/MyPrint.php?16039?001/0035.

[64] Embassy of India, Muscat. India — Oman bilateral economic and commercial relations. https://www.indemb-oman.gov.in/eoi.php?id=trade#:~:text=The%20Agreement%20

focus of India's investments. In Duqm SEZ, a US\$62.7 million project was established by an Indo-Oman JV Sebacic Oman to set up the largest Sebacic acid plant in the Middle East.[65] In addition, Skyline Duqm invested US\$748 million for a tourism complex project in Duqm. ACME India Ltd has signed a deal to invest US\$3.5 billion to build a green hydrogen and green ammonia production complex at Duqm.[66] These investments make Duqm port even more strategically important for India as a ledge to the Indian Ocean.[67]

Due to its strategic position, in 2018, India got access to Duqm for military use and logistical support.[68] Indian Navy could even use a dry dock in the port, which enables it to maintain its vessels without returning them to India.[69] Relatedly, Oman is not only a strategic partner but also the only Gulf country with which Indian armed forces carry out regular bilateral staff talks and exercises.[70] India's goal was to limit China's influence in the Indian Ocean, especially against the 'string of pearls' strategic objective of Beijing, which aims to build up a network of strategically

---

on%20Maritime%20Transport,Muscat%20on%2012%20August%202021; *Oman Observer*. (2019, December 24). Pact inked with India on maritime transport. https://www.omanobserver.om/article/19064/Local/pact-inked-with-india-on-maritime-transport.

[65] Embassy of India, Muscat. *Op. cit.*

[66] *Ibid.*

[67] Valiathan, V. K. (2020, October 1). Oman's strategic Duqm Port and India's opportunities. The Centre for Land Warfare Studies (CLAWS). https://www.claws.in/omans-strategic-duqm-port-and-indias-opportunities/; Chaudhury, D. R. (2020). India's Key West Asian Partner Oman: voice of peace and moderation for centuries. *The Economic Times*, July 7. https://economictimes.indiatimes.com/news/defence/indias-key-west-asian-partner-oman-voice-of-peace-and-moderation-for-centuries/articleshow/76833331.cms.

[68] Ministry of External Affairs, Government of India (2018, March 27). India's outreach to the Middle East and West Asia. https://www.mea.gov.in/distinguished-lectures-detail.htm?739.

[69] Roy, S. (2018, February 13). India gets access to strategic Oman port Duqm for military use, Chabahar-Gwadar in sight. https://indianexpress.com/article/india/india-gets-access-to-strategic-oman-port-for-military-use-chabahar-gwadar-in-sight-5061573/.

[70] *New Delhi Times* (2022, February 14). The strategic significance of the Duqm port in Oman for India. https://www.newdelhitimes.com/the-strategic-significance-of-the-duqm-port-in-oman-for-india/.

located coastal elements including ports.[71] Since China and India have been in an asymmetrical rivalry, India has been utilising asymmetrical measures and instruments. Its developing strategic access in Duqm is one of them. According to the February 2018 India Oman Joint Statement, Oman decided to facilitate 'operational visits by Indian naval ships and aircraft as well as Indian Air Force aircraft to various Omani ports and airports'.[72] To underline the strategic significance of Duqm, in June 2023, National Security Advisor of India, Ajit Doval visited the port where Muscat has particularly 'given access to the Indian Navy to facilitate its presence in the Indian Ocean Region'.[73]

The asymmetrical rivalry on Duqm between China and India is well linked with China–Oman relations. Oman joined the Belt and Road Initiative (BRI) in 2018 and is the first base station of China in the Gulf. Since securing dependable and sustainable energy inflow has been China's priority, developing its presence in Oman was quite necessary, and it would require investments in Oman's maritime capabilities. China's first major investment in the country was Duqm Industrial Park, under a US$10.7 billion agreement.[74] On 25 October 2023, Duqm Hongtong Piping Factory was the first plant in the Sino-Omani Industrial City in Duqm.[75] China's main motivation in investing in Duqm is not necessarily militaristic but commercial. In the specific case of the port, China does not try to expand its military footprint, unlike India. The extent of the threat perception of each side, i.e., China and India, towards the other has been

---

[71] Ashraf, J. (2017). String of pearls and China's emerging strategic culture. *Strategic Studies, 37*(4), 166–181.

[72] Ministry of External Affairs, Government of India (2018, February 12). India Oman Joint Statement during visit of Prime Minister to Oman. https://www.mea.gov.in/bilateral-documents.htm?dtl/29479/India%B1Oman%B1Joint%B1Statement%B1during%B1visit%B1of%B1Prime%B1Minister%B1to%B1Oman.html.

[73] Chaudhury, D. R. (2023). NSA visits Oman's Duqm port where Indian Navy has strategic access. *The Economic Times*, June 29. https://economictimes.indiatimes.com/news/defence/nsa-visits-omans-duqm-port-where-indian-navy-has-strategic-access/articleshow/101348083.cms?utm_source=contentofinterest&utm_medium=text&utm_campaign=cppst.

[74] Xinhua (2018, July 29). Oman to open new terminal for Duqm Airport soon to boost economic zone. http://www.xinhuanet.com/english/asiapacific/2018-08/29/c_137428686.htm.

[75] Duqm Hongtong piping factory opens on October 25 (2021, October 23). https://www.duqm.gov.om/en/sezad/media/news/2021/duqm-hongtong-piping-factory-opens-on-october-25.

imbalanced. As a clear illustration of this asymmetrical rivalry, China does not consider India as a military threat.

Duqm also has a particular significance for China's Maritime Silk Road Initiative (MSRI). China has been investing in the port via a consortium of six Chinese firms called Oman Wanfang. Many members of the consortium are 'from the Ningxia Hui Autonomous Region in north-central China, an area with a large Muslim population that is active in promoting business ties with Arab nations'. Oman Wanfang consortium firms are private and do not receive Beijing's financial aid, but its political backing.[76] Their investments in the SEZ at the port within the framework of MSRI could not only turn Oman into a hub of oil refinery for the Gulf but also increase the Chinese presence in port facilities. This would provide another asymmetrical commercial advantage to China over India.[77] With this advantage, China could extend its influence into the Arabian Peninsula, coastal East Africa and even into Pakistan.[78]

Chinese investments in Duqm would potentially offer Beijing several advantages through which it could get strategic leverage over the US. Firstly, these investments could aid China in establishing a fixed military facility in Duqm with which it can extend its maritime reach by allowing its navy to operate and potentially conduct operations in the Indian Ocean.[79] Secondly, China could increase its economic influence in the region by having a significant stake in Duqm which contributes to the connectivity requirements of the BRI. Thirdly, Duqm's proximity to key oil shipping lanes could potentially offer China greater control or influence over energy resources, which is vital for its energy security

---

[76] Jabarkhyl, N. (2017). Oman counts on Chinese billions to build desert boomtown. *Reuters*, September 5. https://www.reuters.com/article/us-oman-china-investment-idUSKCN1BG1WJ.

[77] Townsend, S. (2017). Oman 'to look east' to China, India for future investment. *Arabian Business*, October 2. https://www.arabianbusiness.com/industries/%20banking-finance/380125-oman-to-look-east-to-china-india-for-future-investment.

[78] Chaziza, M. (2019). The significant role of Oman in China's maritime silk road initiative. *Contemporary Review of the Middle East, 6*(1), 44–57.

[79] Funaiole, M. P., Hart, B., & McElwee, L. (2023, February 3). Dire straits, China's push to secure its energy interests in the Middle East. https://features.csis.org/hiddenreach/china-middle-east-military-facility/.

needs.[80] China's involvement in Duqm could offer obvious strategic advantages, but the extent of these advantages to exert particular leverage over the US remains uncertain.

What is more certain is that the Chinese investments in Duqm significantly contribute to the economic collaboration between Muscat and Beijing. This collaboration has already created several outputs both for China and Oman. The first is the Duqm Industrial Park. The second is the facilitated access for China to markets in the Middle East, Africa, and beyond.[81] The third is the location of Duqm which becomes a strategic node in the BRI by promoting connectivity between Asia, Africa, and Europe.[82] The fourth is that the Chinese partnership aids Oman in diversifying its economic partners and complements its historical ties with the other Gulf countries.[83]

Duqm is also a mini-scene of the US–Iran asymmetrical rivalry. Since the US aims to limit Iran's military and strategic expansion and influence in the Middle East, it followed an India-like pattern in Duqm. In March 2019, Washington signed a 'Strategic Framework Agreement'[84] with Muscat, enabling the US to use the Duqm and Salalah ports. Duqm has the capability to handle the US Navy's aircraft carriers. This facility would increase the US Navy's operational capability, flexibility, and preparedness against Iran. In this asymmetrical rivalry, the US aims to further

---

[80] Baabood, A. (2023, May 24). Why China is emerging as a main promoter of stability in the Strait of Hormuz. https://carnegie-mec.org/2023/05/24/why-china-is-emerging-as-main-promoter-of-stability-in-strait-of-hormuz-pub-89829.

[81] Al-Mamari, S. (2016, July). Establishment of the industrial city Duqm gives us access to many markets in Asia, Africa, and Europe. *Duqm Economist*, (5), 19–21.

[82] Albawaba (2019, June 16). After billions in Chinese investment Oman's Duqm Port could help bypass Hormuz. https://www.albawaba.net/opinion/after-billions-chinese-investment-omans-duqm-port-could-help-bypass-hormuz-1291468.

[83] Smith, S. China's increasing economic presence in Oman: Implications for Oman's economy. https://www.egic.info/china-economic-presence-oman; Xinhua (2021, March 30) China, Oman agree to enhance cooperation, push forward China-GCC free trade talks; http://www.xinhuanet.com/english/2021-03/30/c_139845158.htm.

[84] US Embassy, Oman. (2019, March 24). U.S. statement on the signing of the strategic framework agreement. https://om.usembassy.gov/u-s-statement-on-the-signing-of-the-strategic-framework-agreement/.

88   G. Baba

increase its material power gap against Iran to suppress it in the Persian Gulf and the Arabian Sea. The Agreement gave the US forces a way to bypass Iran's periodical closure of the Strait of Hormuz, a main oil shipping route at the Gulf mouth, to American shipping, which in the past caused tension between the US Navy and the Iranian Revolutionary Guard Corps. An American official, 'speaking on condition of anonymity', underlined the anti-Iranian nature of this agreement by stating that 'we used to operate on the assumption that we could just steam into the Gulf' but now 'the quality and quantity of Iranian weapons raises concerns'. The official added that the agreement 'by improving access to ports that connect to a network of roads to the broader region' would give the US 'military great resiliency in a crisis' with Iran.[85]

The US' attempt to increase its presence in Duqm, in addition to its Fifth Fleet, via an additional Navy destroyer along with fighter jets,[86] provides an example of complex rivalry as a result of two additional circumstances. The first is to counterbalance China's investment-oriented presence in the port. In 2022, the US State Department was aware and concerned about the size of China's investment in Duqm. The Department reported that 'State Grid Corporation of China acquired a 49% stake in the Oman Electricity Transmission Company from Nama Holding' which is 'a government-owned holding company for five electricity transmission and distribution companies'. The report also made a comparison between the US and China's FDIs in 2020 which was RO 2 billion, US$5.2 billion, and RO 773.4 million, US$2 billion, respectively, to imply that the US is still ahead of China.[87] Yet, this gap in investments does not really produce a significant asymmetry in the US–China rivalry. The second is to indirectly bolster India's military position in the port, which conforms to a dyadic-structured rivalry against China and Iran. For this aim, the US

---

[85] Stewart, P. (2019). With an eye on Iran, U.S. clinches strategic port deal with Oman. *Reuters*, March 24. https://www.reuters.com/article/us-usa-oman-military-idUSKCN1R50JD.

[86] US Department of Defense (2023, July 17). DOD increases military presence near Oman. https://www.defense.gov/News/News-Stories/Article/Article/3461167/dod-increases-military-presence-near-oman/.

[87] US Department of State (2023). 2022 investment climate statements: Oman. https://www.state.gov/reports/2022-investment-climatestatements/oman/#:~:text=Oman%20actively%20seeks%20foreign%20direct,removed%20the%20minimum%20capital%20requirement.

deepened its military relations with Oman. Omani authorities have been trying to modernise and expand the country's arsenal primarily with American material. As of 2021, under the Foreign Military Sales System, the US has US$2.72 billion valued at 63 active cases with Oman. The same year, the US allocated US$20.74 million in Title 10 to grant military assistance to Oman. Since 2016, via Direct Commercial Sales, the US exported US$613 million in defence articles and provided US$13 million in Foreign Military Financing and US$12.825 million for International Military Education and Training to Oman. All these elements not only target the goal of enhancing Omani forces' interoperability with US military elements but also deepening their understanding of the US.[88] In other words, these measures are for increasing Oman's dependence on the US and potentially turning it into an alliance in the long run.

Iran's position at Duqm due to its material capabilities gap with the US is a clearer example of an asymmetrical rivalry. Although Iran has been deepening its relations with Oman since 2013 via a memorandum of understanding for the Iranian gas transfer to Oman through a US$6 billion worth of pipeline and also by developing maritime transport fleets, visa facilitations, its investment level, economic and military presence in Oman and particularly in Duqm is nowhere near the US. The sanctions of the West further complicate the completion of Iranian natural gas projects with Oman.[89] Especially with the 2019 Agreement, Iran lost its pressure tool to close the Strait of Hormuz not only because of the developing US military presence in Duqm but also the risk of disrupting a daily transfer of 17 million barrels of crude oil.[90] This obvious material gap between Iran and the US economic and military capabilities leads the former to stay silent in this asymmetrical rivalry on Duqm. It does not get into a

---

[88] US Department of State (2021, June 15). U.S. security cooperation with Oman — Fact sheet. https://www.state.gov/u-s-security-cooperation-with-oman/.

[89] Kalehsar, O. S. (2019). Strategic port deal with US may affect Iran-Oman relations. *The Arab Weekly*, March 31. https://thearabweekly.com/strategic-port-deal-us-may-affect-iran-oman-relations.

[90] Shariatinia, M. (2019). Why Iran is silent about US military deal with neighboring Oman. *Al-Monitor*, April 8. https://www.al-monitor.com/originals/2019/04/iran-oman-duqm-salalah-us-military-bases-china-rivalry.html#ixzz8FDbXgzB4.

direct one-to-one confrontation with the US. Yet, this silence is not an absolute one.

Another component of the complex rivalry on Duqm, i.e., interactions between rivals in dyads but partners on an individual basis, can be observed in Iran's partnership with India which originates from the latter's attempts to increase its influence in the North Arabian Sea and the Persian Gulf. Via this partnership, India aims to develop its presence in Duqm and Chabahar Ports, since these two ports complementarily oversee the Arabian Sea. India has been building Chabahar Port with Iran, the investment of which will reach US$80 million in 2023.[91] The interesting point is that, in this complex rivalry, India was collaborating with Iran which is the most explicit anti-American element in the region. The Iranian Ambassador to New Delhi underlined the value of this collaboration by stating 'we believe India is and was strong and powerful to stand against the pressure of the West... India could easily resist pressure from the US and the West'.[92]

The last element of this complex rivalry regarding Iran's position is its dyadic partnership with China against the US. The 25-year strategic cooperation agreement between Iran and China concluded in March 2021 enabled discounted Iranian oil inflow to China and cheap Chinese consumer goods and investment together with cooperation in the military and cybersecurity realms.[93] Although the agreement does not specifically focus on Duqm, it could be argued that it would provide Iran with

---

[91] Silk Road Briefing. (2023, June 21). India, Iran agree new US$80 million funding to develop Chabahar port. https://www.silkroadbriefing.com/news/2023/06/21/india-iran-agree-new-us80-million-funding-to-develop-chabahar-port/.

[92] The Economic Times. (2023, March 17). Iran pitches for faster cooperation in Chabahar port project. https://economictimes.indiatimes.com/news/india/iran-pitches-for-faster-cooperation-in-chabahar-port-project/articleshow/98733333.cms?utm_source=contentofinterest&utm_medium=text&utm_campaign=cppst.

[93] Islamic Republic of Iran, Ministry of Foreign Affairs. (2021, March 27). Statement on 'Document of Comprehensive cooperation between Iran and China'. https://en.mfa.ir/portal/newsview/632866; Vaisi, G. (2022, March 1). The 25-year Iran-China agreement, endangering 2,500 years of heritage. Middle East Institute. https://www.mei.edu/publications/25-year-iran-china-agreement-endangering-2500-years-heritage.

asymmetrical measures and instruments to deal with the US advantages in the port's vicinity.

Conclusion

Duqm is part of a broader geopolitical context in the Middle East. It's strategically positioned along key global shipping routes, especially in the Indian Ocean, providing access to the Persian Gulf and the wider Middle East region. Its significance lies in its potential as a hub for trade and shipping due to its location and proximity to major markets in Asia, Europe, and Africa. This gives Duqm a peculiar influence on Western and Eastern corridors. On the other hand, factors like infrastructure development, economic partnerships, and political stability always play crucial roles in determining the significance and potential impact of ports like Duqm in regional and global trade. Yet, more importantly, even if they are not traditionally labelled as chokepoints, due to their broader significance within the maritime network, their value continues to rise in the strategic calculations of regional and great powers.

Due to these characteristics and potential, Oman has been focusing on the development of Duqm by both national and international investment projects. Through these projects, the development of the port has become part of Oman's broader vision to diversify its economy, enhance regional connectivity, and establish itself as a key player in global trade and logistics.

These characteristics and features have turned Duqm into a focal point in the rivalries between great and regional powers. The rivalry on Duqm has been a mini-theatre of the asymmetrical and complex rivalry amalgam between China, the US, India, and Iran, both as individual actors and dyads. The asymmetrical rivalries are obvious results of the gaps between the material capabilities of the great and regional powers. The complex rivalries, on the other hand, are the results of the entanglements between the great and regional powers *vis-à-vis* their corresponding dyadic rivals. Neither the India–US nor China–Iran dyads are effectively clinched. They were formed due to regional powers' need for great power protection or support and great powers' need for a regional partner to amplify their presence and achieve an additional economic or strategic advantage. These two patterns of rivalries operate together on Duqm.

The US–India and China–Iran dyadic alliances have not necessarily reduced the asymmetry between the regional and great powers. Although India and the US developed quite a few common points regarding their general aims in the Middle East against the rise of China, when it comes to niche areas, such as Duqm, their priorities might diverge. The US aims for more globally oriented interests whereas India's focus is still regional and national. A similar pattern is also arguable for the Iran–China dyad. The 25-year agreement gives Iran a breathing space *vis-à-vis* the Western sanctions, but it does not necessarily provide overwhelming Chinese military support against the US, since Beijing does not aim to confront the US militarily in the Middle East. Moreover, the projects in the agreement will be heavily carried out by Chinese firms and capital, which would not generate much profit for Iran. Therefore, Iran preferred to work with India, China's regional rival, on the Chabahar port project.

In a nutshell, what makes these asymmetrical and complex rivalry patterns coalesce in Duqm is the role and interests of the extra-regional great powers. They engulf regional powers in a dyadic relationship and make them confront the rival dyad either directly or indirectly. The asymmetrical nature of their rivalry against the great powers makes regional powers accept this dyadic cooperation. As seen in the Iran–India case of Chabahar, the regional powers could generate more economic and strategic profit by working together but this dyad-operated great power rivalry could hinder this inter-regional power collaboration alongside its profit in the long term.

Finally, yet importantly, within these asymmetrical and complex rivalry patterns, Oman's balancing act should also be reassessed. Oman, as a sovereign nation, is navigating multiple alliances and partnerships without significantly leaning towards any one great (or regional) power. This includes maintaining good relations with both the US and China. Muscat needs both great powers' contributions for its economic and strategic development and its influence in the region. Therefore, it would not be wrong to argue that, in addition to the outcomes of asymmetrical and complex rivalries which prevent the dominance of a single power over the port, Muscat will not let any of these great (or regional) powers have an absolutely dominant position in Duqm in order not to lose its bargaining position *vis-à-vis* these powers.

© 2025 World Scientific Publishing Company
https://doi.org/10.1142/9789811294709_0005

Chapter 5

Gwadar: Geopolitics, Development, and Social Change in a Strategic Port City

Atha Tahir

Introduction

This chapter analyses Gwadar's geographical importance in depth. Key aspects of the discussion include its location on the Balochistan coast, proximity to the Strait of Hormuz, physical shape and topography, climate, and access to natural resources. Additionally, the chapter attempts to depict the local grievances about the new developmental projects in the area. The analysis of this aspect demonstrates the question of how the various phases of the political movement of the local fisherfolks disclose the hazardous side of new economic stances in Gwadar. The discussion about local, regional, and global level obstacles to the bilateral megaprojects between China and Pakistan aims to put forward a more inclusive policy interpretation. Most of the previous writings on this area of study ignore the significant aspect of the local grievances over the running development projects in Gwadar. Moreover, this chapter emphasizes the importance of considering native fisherfolks' political grievances in the policy-making processes for a more prosperous implementation of the megaprojects.

Gwadar's geography has made it an appealing port site for centuries yet also isolated it from the major population centres of South Asia. Unlocking Gwadar's potential is a key driver behind massive development projects like the China–Pakistan Economic Corridor (CPEC).

Gwadar is a port city located on the southwestern coast of Pakistan along the Arabian Sea.[1] From the northern infringe, it is covered by Kech and Awaran, and on its western side lies Iran. Lasbela is located on the eastern border of Gwadar and the southern direction is covered by the water bodies of the Arabian Sea. Its strategic location near the Strait of Hormuz has long made it an important port in the region. While Gwadar is a relatively small city today, it has a long and rich history that highlights its strategic importance dating back thousands of years.[2] The meaning of Gwadar is variously interpreted by the locals and in the writings of historians. The foremost conveyed meaning is 'Gwaaty Dar', the gateway of wind.[3]

Gwadar is situated in Balochistan province in western Pakistan.[4] Balochistan covers nearly half of the country's total land area yet has just 5% of its population due to its harsh desert climate.[5] The Makran Coastal Highway links Gwadar to Karachi further east. But the coast itself is otherwise sparsely populated and underdeveloped. Gwadar's location not only gives it a strategic value as a port but also sets natural limits on human settlement and activity.

The concept of littoralisation explains how coasts naturally tend to attract human settlements and economic activity.[6] Yet, aside from some

---

[1]Naz, A. & Ali, F. (2018). Gwadar port: As an economic hub for maritime trade in the world corridor (CPEC). *Journal of Business and Social Review in Emerging Economies, Center for Sustainability Research and Consultancy, 4(1)*, 7. http://www.publishing.globalcsrc.org/jbsee.

[2]Ahmad, A. (2016). Gwadar: A historical kaleidoscope. *Policy Perspectives, 13(2)*, 150–160. https://www.jstor.org/stable/10.13169/polipers.13.2.0149.

[3]Mari, S. M. (2004). Suraj ka shehr Gwadar. Quetta: *Mehrdar Institute of Research and Publication.* www.paknovels.com.

[4]Hussain, R. (2016). Gwadar in Historical Perspective (pp. 1–2). *MUSLIM Institute.* http://www.muslim-institute.org/.

[5]Saleem, A. H. (2017). CPEC and Balochistan. *Institute of Strategic Studies Islamabad, 37(4)*, 118–132. https://www.jstor.org/stable/10.2307/48537575.

[6]Fuerst-Bjeliš, B. & Durbešić, A. (2013). Littoralization and behind: Environmental change in Mediterranean Croatia. *FUNDAÇÃO UNIVERSIDADE DO PORTO –Faculdade*

Gwadar: Geopolitics, Development, and Social Change in a Strategic Port City 95

small fishing villages, the Makran Coast has not seen major development. The arid climate, lack of fresh water, and remoteness from Pakistan's core population centres constrain settlement and agriculture.[7] However, the coast itself allows maritime trade and contact with the wider Indian Ocean world.[8] Rugged hills along the coast also provide security benefits.

While the ocean provides opportunities, Gwadar's coastline also threatens hazards like cyclones.[9] Tsunamis are rare but did affect Gwadar in 1945 and again in 2013. Gwadar's coastline remains vulnerable to future tsunamis and sea level rise. But its coastal location still beckons ambition despite geographical challenges. Port construction requires adapting infrastructure engineering to this sandy, unstable shore.

Until the early nineteenth century, Gwadar had been obscured from the international focus. Right after the endeavour of Pakistan to construct an international port, the city began to attract the international limelight. Furthermore, the city gained the interests of regional and international investors after the involvement of China in the construction of Gwadar deep-sea port. The Chinese concern to initiate CPEC is conceived as a trademark of economic development. Gwadar is the centre of this megaproject. Currently, the coastal city is an important node of the Belt and Road Initiative (BRI) of China due to its strategic location, warm water, and deep-sea features. This significance of Gwadar blesses the mentioned mega-project with a network of land and sea routes by linking China, Central Asia, South Asia, the Middle East, Africa, and Europe.

Moreover, the location of Gwadar near the Persian Gulf and Indian Ocean gives it immense potential as a trade hub and shipping interchange connecting East and West. However, geography has always shaped and constrained human activity in Gwadar. This strategic port city provides a compelling example of how physical geography can influence politics, economics, and society.

---

de Letras da Universidade do Porto, 137. https://www.researchgate.net/publication/271825726.

[7] Saleem (2017). *Op. cit.*

[8] Khan, M. Z. U. & Khan, M. M. (2019). China-Pakistan economic corridor. *Institute of Strategic Studies Islamabad, 39*(2), 68–70. https://www.jstor.org/stable/10.2307/48544300.

[9] Baloch, Z. (2022). Climate change danger to Balochistan coast. *Heinrich Boll Stiftung: The Green Political Foundation.* https://afpak.boell.org/en/2022/05/02/climate-change-danger-balochistan-coast.

The rapid rush of investments in Gwadar increased its significance as a future trade hub. It has generated discussions among national and international business communities to invest in the city. Gwadar's location gives it close maritime access to the strategically vital 'Strait of Hormuz'.[10] This narrow passage connects the landlocked Persian Gulf countries to the Indian Ocean and wider maritime trade routes. The strait sees around 20% of global oil exports pass through its waters. For China, Gwadar provides a significant alternate route for energy imports from the Gulf that avoids the congested 'Malacca Strait'.

Gwadar lies just 260 nautical miles from the Omani coast and 400 miles from the Strait of Hormuz.[11] In the event of conflict or disruption in the strait, Gwadar offers options for maintaining China's oil supply. Its geographic proximity to the Persian Gulf shipping lanes is a major motivation behind China's investments in Gwadar.

However, Gwadar's connectivity to inland regions is still constrained by distance. It lies nearly 500 miles from Pakistan's largest city Karachi. Gwadar is even farther from China's western Xinjiang region which it aims to supply. Vast distances across deserts and mountains make transport infrastructure like roads, railways, and pipelines expensive to build. Solving these geographical challenges is crucial for Gwadar to realise its potential. Its proximity to the Persian Gulf matters little without reliable overland links.

Moreover, the physical shape and topography of Gwadar portray significant knowledge about its inland and coastal importance. The information on the geographic significance of Gwadar lies in its natural features. Gwadar Peninsula's distinctive 'hammerhead' shape jutting into the Arabian Sea gives the port natural shelter and defence. The peninsula extends about 5 miles into the sea culminating at Gwadar. On the peninsula's northern edge lies the Gwadar city centre. Surrounding hills isolate it from the inland regions.

---

[10] Zhao, P. W. G. & Munadi, S. M. (2023). The role of Gwadar in China's maritime strategy: A geostrategic dialogue between Mahan and Mackinder. *Comparative Strategy, 42(4)*, 489–508. DOI: https://doi.org/10.1080/01495933.2023.2219192.

[11] Tanoli, J. R. (2016). Comparative analysis of Gwadar and Chabahar: The two rival pors. *Center for Strategic and Contemporary Research*, 2–3. https://cscr.pk/pdf/rb/RB%20_GwadarvsChabahar.pdf.

Gwadar: Geopolitics, Development, and Social Change in a Strategic Port City 97

This physical isolation provided security to early settlers.[12] But it also constrained Gwadar's growth. The peninsula lacked room to expand inland. Fresh water sources were limited. Moving goods from the port into the interior was obstructed by the hilly topography. Modern engineering efforts like dredging and tunnelling aim to overcome these physical barriers.

The Makran Coastal Range running along Balochistan also constrained human movement and trade.[13] Historically, few major trade routes crossed these mountains. The landscape funnelled trade and settlement towards the coast.[14] Modern infrastructure like highways and railways need to be tunnel through the hills with great effort and expense. Such endeavours are the only way to link Gwadar to Central Asia and China. Overcoming the region's physical geography is thus the key to geoeconomic integration.

Moreover, the climate of Gwadar is also unfavourable to other means of economic generation, such as agriculture and tourism. Gwadar has an arid subtropical climate characterised by scorching summers and mild winters.[15] The average summer high temperature exceeds 95°F. Winters see nighttime lows around 55°F. Rainfall averages just 4–5 inches annually due to the rain shadow effect of inland mountains blocking monsoon rains. Precipitation is sparse even during the winter wet season.

This hot, dry climate historically inhibited large-scale settlement around Gwadar. However, the semi-arid climate does provide benefits for a major port city. Water salinity is lower, reducing ship corrosion compared to humid tropical climates.[16] There is less sediment buildup in port channels due to minimal river outflows. Harsh aridity necessitates modern methods of desalination and irrigation to support Gwadar's growth. Climate projections also warn of rising temperatures worsening water stress in coming decades.

---

[12] Ahmad (2016). *Op. cit.*

[13] Reid, P. (2019). Makran gateways: A strategic reference to Gwadar and Chabahar. *Institute for Defense Studies and Analyses, 23,* 6–17. https://idsa.in/system/files/opaper/makran-gatways-op-53.pdf.

[14] Iftikhar, M. N. *et al.* (2019). The institutional and urban design of Gwadar city. *International Growth Center,* 5–9.

[15] See Quetta: *Planning & Development Department, Government of Balochistan. (2011).* Gwadar-District Development Profile.

[16] *Ibid.*

Access to natural resources is essential for the prosperity of an area that itself lacks this blessing. Natural resources can facilitate boosting the economy via a flourished business and trade. Gwadar's immediate hinterland lacks major natural resources like fresh water, forests, and mineral deposits. This geographical constraint delayed settlement and development.[17]

The wider region, Balochistan, does hold significant minerals, energy, and agricultural resources needed for development. Copper, chromites, and iron ores are found to the north.[18] Coal deposits exist in Balochistan. Oil and gas from Central Asia and Iran can supply port facilities.[19] Solar and wind potential is also substantial. Capturing these resources relies on crossing distances and tricky terrain which Gwadar's infrastructure aims to achieve.

Freshwater access poses problems given low rainfall. But pipelines could supply water pumped from Balochistan's underground aquifers. The Indus River also holds unused flow that could irrigate new cropland. Achieving this, however, requires major cross-country waterworks.

Despite challenges, Gwadar's strategic coastal location beckoned rulers and empires for centuries. Now massive investment aims to finally unlock this potential of the coastal city. But expansion cannot ignore geographic constraints and risks. Climate change also threatens long-term viability.

Its location gives Gwadar major strategic significance on a crowded geopolitical chessboard. This importance has waxed and waned throughout history. The current expansion promises great economic potential but also geopolitical anxieties and local social impacts.

---

[17]Yousaf, T. (2012). Is Gwadar Port an economic haven for Balochistan and Pakistan. *Semantic Scholar.* Corpus ID: 128861266. https://www.semanticscholar.org/paper/Is-Gwadar-Port-an-economic-haven-for-Balochistan-Yousaf/3fdf04dcdf228f136345304fafbe509210194155#citing-papers.

[18]Sadiq Malkani, M. (2020). Revised stratigraphy and mineral resources of Balochistan Basin, Pakistan: An update. *Open Journal of Geology.* DOI: 10.4236/ojg.2020.107036.

[19]Perveen, S. & Khalil, J. (2015). Gwadar-Kashgar economic corridor: Challenges and imperatives for Pakistan and China. *Journal of Political Studies, 22*(2), *351, 366,* 353–355. http://pu.edu.pk/images/journal/pols/pdf-files/1%20-%20SAIMA_v22_2_wint2015.pdf.

Gwadar as a Port Settlement: A Glance from Early History till Present

The Makran region, where Gwadar is located, has been inhabited since ancient times.[20] Archaeologists have found evidence of settlements dating back to the 3rd millennium BCE.[21] The inhospitable desert terrain made permanent settlement difficult, but the coastal region was an important stop for various conquerors and travellers.

Alexander the Great passed through Makran in 325 BCE as he travelled back from India to Babylon.[22] His admiral, Nearchus, led a fleet along the coast while Alexander's army took an inland route. Greek accounts describe the harsh environment of Makran but also mention ports like Gwadar.[23]

After Alexander's death, Makran came under Achaemenid Persian control. It later passed between various regional powers including the Sassanians until the rise of the Rai dynasty in Sindh around 635 CE.[24] The Arabs brought Islam to Makran in the 7th century.[25] For centuries afterwards, Makran remained divided under local rulers.

While Gwadar has recently gained global attention, its strategic location has been recognised for thousands of years. The rocky peninsula was likely home to small fishing settlements since ancient times.[26] Various

---

[20]Nicolini, B. (2013). Maritime Indian Ocean routes: The port of Gwadar/Gwātar. *The Journal of Geography.* Corpus ID: 129921033.

[21]Finkelstein, I. *et al.* (2018). The archaeology and history of the Negev and neighbouring areas in the third millennium BCE: A new paradigm. *Journal of the Institute of Archaeology of Tel Aviv University, 45(1),* 63–88. https://doi.org/10.1080/03344355.2018.1412054.

[22]Mehdi, T. *et al.* (2009, December). South Asia Partnership-Pakistan, Profile of District Gwadar with Focus on Livelihood. *Lahore: Visionaries Division.*

[23]*Ibid.*

[24]Curtis, V. S. & Stewart, S. (2008). The Sasanian era. *The Journal of History.* DOI: 10.5040/9780755696895.

[25]Piacentini, V. (1996). Traces of early muslim presence in Makrān. *Semantic Scholar.* Corpus ID: 163981802.

[26]Beech, M. J. (2001). In the land of the ichthyophagi: Modelling fish exploitation in the Arabian Gulf and Gulf of Oman from the 5th millennium BC to the Late Islamic period. *Environmental Science, Geography, 1,* 40–41. DOI: 10.30861/9781841715773.

conquerors and travellers recorded stopping in the region during antiquity.

The harsh Makran coast saw few permanent settlements, but its bays and inlets offered ships refuge from storms and pirates.[27] Local inhabitants traded fish and other marine goods with merchant vessels passing between the rich Indus Valley civilisations and the Persian Gulf states. Control of Gwadar frequently changed hands between regional powers.

In the following centuries, Gwadar came under the influence of various rulers including the Persians, Arabs, and local chiefs.[28] The port town likely remained a small settlement sustained by fishing and trade.[29] Its location near vital maritime routes gave it strategic value despite regular political turnover. Gwadar provided supplies to ships traversing between the Middle East and the Indian subcontinent.

Medieval sources record that the Portuguese navy attacked and burnt Gwadar in the late 16th century as part of the Portuguese campaign to control the Indian Ocean trade.[30] However, they did not establish a permanent presence. For centuries afterwards, Gwadar remained oriented towards maritime trade under local Baloch rulers while remaining somewhat isolated from major inland empires.

Under Omani rule, Gwadar grew into a fortified port city for the first time.[31] The Omanis constructed a robust fortress and extended Gwadar's coastal defences. For nearly two centuries afterwards, Oman retained control of Gwadar and reoriented its economy towards the Persian Gulf and Arabian Sea trade networks.[32] Thus, it would not be wrong to state that Gwadar's modern emergence began under Omani imperial rule.

In the late 18th century, the fate of Gwadar became contested between the Khanate of Kalat who controlled Balochistan and the Sultanate of

---

[27]Dales, G. F. (2015). Harappan outposts on the Makran Coast. *Published Online by Cambridge University Press Journal Antiquity, 36(142)*. https://www.cambridge.org/core/journals/antiquity.

[28]Fiaz, H. M. *et al.* (2021). Historical review of the beginning and evolution of feudal system and its social and political impact in Saraiki District Dera Ghazi Khan. *Al-Aijaz Research Journal of Islamic Studies & Humanities*. https://doi.org/10.53575/u22.v5.03. (21)236-245.

[29]Naz & Ali (2018). *Op. cit.*

[30]Nicolini (2013). *Op. cit.*

[31]Yousaf, T. (2012). *Op. cit.*

[32]*Ibid.*

Muscat on the Arabian Peninsula. This affair originated decades earlier in 1783.

That year, a prince of Muscat named Said bin Sultan had fled civil war in Oman and received refuge in Gwadar from the ruler of Kalat, Mir Nasir Khan. It was intended as a temporary arrangement until the civil war in Oman ended.

Several years later, Said bin Sultan emerged victorious in Oman and became the Sultan. Yet he refused to return Gwadar as promised to Kalat.[33] Gwadar thereby came into control of Muscat though Kalat insisted this was supposed to be temporary.

Tensions escalated in the early 19th century as the successor to Nasir Khan demanded Gwadar's return while Muscat refused. The British Empire took interest as its own power grew in the region. Seeing an opportunity, Muscat signed an agreement with Britain in 1839 to make Gwadar a protectorate of the British Empire. This consolidated Muscat's control of Gwadar against Kalat's claims.

The contestation continued for over a century between Kalat and Muscat over Gwadar's status.[34] The Khan of Kalat argued Gwadar had only been temporarily lent, not permanently ceded to Oman's sultans. But the British insisted Gwadar should remain an Omani territory under British protection.

This issue finally reached an inflection point around 1947 as the British Empire prepared to withdraw from South Asia. The new state of Pakistan demanded that Britain return Gwadar or compel Oman to do so. Britain, however, hoped to retain influence in Gwadar and was reluctant to undermine Oman.

After further pressure from Pakistan, an agreement was finally signed in 1958, transferring Gwadar from Oman to Pakistan for a payment of 3 million pounds. On September 8, 1958, Pakistan officially took control of the Gwadar enclave nearly two centuries after Oman had first gained it. This allowed subsequent investment to finally develop Gwadar into a modern deep-water port.

Thus, Pakistan had to struggle for over a decade after independence to regain Gwadar from Omani control. This extended dispute originated in the late 18th century when Gwadar was used as a refuge by an Omani

---

[33] Ahmad (2016). *Op. cit.*

[34] *Ibid.*

prince. Though intended as temporary, Gwadar became an Omani territory and later a British protectorate for nearly 200 years before finally returning to Pakistani sovereignty.

This early history shows Gwadar's strategic location attracted imperial interest since antiquity. Its geography destined it to be a maritime port settlement despite political fluctuations. Each new ruler sought to control Gwadar given its access to Indian Ocean trade routes. However, it would take major powers like Oman and later Pakistan to invest the resources needed to transform Gwadar from a backwater fishing village into a globally important deep-water port.

Maritime strategic locations strengthen trade and defence capabilities of regions and remain pivotal for state power ambitions. Although beneficial economically, CPEC faces security hurdles and regional tensions. It is significant to note Gwadar's geopolitical importance and interests of major powers related to its strategic feasibility.

Gwadar's strategic location has maintained a recurring prize for regional powers across history. Its geography along the Balochistan coast proximal to the Strait of Hormuz and Indian Ocean shipping lanes gives Gwadar economic and military significance. Possession of Gwadar allows projection of naval power and maritime trade access.

Modern infrastructure now seeks to unlock Gwadar's potential as a transshipment hub linking regions as distant as China to Africa. Its deep-water port, highways, pipelines, and rail links aim to tap nearby resources and enable geoeconomic integration across Asia. However, Gwadar's geography has always been a double-edged blade.

On one hand, its coastal placement, harbour, and proximity to the Arabian Sea and Persian Gulf made it a desirable port settlement since ancient times. But the harsh climate, water scarcity, isolation from South Asia's population centres, and surrounding hills also constrained Gwadar for centuries. The prosperity of Gwadar requires immense resources to overcome these enduring geographic challenges.

Imperial powers like the Omani sultans and British Empire saw Gwadar's value despite its isolation. But only modern technology and infrastructure can fully harness Gwadar as a trade gateway between regions. Pakistan had to struggle for a decade after independence to regain Gwadar and start developing it. Now China sees Gwadar's location as giving unique access to Middle Eastern energy, African markets, and western China.

Gwadar: Geopolitics, Development, and Social Change in a Strategic Port City 103

Gwadar's geography is both an opportunity and obstacle. Pakistan and China are making a massive investment in roads, rail, pipelines, and industry. The failure of the past ventures poses challenges on the success of these multilateral economic stances. But sustainability will require prudence given the region's various challenges, including water stress, climate change, earthquakes, and local disenfranchisement.

Gwadar's coastal position near vital shipping channels has made control of the region strategically and economically desirable for great powers across history. But geography has also posed barriers that past civilizations failed to fully overcome. Only modern technology can enable tapping Gwadar's potential while overcoming its historic isolation. The port's geography remains pivotal, for good or ill.

After having a glance over the various historical settlements and strategic manipulations of Gwadar, the following paragraphs shed light on its dormant period right after the withdrawal of the British Empire from the region and the regained control of Pakistan on Gwadar from the Sultanate of Muscat. Gwadar remained underdeveloped for decades after independence.

Although Pakistan gained control of Gwadar from Oman in 1958 after considerable diplomatic struggle, the area remained largely underdeveloped and neglected for several decades afterwards. Despite regaining the previous position of Gwadar after a long journey of diplomatic/political struggle, Pakistan put the least focus on this geographically significant city. Its historical status was restored by administering it as part of Balochistan province. But the port infrastructure was as basic as before, and transportation links were lacking despite its valuable feature strategic location. Gwadar remained an isolated, remote settlement accessible only by Makran Coastal Highway linking to Karachi. Port infrastructure was lacking because there was no capacity for major shipping in the significant coastal city. The government failed to integrate Gwadar with the rest of the country through improved transportation, communications, or energy infrastructure. It was an extended dormant period where the region saw little progress. Turning Gwadar into a functioning deep-water port required renewed policy interest and massive investment that only materialised decades later.

Lack of development kept Gwadar a small fishing town with little economic activity or population growth. Islamabad devoted few resources to upgrade the port, build connectivity, or establish industry in the area after reacquiring it. Gwadar saw marginal public infrastructure investment for decades following independence.

It was not until the 1990s that the Pakistani government seriously considered Gwadar's potential as a deep-sea port. In 1991, Pakistan formally conceived plans for a major port at Gwadar to be built with foreign assistance.[35] However, the project moved slowly for many more years. China ultimately became involved in the early 2000s.[36] In 2002, Pakistan signed an agreement with China for the construction of the first phase of a new port at Gwadar.[37] This port was inaugurated in 2008.[38]

The development of Gwadar Port in Pakistan was a major component of China's plan to expand its transportation links and economic influence to the west and southwest.[39] Strategically located on the Arabian Sea near the mouth of the Persian Gulf, Gwadar provided western China with access to warm-water ports and the global maritime trade network.

Construction of Gwadar Port started in 2002 with heavy investment from China, as part of a broader effort by China to develop transportation corridors linking its western regions with Central Asia, South Asia, and the Middle East.[40] Gwadar was seen as the hub of this emerging network, connecting China to the Indian Ocean and Arabian Sea through pipelines, roads, and railways across Pakistan.

China provided significant funding and technical assistance for developing Gwadar, including dredging the port and building new berths and cargo handling facilities. This allowed Gwadar to handle large cargo ships and oil tankers from China and elsewhere. Gwadar also had the potential to serve as a key link in China's energy security, by receiving oil shipments from the Middle East.

---

[35] Hassan, A. (2005). Pakistan's Gwadar Port — prospects of economic revival. *Conference Proceedings*. Corpus ID: 128657849.

[36] Conrad, P. B. (2017). China's access to Gwadar Port: Strategic implications and options for India. *Maritime Affairs: Journal of the National Maritime Foundation of India, 13(1)*, 55–62, 55. http://dx.doi.org/10.1080/09733159.2017.1317123.

[37] *Ibid.*, 55–56.

[38] *Ibid.*

[39] Conrad (2017). *Op. cit.*

[40] *Ibid.*

In essence, Gwadar Port enabled China to bypass the longer route through the Strait of Malacca and have direct access to the Indian Ocean.[41] This made it a strategic gateway for China's imports and exports to grow. With its infrastructure investments in Gwadar, China aimed to develop it as the centrepiece of the CPEC and a significant node in China's BRI.

Gwadar as a Strategic Node in China's Belt and Road Initiative

The BRI, also known as One Belt One Road, is a multibillion-dollar project launched by China in 2013 to improve connectivity and cooperation between China and the rest of Asia, Europe, Africa and Oceania.[42] It is based on two main components: the Silk Road Economic Belt and the 21st Century Maritime Silk Road.

The Silk Road Economic Belt focuses on land-based infrastructure development, including highways, railways, pipelines and power grids stretching from China through Central Asia, Iran, Turkey and ultimately to Europe.[43] The aim is to boost economic development in China's western regions by linking them with Central Asian and European markets.

The 21st Century Maritime Silk Road component centres on developing maritime routes and port infrastructure from China's eastern coast through Southeast Asia to the Indian Ocean, the Middle East, East Africa, and the Mediterranean. This will enhance China's access to overseas energy resources, markets and production centres.

The BRI has both economic and strategic motivations. Economically, it will open up new trade routes, markets and investment opportunities for Chinese companies as transport infrastructure is developed across Eurasia and the Indian Ocean. Strategically, it will extend China's diplomatic influence and soft power in regions blanketed by the project.

---

[41] *Ibid.*

[42] Long, D. (2021). مبادرة الحزام والطريق: نشأة وأهداف/The Belt and Road Initiative: Origin and objectives. *Chinese and Arab Studies*, *1*(1), 81–89. https://doi.org/10.1515/caas-2021–2008.

[43] Zhu & Zi-jun. (2014). Silk Road Economic Belt Underway.

Gwadar Port in Pakistan is a major pilot project and linchpin of the CPEC which provides China land and sea access from its western regions to the Arabian Sea and Strait of Hormuz.[44] Development of Gwadar is intended to make it a regional transportation, trade and energy hub.

China is funding most of the Belt and Road projects through its policy banks, with over US\$200 billion already invested across Asia, Africa and Europe.[45] BRI provides opportunities for China's construction, engineering, logistics and telecom firms to gain contracts overseas, boosting China's exports. However, many recipient countries also worry about debt burdens and over-reliance on China.

In total, the BRI spans 4.4 billion people across more than 60 countries that account for 60% of the world's population and over 30% of global GDP.[46] It is one of the most ambitious infrastructure development programs ever conceived, with massive implications economically and geopolitically.

The strategic junction of Gwadar helps accelerate the BRI aims to improving connectivity and cooperation between China and the rest of Eurasia through infrastructure development. Gwadar Port in Pakistan is a centrepiece of the CPEC. Strategically situated on the Arabian Sea near the Strait of Hormuz, Gwadar provides western China with an easier maritime trade route and access to the Indian Ocean.

China has heavily invested in developing Gwadar, including dredging work to enable berthing of large ships, building new port terminals and cargo handling facilities. This allows Gwadar to handle most of Pakistan's sea-borne trade, providing an alternative to Karachi port which currently accounts for 90% of sea-borne trade.[47]

---

[44] ul Munir, F., Ihsan, N., & Sanaullah. (2021, September). Strategic and economic importance of Gwadar for China and other regional and Western States. *Global Economics Review.* DOI: 10.31703/ger.2021(vi-iii).03.

[45] Chan, S. (2017). The Belt and Road Initiative: Implications for China and East Asian economies. *The Copenhagen Journal of Asian Studies, 35*(2). https://doi.org/10.22439/cjas.v35i2.5446.

[46] Jing, C. *et al.* (2020). Population, urbanization and economic scenarios over the Belt and Road region under the shared socioeconomic pathways. *Journal of Geographical Sciences, 30*, 68–84. https://doi.org/10.1007/s11442-020-1715-x.

[47] Naseem, N. (2014). Geopolitical value of Gwader for the region (Mainly for Pakistan, China and the region). *South Asian Studies: A Research Journal of South Asian Studies, 29*(2), *519–530.* http://pu.edu.pk/images/journal/csas/PDF/11._Geopolitical_value_of_Gwader_v29_no2_2014.pdf.

New railways and roads linking Gwadar with Pakistan's transport network are also being built with Chinese assistance. A railway line will connect Gwadar to Quetta and merge with Pakistan's main railway at Dalbandin.[48] The Makran Coastal Highway from Gwadar to Karachi is also being upgraded.

Once fully operational, Gwadar is presumed to act as a gateway for trade between China, Pakistan, Afghanistan, Iran and other Gulf countries. It may become a new Eurasian land and maritime bridge facilitating China's economic integration with South Asia, Central Asia and the Middle East.

However, realizing Gwadar's potential requires massive upgrades of Pakistan's national transport infrastructure. Issues of electricity, water and connectivity infrastructure for Gwadar need to be resolved. There are also concerns over local Baloch rights, and whether Gwadar's prosperity benefit them. This phenomenon is explained in the further pages.

The China–Pakistan Economic Corridor: Strategic Rationales and Local Impacts in Gwadar

The CPEC is a 3,000-kilometre corridor connecting China's Xinjiang region to Pakistan's Gwadar Port on the Arabian Sea. CPEC is considered a flagship project of China's BRI, aimed at improving trade connectivity between China, Pakistan, Central Asia, and beyond.[49]

The total value of CPEC projects is estimated at around US$62 billion.[50] Major infrastructure projects under CPEC include highways, railways, power plants, and the development of Gwadar Port. Once completed, CPEC will provide China with a shorter trade route that bypasses the Strait of Malacca. Currently, China imports most of its oil through the Strait which takes 2–3 months for shipments to reach

---

[48] Singh, S. & Magray, J. M. (2017, July). China-Pakistan economic corridor (CPEC), its impacts on Pakistan economy. *International Journal of Innovative Research and Advanced Studies (IJIRAS)*, *4*(7). http://www.ijiras.com/2017/Vol_4-Issue_7/paper_2.pdf.

[49] Wang, L. (2017, September 6). Opportunities and challenges of the China-Pakistan economic corridor (CPEC) and implications for US Policy and Pakistan. *Asia Pacific Bulletin No. 395*. https://scholarspace.manoa.hawaii.edu/bitstream/10125/48534/1/apb%20no.395.pdf.

[50] *Ibid.*

Shanghai. The overland CPEC route will reduce this distance to less than 5,000 kilometres and the transport time to just 10 days.[51]

For Pakistan, CPEC offers significant economic potential. Infrastructure projects are expected to help alleviate Pakistan's energy crisis and improve connectivity between major cities and trade routes. The upgrades to Gwadar Port could make it an important regional shipping hub. CPEC may also generate hundreds of thousands of jobs in Pakistan through power plant, road, and port construction projects.

However, CPEC has raised some concerns within Pakistan. In Gwadar, a large section of the fishing community worries that port restrictions and displacements will impact their livelihoods.[52] There are also worries that workers from other regions may be favoured for CPEC jobs and that local Baloch people may get benefit. The major grievances of the fishery community of Gwadar are discussed in the down pages. Environmentalists have warned about the impacts of coal power plants and other several factors planned under CPEC.

Overall, while CPEC represents major Chinese investment in Pakistan, its benefits at the local level remain uncertain. More inclusive development and resettlement policies may be needed to ensure CPEC improves livelihoods for people in affected regions like Balochistan. Managing environmental impacts is also critical for ensuring sustainable long-term growth through CPEC projects.

The development of infrastructure in Gwadar accelerated after 2013 when China and Pakistan agreed to cooperate on the CPEC.

Between 2013 and 2022, China has pledged over US$50 billion for CPEC projects including Gwadar. The port is now being operated by a Chinese state-owned company. Gwadar's potential is enormous, though realising CPEC's full vision will take many more years of work. Moreover, it has been revealed in the initial documents that CPEC transforms Gwadar into a strategic hub.

---

[51] Uddin, I. (2019, February). The role of China-Pak economic corridor (CPEC) in logistic system of Pakistan's and China's. *Journal of Management Info, 6(1)*, 48–50. DOI: 10.31580/jmi.v6i1.469.

[52] Anwar, M. *et al.* (2022). Impact of CPEC project on socio-economy of fishery community in Gwadar: A case study of Gwadar West Bay fishery community. *Global Economics Review*. https://doi.org/10.31703/ger.2022(vii-ii).06.

Gwadar: Geopolitics, Development, and Social Change in a Strategic Port City 109

As part of CPEC, China has funded over US$250 million to expand Gwadar Port.[53] This has enabled the port to handle large bulk carriers and container ships. China is also constructing supporting infrastructure like expressways, an international airport, and industrial zones.

Gwadar provides strategic depth for China's naval power projection into the Arabian Sea and Persian Gulf.[54] While not overtly stated, many analysts believe China may seek a naval base at Gwadar in the future as its global military footprint expands.[55] Even if no permanent base is established, Chinese warships are likely utilise Gwadar's deep-water berths.

For Pakistan, developing Gwadar is hoped to make the city a new economic hub and gateway for trade and other political, economic, and defence purposes. The then concerned government officials claimed that CPEC projects around Gwadar alone have created over 30,000 jobs since 2015, with more expected as investment accelerates.[56]

Massive Chinese investment seeks to transform Gwadar from a remote fishing village into a globally important port, an industrial centre, and a core point of regional connectivity. It remains to be seen whether such hyper-development is economically sustainable. But strategically, an upgraded Gwadar may be pivotal for both Pakistan and China if CPEC lives up to its potential.

In addition to the above-discussed aspects, it is necessary to bring into discussion the regional concerns and threats to Sino–Pakistan bilateral megaprojects. The regional rivalry states to Pakistan and the global economic and technological competition with China raise serious concerns about the development projects running between both ties.

India sees CPEC passing through disputed Kashmir territory and fears it can cement Chinese presence in the region.[57] There are concerns that China aims to surround India by deepening ties with India's neighbours.

---

[53] Singh & Magray (2017). *Op. cit.*

[54] ul Munir *et al.* (2021). *Op. cit.*

[55] *Ibid.*

[56] Raza, H., Mohiuddin, Z. A., Zaidi, S. S. Z. & Osama, A. (2018). CPEC: Pakistan-China cordial ties — A boost to Pakistan's economy. *Journal of Accounting, Business and Finance Research*, 2(1), 1–6. https://doi.org/10.20448/2002.21.1.6.

[57] Wagner, C. (2016). The effects of the China-Pakistan Economic Corridor on India-Pakistan relations.

The US views CPEC as China's influence expansion in the Indian Ocean region which threatens American interests.[58] There are suspicions about China's naval ambitions in Gwadar.

For Iran, CPEC is a rival initiative to its Chabahar port so there is potential for competition between Gwadar and Chabahar to handle trade from Central Asia and Afghanistan.[59] Other regional players like Saudi Arabia and UAE also have apprehensions about China expanding its footprint in Balochistan and the Arabian Sea region.

The bilateral endeavours of development projects between China and Pakistan have also raised serious concerns and mass political resistance among the natives of Gwadar and the nationalist political organizations of the province. In Balochistan, Baloch nationalists oppose CPEC viewing it as an exploitation of local resources which benefits only the outsiders.[60] There are concerns about changing demographics due to the influx of non-Baloch labourers and investors.

The local fishermen community in Gwadar worries about losing access to fishing grounds due to port construction.[61] Their mass protests, in recent years, have conveyed demands to be included in CPEC development that are currently being violated. In Gilgit-Baltistan, there are concerns that CPEC projects are being built on disputed territory claimed by India. Locals demand to restore their lost status first, constitutional rights, and economic benefits.

The security threat from Baloch insurgent groups like Balochistan Liberation Army and Balochistan Liberation Front carries risks of attacks on Chinese workers and CPEC installations in Balochistan and

---

[58] See Ali, S. M. (2020, 1 December). The U.S.-China strategic rivalry and its implications for Pakistan. https://www.stimson.org/2020/the-u-s-china-strategic-rivalry-and-its-implications-for-pakistan/.

[59] Khan, K. H. & Omidi, A. (2023). China-India counterbalancing measures through international corridors and ports: The focus on Chabahar and Gwadar Ports. *Journal of Liberty and International Affairs, 9*.

[60] Wani, S. A. (2021, November). *The Baloch insurgency in Pakistan and the Chinese connection. 17*(22), 82–99. https://www.researchgate.net/publication/355874064.

[61] Talpur, A. R. *et al.* (2023, July-September). Development of Gwadar Port: A plight for fisherfolk community. *Journal of Development and Social Sciences, 4*(3). http://dx.doi.org/10.31703/gssr.2018(III-II).01.

beyond.[62] In recent years, these organisations have carried out several attacks even in the security-tight city of Gwadar. Several news confirms hundreds and thousands of attacks of the nationalist militant organisations on CPEC's machinery, working labourers, patrolling personnel, and the infrastructure. So at both the regional and local level, CPEC faces challenges that need astute diplomacy and inclusive development policies to address.

The Strategic Value of Gwadar: Geography, Resources, and Regional Interests

First, Gwadar provides Pakistan with a deep-sea port near the Strait of Hormuz, through which much of the world's oil transits. This allows Pakistan to project naval power in the Arabian Sea and the Middle East. It also gives access for trade connections to Central Asia and western China. The regional connectivity for trade purposes has always remained a vital concern, mainly, for the developed/industrial countries. Comparing the previous era of China's trade route affairs with the post-Gwadar Port era reveals a bunch of information regarding the importance of this new connecting point.

Second, Gwadar is seen as an energy transit hub for Central Asian oil and gas fields. Pipelines from landlocked Caspian fields can be terminated at Gwadar for maritime shipments. This motivates Pakistan's plans for rail, road, and pipeline links between Gwadar and Central Asia.

Third, Gwadar provides strategic depth versus India, ensuring alternative naval access if tensions shut Persian Gulf ports nearer India. Analysts believe China funded Gwadar to monitor Indian naval activity and shipping lanes.

Fourth, Gwadar enables China to secure oil and gas supplies by diversifying transit routes that avoid the Malacca chokepoint near India and Southeast Asia.

---

[62] See Younus, U. & Ahmed, R. (2022, 24 May). Attacks on Chinese nationals in Pakistan risk creating rifts. https://newlinesinstitute.org/state-resilience-fragility/attacks-on-chinese-nationals-in-pakistan-risk-creating-rifts-2/.

Last, Gwadar projects Pakistani influence deeper into the Arabian Sea and Middle East, countering Iran's Chabahar port. Some even predict Gwadar as an alternative regional shipping hub rivalling Dubai.

Gwadar holds enormous strategic value for Pakistan and allies like China in projecting power, securing energy access, countering regional rivals, and expanding trade influence. This drives the mega-projects despite high costs and local opposition. The strategic location fuels ambitions for Gwadar as a world-class port and city. Gwadar increases the strategic, economic, political, and defence significance of Pakistan at global level.

The Geopolitics of Port Development: Gwadar's Emerging Role and Regional Responses

The development of Gwadar Port is seen by some analysts as having negative geopolitical implications. For India, the CPEC passing through disputed Kashmir is unacceptable.[63] Expansion of the port at Gwadar also has military overtones. Some in the United States see Gwadar as part of China's 'string of pearls' strategy to surround India and project power in the Indian Ocean.[64]

Pakistan stands to benefit economically from transit fees and expanded maritime trade. Still, the geopolitical situation likely to make some powers wary of rapid development at Gwadar. Managing these regional anxieties will require diplomatic engagement by all parties.

Economically, Gwadar can emerge as a transshipment hub serving Central Asia, the Gulf, and China's western regions. It can boost trade, industrial development, and revenue generation for Pakistan. For China, it secures oil supplies and opens alternate routes for its exports. But whether the local Baloch population benefits yet remains to be seen.

---

[63] See Does the China-Pakistan economic corridor worry India? https://www.aljazeera.com/features/2017/2/23/does-the-china-pakistan-economic-corridor-worry-india.

[64] Kardon, I. B. et al. (2020). China Maritime Report China Maritime Report No. 7: Gwadar: China No. 7: Gwadar: China's Potential Strategic Strongpoint in Pakistan. U.S. Naval War College U.S. Naval War College Digital Commons. https://digital-commons.usnwc.edu/cgi/viewcontent.cgi?article=1006&context=cmsi-maritime-reports.

Gwadar: Geopolitics, Development, and Social Change in a Strategic Port City   113

Militarily, while Pakistan and China assert Gwadar is purely commercial, its dual-use potential cannot be discounted given the strategic ties between the two countries. China likely aims to expand its naval reach to monitor and secure its sea lines of communication. For Pakistan, the Chinese presence at Gwadar acts as a deterrent against regional adversaries.

Politically, Gwadar cements the Sino–Pakistan nexus and can help integrate South Asia through trade. But the increasing Chinese influence in Pakistan has also raised concerns in India. The US too sees Chinese expansion into the Indian Ocean region as a threat to its interests.

Within Pakistan, Gwadar's success depends on addressing Baloch grievances over rights and development. The disputed status of Gilgit-Baltistan also has legal implications as it lies on the CPEC route.

Overall, while Gwadar has major economic potential, its location makes it a geopolitical flashpoint. Managing regional tensions and balancing superpower rivalry over Gwadar is a serious concern depending on Pakistan's diplomatic skills.

Coastal Livelihoods, Mega-Projects, and Environmental Change in Gwadar

Along with geopolitical issues, Gwadar's development faces environmental and socioeconomic challenges. The pace of expansion risks environmental degradation if not properly managed. There are concerns about threats to fisheries, climate, beaches, and marine ecosystems. Expanding industry and shipping could also worsen air and water pollution around Gwadar.

Rapid growth driven by CPEC can disrupt communities if local residents are not included equitably in opportunities. There are risks of economic and social inequality emerging. Government policy needs to focus on sustainable development and investing in health, education, and livelihoods for Balochs. Port construction has already impacted most of the fishing villages. The mass political mobilisations of fisherfolks in Gwadar in the earlier months of 2020[65] along with the previous phases of political movements depict the exclusion of fisherfolks from the

---

[65] Baloch, B. & Muhammad, A. N. (2022, 26 December). Gwadar's Haq Do Tehreek — Genuine movement or political ambition? *Dawn.* https://www.dawn.com/news/1728328.

development charter/policies of concerned authorities. The grievances of fisherfolks' political movement include their displacement from sea sites and living slums. In addition to this, they demand to restrict the big trawlers causing hazards to the sea environment/lives. The protests took the shape of a continuous movement which was then named 'Gwadar Bachao Tehrik' (Save Gwadar Movement) and 'Haq Do Tehrik' (People's Rights Movement).

However, the political slogans of fisherfolks' movements respond to the question of how the Pakistani government's plans to develop the coastal town of Gwadar into a major port city and industrial hub have impacted the local fishermen community. Initially, the fishermen had hopes and desires for socioeconomic development from the mega development projects. The natives revealed their hopes and did not resist in the initial phases of the bilateral agreements of constructing Gwadar Port. People only took to the streets when they suffered consequences and when their hopes of socioeconomic development were ignored in the development processes. On one hand, the promise of Gwadar becoming a modern port city incited desires and hopes among the fishermen for a better future. They dreamed their children could get quality education and good jobs rather than remain poor fishermen. The real estate boom also presented opportunities to make money by selling lands. Some fishermen willingly relocated from the old Mulla Band neighbourhood to make way for the port construction, in exchange for monetary compensation and land in the new town.

However, as the projects progressed, threats and anxieties emerged. The construction disrupted and polluted fishing areas, limiting fishermen's access to the sea which is vital for their livelihoods. The compensation and amenities promised by the government did not fully materialise in the new town, leaving relocated residents struggling. Militarisation of Gwadar by security forces to protect the projects also stifled local mobility and access to public spaces. Fishermen were mistreated by soldiers when fishing near the port.

Furthermore, the fishermen felt marginalised as profits from land deals went to wealthy outsiders, while their demands for livelihood protection were ignored.[66] The projects proceeded without much consultation

---

[66] *The Express Tribune* (2023, 10 November). Fishermen's livelihood hit by illegal trawling. https://tribune.com.pk/story/2445736/fishermens-livelihood-hit-by-illegal-trawling.

Gwadar: Geopolitics, Development, and Social Change in a Strategic Port City   115

with locals. This led to resentment as lands were appropriated from fishermen who had lived there for generations. Politically, local Baloch nationalist leaders who criticised the potentially exploitative projects were suppressed.

While mega-development projects fuelled modern aspirations, they threatened fishermen's livelihoods, autonomy over local spaces, and sense of belonging. Lack of consultation, broken promises of benefits, and appropriation of lands without consent were major grievances. The fishermen mobilised to demand rights but faced restrictions from security forces and indifference from authorities.

It is also imperative to bring into discussion the several ways in which the mega development projects in Gwadar caused environmental damage with hazardous impacts on the local population. A major issue was the disruption of local fisheries due to pollution, restriction of access, and overfishing. Construction of the port disturbed fishing areas along the coastline which were vital habitats and breeding grounds for fish stocks. Fishermen's access to their previously owned boat centre was also limited by security cordons around the port. Illegal mass trawling by commercial fleets decimated fish populations. These factors severely threatened the sustainability of small-scale local fishing.

Additionally, the projects interfered with the natural drainage patterns and flood flows in the area.[67] Construction activity filled in wetlands and blocked stormwater flows to the sea, worsening the impact of cyclones and monsoons. For example, Cyclone Phet inundated neighbourhoods when drainage channels were blocked by newly built walls and roads.

The influx of outsiders and vehicles in the small congested city has further degraded its environment. Trash management was poor, polluting land and sea. Diesel smuggling led to oil spills. Untreated sewage was discharged into coastal waters near populated areas. The population rise and real estate boom outstripped civic capacities to manage waste and sanitise the urban environment.

Overall, the mega projects severely disrupted the local ecology that had sustained fishing livelihoods and moderated seasonal storms. Uncontrolled construction interfered with natural hydrological patterns,

---

[67]Memon, N. (2015, July). Climate Change and Natural Disasters in Pakistan, 5th edn. *Stengthening Participatory Organization.*

worsening floods. The environmental effects compounded economic losses for fishermen and health risks for residents. Lack of ecological impact assessments and insufficient investments in managing the environmental changes exacerbated the hazards.

Conclusion

In a nutshell, it is concluded that the deep-sea port at Gwadar in Pakistan's Balochistan province holds immense economic and strategic potential but also faces significant challenges at local, regional, and global levels. Developing Gwadar is a priority for China under BRI as it provides western China with access to the Arabian Sea and Strait of Hormuz.

China has invested heavily in Gwadar. The funding is focused on the upgradation of port and also road/rail links connecting China to Pakistan's transport network. Once fully operational, Gwadar can boost Pakistan's exports, serve as an energy transshipment hub, and provide China an alternate route for oil supplies avoiding the Malacca Strait.

However, both regional tensions and local grievances pose threats to Sino–Pakistani realisation of Gwadar's potential. Regionally, India sees Gwadar as a Chinese foothold in its backyard and fears geographic encirclement. The US too views Chinese presence in Gwadar as a challenge to its regional interests. There are also concerns about China's long-term naval ambitions.

Locally in Balochistan, Baloch nationalists oppose Chinese investments viewing it as exploitation of resources with limited benefit for locals. Unless Baloch grievances over rights and development are addressed, insurgent attacks on CPEC projects could persist. Protests by Gwadar's fishermen over loss of access also highlight the need for inclusive development.

Pakistan needs to leverage Gwadar as a bridge between regions and not an arena for new rivalries. Ensuring equitable distribution of economic gains, expanding local stakeholding, and providing constitutional rights and protections are necessary policy stances for the implementation of the bilateral megaproject. Deft regional diplomacy is required to alleviate India and US suspicions regarding China–Pakistan strategic motivations on Gwadar.

While Gwadar holds major promise as a hub of regional connectivity and engine of growth for Pakistan, it also remains hostage to regional tensions and local discontent. Pakistan's ability to balance superpower competition and take into account the local political grievances will determine whether Gwadar emerges as a geostrategic asset or liability.

© 2025 World Scientific Publishing Company
https://doi.org/10.1142/9789811294709_0006

Chapter 6

Chabahar: Geoeconomic Hopes and Geopolitical Games

Deepika Saraswat

Introduction

Chabahar port, located in the Gulf of Oman outside the chokepoint of the Strait of Hormuz, is Iran's only oceanic port. Further, its location at the crossroads of energy trading routes, proximity to land-locked Afghanistan and Central Asia, and direct access to the Indian Ocean have led Iranian policymakers to envisage it as a major regional transshipment hub. Iran's geoeconomic plans for Chabahar can be traced to the early 1990s, when to attract foreign investment and promote regional trade, Iran launched Free Trade-Industrial Zones (FTZs) near its strategic ports in the Persian Gulf. Two FTZs were created in Kish and Qeshm islands in the Persian Gulf and one on Chabahar the Makran coast.[1] These FTZs, with their good access to international waters, and favourable economic environment through various deregulations and concessions on labour, environmental protection, and tax-free imports, were seen as vehicles for a gradual and selective economic liberalisation integrating Iran with the globalising

---

[1] Azar, B. (2022, August 17). Failed promises in Iran's free trade zones. *Fikra Forum*. https://www.washingtoninstitute.org/policy-analysis/failed-promises-irans-free-trade-zones.

world economy.[2] It was hoped that they will attract foreign direct investment, promote a diversified industrialisation base and non-oil exports, and help address underdevelopment of the south-eastern region of the country.[3] Chabahar was envisaged as the third major hub for petrochemical industries in Iran after Bandar-e Emam Khomeyni and Assaluyeh.[4] But as a result of the tightening of the US sanctions in the mid-1990s, Indian firms hired to develop the port were able to partially build the port facility.[5] Experts point to the realities of Iranian economic system, with its weak foundations of industrial capitalism, ambivalence towards Iran's position in the international economy, and intensive regional competition in the Persian Gulf over foreign investment and capital as factors relegating Kish and Qeshm playing the role of import destinations serving Iranian consumer market.[6] Chabahar also suffered from a lack of hinterland connectivity and a viable commercial ecosystem around it. But given India's early role, India has been central to the Chabahar port project.[7]

At the turn of the century regional developments such as the US overthrow of the Taliban government in 2001, subsequent convergence of interest between Iran and India in fostering independent state-building in Afghanistan, and India's quest for overcoming Pakistan's refusal of its 'natural' overland access to Afghanistan created a buzz around Chabahar as a potential hub connecting landlocked Afghanistan and Central Asia with the Indian Ocean. However, any real progress at the port had to wait until the lifting of the international economic sanctions on Iran and the

---

[2] Hakimian, H. (2011, November). Iran's free trade zones: Back doors to the international economy? *Iranian Studies, 44*(36), 851–874.

[3] *Tehran Times*. (2023, April 28). Iran, Uzbekistan negotiate establishment of joint free zone. https://www.tehrantimes.com/news/484061/Iran-Uzbekistan-negotiate-establishment-of-joint-free-zone.

[4] Joshi, N. (2018, July-September). Strategic significance of Chabahar for India and the region. *Journal of the United Service Institution of India CXLVIII*, no. 613. https://www.usiofindia.org/publication-journal/strategic-significance-of-chabahar-for-india-and-the-region.html.

[5] Fars News Agency. (2014, October 19). India approves plan to develop Iran's Chabahar port. https://www.farsnews.ir/en/news/13930727000697/India-Apprves-Plan-Develp-Iran39-s-Chabahar-Pr.

[6] Hakimian (2011). *Op. cit.*, 852.

[7] Pant, H. V. (2018, March 3). India-Iran cooperation at Chabahar port. *CSIS Briefs*. https://csis-website-prod.s3.amazonaws.com/s3fs-public/publication/180717_Pant_IndiaIranCooperation.pdf.

signing of trilateral Chabahar Agreement between Iran, India, and Afghanistan in May 2016. This chapter seeks to analyse how Iran's geoeconomic aspirations for Chabahar port and approach towards cooperation with India *vis-à-vis* the port have transformed in tandem with the broader Iranian strategies of navigating the changing regional and international geopolitical dynamics. After a brief historical and geopolitical background of Chabahar and Makran coast, it discusses three different phases of Iranian geoeconomic and geopolitical discourse *vis-à-vis* Chabahar.

The first phase started in 2003 when India and Iran made an initial trilateral agreement together with Afghanistan to develop the Chabahar route through Milak, Zaranj, and Delaram in Afghanistan to advance regional trade and transit to Afghanistan and Central Asia.[8] During this phase, Iran and India cooperated on several hinterland connectivity projects in Iran and Afghanistan with the aim of providing Afghanistan with alternative access to international markets via Chabahar reducing Pakistan's leverage over Afghanistan. The second phase started with Iran, India, and Afghanistan signing a Trilateral Agreement in 2016 to establish an International Transport and Transit Corridor through Chabahar port. During this phase, Iran hailed Chabahar port as the 'symbol of cooperation' with India, which saw the port as a strategic investment and counter to China's development of Gwadar as the centrepiece of China–Pakistan Economic Corridor. However, as India successfully negotiated with Washington to give exemptions from sanctions for the development of infrastructure at Chabahar Port, it stopped oil imports from Iran in compliance with the economic sanctions re-imposed by the Trump Administration. Subsequently, Iran turned to a 'Look East' policy prioritising cooperation with its neighbouring countries and China, while adopting a strategy of playing off India and China against each other. Tehran also sought to allay perception of Chabahar being a rival to Gwadar. This phase came to an end with the Taliban's overthrowing of the US-backed Islamic Republic of Afghanistan in August 2021. The third phase can be traced to the approval of Iran's full membership of the Shanghai Cooperation Organisation in September 2021. As Iran sought to downplay competitive

---

[8]Ministry of External Affairs of India. (2003, January 25). The Republic of India and the Islamic Republic of Iran 'The New Delhi Declaration.' https://mea.gov.in/outoging-visit-detail.htm?20182/The+Republic+of+India+and+the+Islamic+Republic+of+Iran+quotThe+New+Delhi+Declarationquot.

dynamics in the Eurasian connectivity, it also engaged in re-branding of Chabahar port as a 'symbol of cooperation' among the SCO member states. During this phase, Iran and India's efforts to encourage Central Asian states, especially Uzbekistan, to utilise Chabahar have received a fillip as these countries seek to diversify their transit routes in the aftermath of the Russia–Ukraine war and Western sanctions on Russia. Further, as the International North–South Transport Corridor (INSTC) gains in importance for international freight transit between Russia, Iran, and India, Chabahar is being integrated with an eastern route of the INSTC.

Chabahar: Historical and Geopolitical Background

Chabahar port is located on the Makran coast, which runs along Iran's Hormozgan and Sistan-Baluchestan provinces, the Gwadar Bay in Pakistan's Balochistan province, and up to Lasbela district near Karachi port.[9] The Makran coastal region has a semi-dessert climate, rugged topography, and sparse population. As a result, despite its location on the open sea, historically the coast did not see the growth of ocean-facing emporia.[10] It was the port of Karachi located on the mouth of the Indus River, which, from the time it was under the control of Indo-Scythian tribes or the Saka kingdoms, channelled trade from Bactria, the neighbouring parts of Central Asia, and China to the Roman Empire.[11]

In modern times, geopolitical importance of Makran coast finds a mention in the works of the late 19th-century geopolitical thinkers, who used geography as 'aid to statecraft' in the context of the inter-imperial rivalries among European powers and explained world politics in terms

---

[9]Mollazehi, P.-M. (2016, June 14). From Gwadar to Chabahar, the Makran coast is becoming an arena for rivalry between powers. *The Wire*. https://thewire.in/south-asia/from-gwadar-to-chabahar-the-makran-coast-is-becoming-an-arena-for-rivalry-between-powers.

[10]Reid, P. (2019, August). Makran gateways: A strategic reference for Gwadar and Chabahar. *IDSA Occasional Paper*, 53. https://idsa.in/occasionalpapers/makran-gatways-op-53.

[11]Stobdan, P. (2015). Central Asia: India's Northern exposure. *Institute for Defence Studies and Analyses*. https://www.idsa.in/monograph/CentralAsiaIndiasNorthernExposure_pstobdan_44; Mishra, R. K. (2020). The 'Silk Road': Historical perspectives and modern constructions. *Indian Historical Review, 47*(1), 21–39.

of a land-sea dichotomy.[12] A. T. Mahan and Halford J. Mackinder, who were the founding thinkers of Anglo–American geopolitical tradition, considered the geostrategic importance of the Eurasian littoral — which includes Makran — in the broader context of the struggle for primacy between continental and maritime powers. Mahan, an American naval historian, had articulated 'sea power' as a model of statehood premised on the control of strategically significant chokepoints and harbours, as opposed to the annexation of large territories.[13] Mackinder, a British geographer, in his 'Heartland thesis' warned Britain, a classical maritime-based power, about the dangers of a Eurasian interior unified by a single power and becoming 'inaccessible to oceanic commerce'. He argued that efficient overland connectivity in the wake of the railway revolution of the 19th century will extend Russian continental hegemony over the Eurasian landmass and littoral, potentially challenging the dominance of the oceanic empires.[14] Russian Empire's spectacular territorial expansion in Eurasia beginning with its annexing of much of Trans-Caucasia from Iran's Qajar rulers in the Treaty of Turkmenchay (1828) and into Khanates of Turkestan in Central Asia during the second half of the 19th century alarmed Britain. Following the success of their Mediterranean campaign of 1798, the British negotiated the first of a series of agreements with the local rulers along the Persian Gulf and during the course of the 19th century, the entire coastal route to India had assumed the form of a virtual British protectorate.[15] However, Iran and Afghanistan were allowed to maintain their nominal sovereignty as a buffer against Russian expansionism.

As a result of Anglo–Russian rivalry, Iran's plans for development of railways, arguably the great benchmark of 19th-century economic progress, were stalled except for short sections extending from the Russian frontier in the north and British frontier in the south-east which were obviously constructed with British and Russian commercial and strategic

---

[12]Okunev, I. (2019, July 19). West/Non-West: Funhouse mirror of world politics. *Russian International Affairs Council.* https://russiancouncil.ru/en/analytics-and-comments/analytics/west-non-west-funhouse-mirror-of-world-politics/.

[13]Reid, P. (2022, June). Mahan and Mackinder: Addressing the false dichotomy in the Eurasian pivot theory. *MP-IDSA Occasional Paper* No. 59, 30. https://www.idsa.in/system/files/opaper/op-59-mahan-and-mackinder_0.pdf.

[14]*Ibid.*

[15]Fromkin, D. (1980). The great game in Asia. *Foreign Affairs, 58*(4) (Spring), 936–951.

interests in mind.[16] For Russia, its commercial interests in northern Iran benefited from the geographical isolation of the region. Moscow saw overland connectivity to the Gulf coast in terms of strategic exposure to Britain, which had naval supremacy in the Persian Gulf. Britain, for its part, was concerned that a railway extending from Russia to Indian Ocean littoral or for that matter Germany's Berlin–Baghdad Railway will facilitate continental hegemony over the Eurasian littoral threatening its naval primacy.[17] When Reza Khan Pahlavi constructed the 1,392-kilometres long Trans-Iranian Railway in the 1930s, it stretched from the Caspian harbour city of Bandar-e Shah (today Bandar-e Torkaman) and Bandar-e Shahpur (today Bandar-e Emam Khomeyni) in Khuzestan province near Iraq border rather than ports of Bandar Abbas or Chabahar on the southern coast of Iran. These two terminals were selected for their location being as far as possible from Russian and British territories, respectively.[18]

It was against the backdrop of the Iran–Iraq War (1980–1988), which saw targeting of civilian shipping and oil tankers plying the Persian Gulf and exposed Iran's vulnerability in relying on seaports in the vicinity of Iraq, that Iranian policymakers took note of both strategic and geoeconomic potentials of the Chabahar port.[19] Also, towards the late 1990s, Iran found convergence with Russia and India in developing north-south connectivity between Central Eurasia and Indian Ocean via Iranian territory. Following the collapse of the Soviet Union and the emergence of independent landlocked states in Central Asia and the Caucasus, United States and European Union had pursued a zero-sum approach to connectivity between Europe and Asia. As they sought to consolidate independence of these fledgling smaller republics in Russia's immediate backyard and promote Western orientation in their economy and thus foreign policy, their flagship east-west connectivity project Transport Corridor Europe-Caucasus-Asia (TRACECA) bypassed Russia and side-lined Iran.[20]

---

[16]Lemańczyk, S. (2013, March). The Transiranian railway — History, context and consequences. *Middle Eastern Studies, 49*(2), 238.

[17]Reid (2022). *Op. cit.*

[18]Lemańczyk (2013). *Op. cit.*, 239.

[19]https://www.nonproliferation.org/wp-content/uploads/npr/81ali.pdf; Pant, H. V. & Mehta, K. (2018). India in Chabahar. *Asian Survey, 58*(4), 665.

[20]Abilov, S. & Hajiyev, B. (2021). The European Union–Azerbaijan high-level transport dialogue: A timely reaction to the structural changes? *Journal of Eurasian Studies, 13*(1), 37.

Russia, after realising that the Yeltsin-era attempts at liberalising Russia's economy and seeking integration into the West had not borne desired fruits, made renewed efforts to strengthen ties with its traditional partners in the East including India.[21] For India, ties with Central Asia in the decade since the collapse of the Soviet Union had suffered considerably.[22] It therefore signed on to the idea of north-south connectivity with Russia and Central Asia and via Iran.[23] Further, multilateral efforts led by two leading non-Western powers that is Russia and India to implement a transcontinental land-sea transport corridor also fit well within their vision of a multipolar world in the 21st century and appealed to Iran.

By the end of the first decade of the 21st century however, it was the rivalry between China and India that would revive the geopolitical importance of Chabahar. David Brewster notes that historically, two geographical constraints of the Indian Ocean, namely the absence of connection between the interior of the Eurasian continent and Indian Ocean littoral through navigable rivers, and that the access to the ocean is through a few narrow entry-exit points, have contributed to the domination of this ocean by a succession of extra-regional maritime powers.[24] This unique geography drives competition for control over those chokepoints and the sea lanes between them. By corollary, these two geographic factors have also had the effect of virtually excluding Eurasian land powers such as China and Russia from projecting their naval power in the Indian Ocean. However, since the turn of the century, rising Asian powers China and India in their competitive pursuit of previously untapped markets and resources and to project power have been developing deep-water ports and overland transport corridors as their independent or alternative links between the Eurasian interior and Indian Ocean.[25] For instance, over the last two decades, China has developed a substantial portfolio of

---

[21] Rudnitsky, A. (1999, April–June). Russia and India: In search of a new strategy. *World Affairs: The Journal of International Issues, 3*(2), 83.

[22] *Ibid.*, 82.

[23] Sahakyan, M. D. (2020). Rebuilding interconnections: Russia, India and the international North-South transport corridor. *Asia Global Online.* https://hal.archives-ouvertes.fr/hal-02980041/document.

[24] Brewster, D. (2017). Silk Roads and Strings of Pearls: The strategic geography of China's new pathways in the Indian Ocean. *Geopolitics, 22*(2), 269–291.

[25] Daniels, R. (2013). Strategic competition in South Asia: Gwadar, Chabahar, and the risks of infrastructure development. *American Foreign Policy Interests, 35*, 93–100.

investments in the Indian Ocean littoral. Some are port facilities on which China relies for its maritime trade, while others are oceanic terminals for trade and transport corridors stretching to the Chinese interior.[26] India for its part does not see Chinese infrastructure development in purely geoeconomic terms but aimed at strategic encirclement of India. At the same time, it sees Chabahar as crucial to developing its independent access to Afghanistan and Central Asia bypassing Pakistan. The new-found strategic and geoeconomic significance of Chabahar is therefore attributed to its geographical location outside the chokepoint of the Strait of Hormuz and as a suitable gateway connecting the Eurasian interior to the Indian Ocean.

Iranian leadership for their part has been determined to tap into the unrealised geoeconomic and geopolitical potential of the Makran coast and the Gulf of Oman. Supreme Leader Ayatollah Ali Khamenei, who sets the general direction for Iran's security and development policies, gave his own dictum on the geoeconomic and strategic potential of Makran and the Gulf of Oman. He described the Makran coast as an 'undiscovered treasure', as he acknowledged that Iran had focused all of its attention on the Persian Gulf and ignored 'our enormous wealth in the Sea of Oman'. The Sea of Oman, he noted, was 'the backbone of the Persian Gulf and determines its fate.'[27] The Special Plan for Development of Makran Region was finally approved in December 2016. It identified Makran as a 'developing region', ideal for becoming a commercial hub in southern Iran.[28]

First Phase: Iran and Iran Develop Hinterland Connectivity to Afghanistan

The New Delhi Declaration made during Iranian President Mohammed Khatami's visit to India in January 2003 noted that the two countries' growing strategic convergence in Afghanistan and the wider region needs to be underpinned with a strong economic relationship. They also agreed

---

[26]Brewster, D. (2016, May 31). Chabahar: India's new move in the great Indian Ocean port race. *The Interpreter.* https://www.lowyinstitute.org/the-interpreter/chabahar-india-s-new-move-great-indian-ocean-port-race.

[27]Jalili, S. (2017, May 31). Iran Makran coast strategic plan gets underway. *Financial Tribune.* https://financialtribune.com/articles/economy-domestic-economy/65718/iran-makran-coast-strategic-plan-gets-underway.

[28]*Ibid.*

Chabahar: Geoeconomic Hopes and Geopolitical Games   127

to broad-base their cooperation in the oil and gas sector, boost non-oil trade, and jointly develop Chabahar port complex and free trade zone.[29] It also referenced a trilateral agreement between governments of India, Iran, and Afghanistan to develop the Chahbahar route through Milak on the Iran–Afghanistan border in Sistan and Balochistan province to Zaranj and Delaram in Afghanistan's Nimruz province. The route would facilitate regional trade and transit, including India's access to Afghanistan and Central Asia bypassing Pakistan. Pakistan on the one hand impedes India's overland transit to Eurasia, and on the other, it has maintained near monopoly over transit routes to landlocked Afghanistan. India realised that transport and transit cooperation with Iran can significantly diminish both these leverages wielded by Pakistan against India and support independent state-building in Afghanistan, an outcome favoured by both Iran and India. Both India and Iran hoped that the Chabahar route would provide alternative access to the Karachi–Kandahar Road until then Afghanistan's only current roadway to international markets.[30] In doing so they would also deny Pakistan the ability to use this dependence as leverage to pressurise the Afghan government.[31] Tehran's twin objective was to ensure the security of its more than 900-kilometres border with Afghanistan while utilising it to promote Iran's regional trade with Central Asia and beyond. The envisaged Chabahar route connects Iran to Afghanistan at two border points: one at Milak crossing which facilitates access to Zaranj–Delaram Highway and another at Khorasan province's Dogharoun crossing providing access to Herat.

Mohsen Milani notes that 'one of the main objectives of Iran is to create an "economic sphere of influence" in Afghanistan, with the ultimate goal of becoming the hub for the transit of goods and services between the Persian Gulf, Afghanistan, Central Asia, China, and India.'[32] Iran was one of the largest donors at the 2002 Tokyo International Conference on Reconstruction Assistance to Afghanistan. It dedicated bulk of its assistance to building infrastructure including new border crossings and roads in western Afghanistan, which shares strong historic

---

[29] Ministry of External Affairs of India. (2003). *Op. cit.*

[30] Milani, M. M. (2006). Iran's policy towards Afghanistan. *Middle East Journal, 60*(2), 252.

[31] Srivastava, D. P. (2022, August 18). India-Iran ties: A former ambassador writes. *ICWA Guest Column.* https://www.icwa.in/show_content.php?lang=1&level=1&ls_id=7780&lid=5187.

[32] Milani (2006). *Op. cit.*, 251.

and cultural ties with Iran.[33] In 2005, Iran opened the 122 kilometres Dogharoun–Herat Highway, a US$60 million project built by Khatam-al Anbiya, the construction arm of the Islamic Revolutionary Guard Corps (IRGC). Over the years it will become one of the major import-export gateways to Afghanistan. Dogharoun Special Economic Zone located at the zero point of Iran–Afghanistan border has emerged as a key hub for trade with Afghanistan and also to Central Asian countries.[34] Iran announced its biggest project in Afghanistan in 2007, allocating US$75 million for constructing railway line from Khaf in north-eastern Iran to Herat. Khaf–Herat railway project was part of the trilateral agreement between Iran, Afghanistan, and India to develop the Chabahar route and also the larger East-West Five Nations Railway Corridor between China and Europe.[35] In December 2020, Tehran inaugurated a 140-kilometres section from Khaf to Ghoryan in western Afghanistan, while the last section from Ghoryan to Herat, financed by Italy, was 80% complete.[36]

In 2009, India completed the construction of the 215-kilometres long Zaranj–Delaram Road at the cost of US$150 million.[37] This strategic highway feeds into the 2,200 kilometres two-lane metalled highway called the 'garland road' connecting the major cities of Afghanistan. India also upgraded the road from Zaranj to Chabahar. When India was offered participation in the development of Chabahar port during President Khatami's visit to India in 2003, the work was assigned to a private sector company, which formed a joint venture with Indian Railway Construction Limited (IRCON).[38] However, soon after, transparency concerns about Iran's civilian nuclear program and imposition of international economic sanctions stalled any serious discussion between India and Iran regarding Chabahar port.

Chabahar was brought back to government track negotiations by 2011.[39] In August 2012, on the sidelines of the Non-Aligned Movement

---

[33] Bizaer, M. (2021, January 4). Iran's railway ambitions go beyond Afghanistan. *Atlantic Council.* https://www.atlanticcouncil.org/blogs/iransource/irans-railway-ambitions-go-beyond-afghanistan/.

[34] Dogharoon Special Economic Zone. https://dogharoon.ir/home-2/.

[35] *Ibid.*

[36] *Ibid.*

[37] Pandey, A. (2013, July 26). India ponders future role in Afghanistan. *Voice of America.* https://www.voanews.com/a/india-ponders-future-role-in-afghanistan/1710748.html.

[38] Srivastava (2022). *Op. cit.*

[39] *Ibid.*

Summit in Tehran, which was attended by then Indian Prime Minister Manmohan Singh, a trilateral meeting of India, Iran, and Afghanistan at the level of Deputy Foreign Ministers or Foreign Secretaries was held on Iran's initiative. One of the key agendas was to look into the report by the Indian Ports Association (IPA) on various commercial activities which could be taken up through the port.[40] Iran saw Chabahar as a lifeline that helps it break through US-sponsored isolation.[41] At the same time, it hoped that cooperation with India on Chabahar will lead New Delhi to support Iran in countering the US policy of containment of Iran. The United States for its part has tolerated India's involvement in developing Chabahar as part of a trade and transit to Afghanistan, especially as it expected India to play a role in the US New Silk Road initiative of supporting continental corridors linking Afghanistan with neighbouring Central Asia, India, and Pakistan, a region it dubbed as 'Greater Central Asia'.[42] But it was only after the Rouhani administration reached an interim nuclear agreement with six major powers in 2013 that negotiations on Chabahar between India and Iran picked up momentum. The MOU for India's participation in Chabahar port was signed by then Minister for Shipping Nitin Gadkari on May 6, 2015.[43]

Second Phase: From Cooperation with India to Playing off India and China

During Indian Prime Minister Modi's visit to Tehran in May 2016, leaders of India, Iran, and Afghanistan signed the Trilateral Agreement on the establishment of an International Transit and Transport Corridor, also called the Chabahar Agreement.[44] Under the agreement, India committed

---

[40] *The Times of India*. (2012, August 25). India-Iran-Afghanistan trilateral meeting to be held in Tehran, trade tops agenda. https://timesofindia.indiatimes.com/india/india-iran-afghanistan-trilateral-meeting-to-be-held-in-tehran-trade-tops-agenda/articleshow/15692480.cms.

[41] Daniels (2013). *Op. cit.*

[42] The Jamestown Foundation. (2011, November 14). Central Asia, Afghanistan and the New Silk Road: Political, Economic and Security Challenges. https://jamestown.org/wp-content/uploads/2011/11/Afghan_Silk_Road_conf_report_-_FULL.pdf.

[43] Srivastava (2022). *Op. cit.*

[44] Agreement on the Establishment of an International Transport and Transit Corridor among the Governments of the Republic of India, Islamic Republic of Afghanistan, and Islamic Republic of Iran. https://www.mea.gov.in/Portal/LegalTreatiesDoc/016P2941.pdf.

to invest US$500 million in Phase-1 including US$150 million line of credit by India's Exim Bank to Iran's Maritime and Ports Organisation for making jetties and berths at Chabahar and a capital investment of US$85.21 million by India Ports Global Private Limited (IPGPL), a joint venture between the Jawaharlal Nehru Port Trust and the Kandla Port Trust, as part of a deal with an Iranian company to equip and operate two container and multipurpose terminals at the Shahid Beheshti–Chabahar Port Phase-1.[45] While an annual revenue expenditure of US$22.95 million will start when India takes over Shahid Baheshti on a 10-year lease. Also, Indian Railway Construction Limited (IRCON) signed a MoU with Iran's Construction, Development of Transport Infrastructure Company (CDTIC) to provide requisite services for the construction of the Chabahar–Zahedan railway line as part of the transit and transportation corridor.[46]

In October 2017, less than two months after the US Strategy on Afghanistan and South Asia had called on India to play a bigger role in stabilising Afghanistan, India sent a shipment of wheat assistance for Afghanistan through Chabahar, marking the operationalisation of the port.[47] The shipment was seen as the US nod of approval for India's engagement in Chabahar and demonstrated that the port is a viable and secure alternative for promoting regional connectivity among India, Iran, and Afghanistan.[48] In December 2017, Iranian President Hassan Rouhani

---

[45] *Hindustan Times*. (2016, May 24). India, Iran and Afghanistan sign Chabahar port agreement. https://www.hindustantimes.com/india/india-iran-afghanistan-sign-chabahar-port-agreement/story-2EytbKZeo6zeCIpR8WSuAO.html.

[46] Press Information Bureau. Chabahar Port. https://pib.gov.in/PressReleasePage.aspx?PRID=1558480.

[47] Roche, E. India sends 1st wheat shipment to Afghanistan via Chabahar port. *Mint*. https://www.livemint.com/Politics/lxmYQHtlukr2FFkYG3ZqoI/Indias-first-wheat-shipment-leaves-Irans-Chabahar-port-for.html; Trump White House. (2017, August 21). Remarks by President Trump on the strategy in Afghanistan and South Asia. https://trumpwhitehouse.archives.gov/briefings-statements/remarks-president-trump-strategy-afghanistan-south-asia/.

[48] Kapoor, S. (2018, January). A shadow over Chabahar's fate. *Observer Research Foundation*. https://www.orfonline.org/wp-content/uploads/2018/01/ORF_SpecialReport_55_Chabahar.pdf; Ministry of External Affairs. (2018, January 3). Question No.2723 Development Of Chabahar Port. https://www.mea.gov.in/lok-sabha.htm?dtl/29311/question+no2723+development+of+chabahar+port.

inaugurated the newly extended berth under the first phase of Chabahar.[49] In the same month, Chinese Foreign Minister Wang Yi hosted the first trilateral meeting between the foreign ministers of China, Pakistan, and Afghanistan, where he proposed to extend the China–Pakistan Economic Corridor (CPEC) to Afghanistan.[50] The timing of Beijing's proposal underscored longstanding China–Pakistan strategy to gain influence over Afghanistan's mineral resources and transit routes. Yet, Wang Yi framed his proposal within the Belt and Road Initiative (BRI) narrative of promoting regional connectivity cooperation as he said that 'China hoped the economic corridor (CPEC) could benefit the whole region and act as an impetus for development.'[51] The alignment between China and Pakistan in Afghanistan also stems from their shared perception of Chabahar as part of India's efforts to create a rival connectivity network sidestepping Pakistan and counter-balance the CPEC.[52] Further, Beijing by talking up about the extension of the CPEC to Afghanistan hoped to mend the strained ties between Kabul and Islamabad over the latter's support for Taliban so that they could better tackle the spread of Islamic militancy from Af-Pak region to China's Western province of Xinjiang.

In December 2018, just before the snapback of the US sanctions, India took over the operations of a part of Shahid Beheshti Port.[53] Subsequently, New Delhi was able to negotiate limited sanctions exemptions for the Chabahar port and the associated railway line. The two projects were key to India's direct connectivity with Afghanistan, especially as the Trump administration's Afghan policy called on India to play an active role in stabilising the country. But despite India earmarking US$85 million for procuring equipment, it faced challenges in attracting

---

[49] *Tehran Times*. (2017, December 3). Strategic Chabahar port development plan inaugurated. https://www.tehrantimes.com/news/419011/Strategic-Chabahar-port-development-plan-inaugurated.

[50] Blachard, B. (2017, December 26). China, Pakistan to look at including Afghanistan in $57 billion economic corridor. *Reuters*. https://www.reuters.com/article/china-pakistan-afghanistan-idINKBN1EK0EQ/.

[51] *Ibid.*

[52] *The Dawn*. (2017, June 26). India's expanding trade ties a strategy to counter balance CPEC: Chinese daily. https://www.dawn.com/news/1341911.

[53] Press Information Bureau. (2019, January 7). India takes over operations of part of Chabahar Port in Iran. https://pib.gov.in/Pressreleaseshare.aspx?PRID=1558896.

132   D. Saraswat

international bidders, which delayed the full-scale operation of the port.[54] In 2020, India had to cancel a US$30-million contract with Shanghai Zhenhua Heavy Industries for heavy cranes because of delays by the Chinese company in supplying the equipment ordered in 2017. In January 2021, Italian firm Italgru S.r.l. supplied first consignment of heavy equipment, including two 140-tonne mobile harbour cranes first from the US$25 million contract for six such cranes.[55] The second consignment of heavy equipment, including two 100-tonne mobile cranes, was delivered two months later in March.

A major challenge for India–Iran cooperation in Chabahar came in July 2020; when citing delays from the Indian side, Iran decided to go alone in developing the Chabahar–Zahedan railway line. Washington had given limited sanction exemptions on the condition that Iran's IRGC, which had been put on the US State Department list of Foreign Terrorist Organizations in April 2019, does not participate in the port project.[56] As a result of Tehran's insistence that Khatam-al Anbiya Construction Headquarters be entrusted with the civil work, New Delhi became circumspect about its role in the construction of the strategic railway line.[57] India's exit from the project raised alarm in India, especially as the news coincided with reports that Iran and China were negotiating a 25-year comprehensive strategic cooperation agreement. Earlier, Iranian Foreign Minister Javad Zarif, during a visit to Pakistan, had proposed to connect Chabahar with the Gwadar Port, in effect linking with the CPEC, the 'flagship project' of BRI.[58] Given India's principled opposition to the

---

[54]Laskar, R. H. (2020, February 4). Chabahar port plan gets big boost as govt hikes outlay. *Hindustan Times.* https://www.hindustantimes.com/india-news/chabahar-port-plan-gets-big-boost-as-govt-hikes-outlay/story-sZLStXRyccJzzHiFiQ3UuO.html.

[55]Laskar, R. H. (2021, March 23). India delivers second batch of heavy equipment to Chabahar port. *Hindustan Times.* https://www.hindustantimes.com/india-news/india-delivers-second-batch-of-heavy-equipment-to-chabahar-port-101616493174886.html.

[56]Jha, L. K. (2019, December 19). US grants India 'narrow exemption' from sanctions to continue Chabahar port development in Iran. *The Print.* https://theprint.in/diplomacy/us-grants-india-narrow-exemption-from-sanctions-to-continue-chabahar-port-development-in-iran/337733/.

[57]Mohan, G. (2021, July 21). Real reason why India sits out of Iran's Chabahar-Zahedan rail link project. *India Today.* https://www.indiatoday.in/india/story/iran-chabahar-zahedan-rail-link-project-india-1702928-2020-07-21.

[58]Bhaumik, A. (2019, May 28). Iran goes to Pakistan with Chabahar link plan. *Deccan Herald.* https://www.deccanherald.com/national/iran-goes-to-pakistan-with-chabahar-link-plan-736492.html.

CPEC, which runs through Gilgit-Baltistan in Pakistan-occupied Kashmir violating Indian sovereignty, Tehran's proposal was widely seen as a response to India's compliance with the US sanctions by stopping crude imports from Iran. Further, Iranian proposal ran counter to India's strategic objectives of countering China's strategic investment in Gwadar and the expanding Chinese influence across the African and Asian shores of the Indian Ocean.[59] Iran's growing strategic convergence with China and Russia was also on display in their trilateral naval exercise 'Maritime Security Belt' in the Gulf of Oman in December 2019. Coming amid rising Iran–US tensions and close on the heels of the US-led maritime coalition's Operation Sentinel sending warships to escort Gulf shipping, the trilateral exercise underscored China and Russia's stakeholdership in ensuring security in the crucial waterway and their diplomatic-political support of Iran.[60] Nevertheless, Iran's Port and Maritime Organisation (PMO) sought India's cooperation in procuring the equipment to run the railway line and activate the US$150 credit line to pay for equipment procurement, which had been promised by New Delhi during President Rouhani's visit to India in 2018.[61]

Against the backdrop of the electoral defeat of the incumbent US President Donald Trump by Joe Biden, who was keen to re-engage Iran on the nuclear issue, India and Iran intensified their diplomatic outreach to Central Asian countries, especially Uzbekistan to participate in Chabahar and the INSTC.[62] Soon after a virtual summit was held between Indian

---

[59]Grare, F. (2018, July 31). Along the road: Gwadar and China's power projection. European Union Institute for Security Studies. https://carnegieendowment.org/2018/07/31/along-road-gwadar-and-china-s-power-projection-pub-77217.

[60]Al-Jazeera. (2019, November 7). US-led coalition launches operation to protect Gulf waters. https://www.aljazeera.com/news/2019/11/7/us-led-coalition-launches-operati; Saraswat, D. (2022, July 7). Iran's ties with China: Synergising geoconomic strategies. *Arab Center for Research and Policy Studies*. https://www.dohainstitute.org/en/Lists/ACRPS-PDFDocumentLibrary/iran-ties-with-china-synergising-geoconomic-strategies.pdf.

[61]Haidar, S. (2021, November 7). Months after starting Chabahar rail project without India, Iran seeks equipment. *The Hindu*. https://www.thehindu.com/news/national/months-after-starting-chabahar-rail-project-without-india-iran-requests-help-with-equipment/article33048813.ece.

[62]Press Information Bureau. (2020, December 14). First trilateral working group meeting between India, Iran and Uzbekistan on joint use of Chabahar Port. https://www.mea.gov.in/press-releases.htm?dtl/33295/First+Trilateral+Working+Group+Meeting+between+India+Iran+and+Uzbekistan+on+joint+use+of+Chabahar+Port.

Prime Minister Narendra Modi and President of Uzbekistan Shavkat Mirziyoyev on December 11, 2020, India, Iran, and Uzbekistan had their first Trilateral Working Group Meeting on the joint use of Chabahar Port.[63] Uzbekistan is a doubly landlocked country, which has the distinction of sharing borders with Afghanistan and all other Central Asian countries. As a result, Uzbekistan is key to Iran and India's plans for Central Asian states to use the Chabahar route. Further, Uzbekistan built a 75-kilometre railway line between the northern Afghan city of Mazar-i-Sharif and Hairatan town at the Uzbek-Afghan border in 2011, with US$1.5 billion in finances from Asian Development Bank.[64] In December 2017, Mirziyoyev signed an agreement with then Afghan President Ashraf Ghani, to build a route from Mazar-i-Sharif to Herat in the west, which will be connected with the 628-kilometres Chabahar–Zahedan rail track along the Iran–Afghanistan border.[65]

Following Taliban's return to power in Afghanistan in August 2021, India closed its embassy in Kabul and consulates in Kandahar and Mazar-i-Sharif. The uncertainty surrounding the future of India's development cooperation with Afghanistan also raised a question mark on Chabahar's utility in facilitating India's access to Afghanistan. However, amidst worsening humanitarian conditions in Afghanistan, India has continued to use Chabahar to send wheat and humanitarian assistance to Afghanistan in partnership with the UN World Food Programme.[66] More importantly, India recalibrated its approach to Chabahar by pushing to link it with an eastern branch of the INSTC. The Iranian section of the branch runs from Chabahar to Sarakhs on the Iran–Turkmenistan border. At the 3rd meeting of the India–Central Asia Dialogue at the level of foreign ministers, organised virtually in December 2021, participants emphasised on optimum usage of the INSTC as well as Ashgabat Agreement to

---

[63] *Ibid.*

[64] Wani, A. (2020, December 14). The potential for transformative India-Uzbekistan bilateral relations. *Observer Research Foundation.* https://www.orfonline.org/expert-speak/the-potential-for-transformative-india-uzbekistan-bilateral-relations/.

[65] Eurasianet. (2023, May 15). Uzbekistan hosts HQ for trans-Afghan train project. https://eurasianet.org/uzbekistan-hosts-hq-for-trans-afghan-train-project.

[66] Kapparath, M. (2023, June 13). India sends food aid to Afghanistan on humanitarian grounds, upon Taliban's request. *Forbes India.* https://www.forbesindia.com/article/news/india-sends-food-aid-to-afghanistan-on-humanitarian-grounds-upon-talibans-request/85659/1.

enhance connectivity between India and the Central Asian countries and welcomed India's proposal to include Chabahar Port within the framework of INSTC.[67] As Central Asian countries seek to deepen economic cooperation with India, a sea-based trading route through Chabahar becomes important. However, Iran did its recalibration *vis-à-vis* Chabahar in the light of the changes in Afghanistan and prioritisation of its Look East policy with the onset of the hardliner presidency of Ebrahim Raisi. Chabahar was now considered integral to the Eastern engagement policy prioritising trade and economic ties with eastern powers, especially China, and Russia and Iran's neighbourhood in Asia.[68]

Third Phase: Chabahar as 'Symbol of Cooperation' among SCO Members

After Iran's application for full membership of the Shanghai Cooperation Organization was approved at the 21st Council of the Head of the State meeting in Tajikistan in September 2021, Iranian leaders laid great emphasis on the associate economic dimension in terms of pushing for de-dollarisation of trade, alternate banking, and financial arrangements that will help collectively counter Western economic sanctions.[69] Mohsen Rezaei, Vice President for Economic Affairs, hailed Iran's membership as 'an important step to turn Iran into an economic corridor between East and West and North and South Eurasia.'[70] Iran's new geoeconomic vision for Chabahar Port was offered by President Ebrahim Raisi in his maiden speech at the SCO.[71] Raisi projected Iran as the link between major infrastructure projects in Eurasia, namely the INSTC and the BRI. Notably, he

---

[67] Ministry of External Affairs. (2021, December 19). Joint statement of the 3rd meeting of the India-Central Asia dialogue. https://www.mea.gov.in/bilateral-documents.htm?dtl/34705/Joint_Statement_of_the_3rd_meeting_of_the_IndiaCentral_Asia_Dialogue.

[68] Aliasgary, S. & Ekstrom, M. (2021, October 21). Chabahar Port and Iran's strategic balancing with China and India. *The Diplomat.* https://thediplomat.com/2021/10/chabahar-port-and-irans-strategic-balancing-with-china-and-india/.

[69] Khajehopour, B. (2023, March 8). Will transit become Iran's new top revenue generator? *Amwaj Media.* https://amwaj.media/article/will-transit-become-iran-s-new-top-revenue-generator.

[70] http://www.news.cn/english/2021-09/19/c_1310198050.htm.

[71] Islamic Republic of Iran Ministry of Foreign Affairs. (2021, September 17). President Raisi addressing 21st SCO Summit. https://en.mfa.ir/portal/NewsView/652104/President-

136 D. Saraswat

did so within a broader vision of development-oriented connectivity and a vision of networked, cooperative regional order:

> Peace and development are achieved through the cooperation and coordination of key countries in the region. In this direction, the formation and strengthening of infrastructure bonds between different countries is important and necessary. The One Belt-One Road Initiative, the Eurasian Economic Union and the North-South Corridor, as key projects in the field of infrastructural links, can play a role in strengthening the common interests of developing countries and strengthening peace in the region. These projects are not competitors, but complement each other. Iran is the link between the above three infrastructure projects.[72]

As Raisi sought to put Iran above the geopolitical fray, he also rebranded Chabahar. He argued that 'Chabahar has the capacity to become an exchange centre for several member and neighbouring countries in a special way, which with the efforts of members can be a symbol of cooperation of all members of the Shanghai Organisation.' Iran's key objective is to avoid getting caught up in the zero-sum geopolitical rivalries between major Eurasian actors, that is, China, India, and Russia. As much as Iran has been public about its frustration with India over slow pace of progress in Chabahar, it is also aware of the asymmetric nature of its economic and trade ties with China. Arguably, Iran seems to be falling back on its time-tested, but risky strategy of playing off rival major powers against each other to garner benefits for Iran. Iran could threaten to side more closely with one country if it doesn't gain greater concessions from the other.[73] Tehran also seeks to leverage the extant multipolar dynamics in Eurasia to enhance its own interests and status, while promoting a horizontal, de-centred, multipolar order in Asia conducive to Iran's long-term interests.

In August 2022, India's Minister of Ports, Shipping and Waterways Sarbananda Sonowal visited Chabahar and handed over six mobile harbour cranes to Indian Ports Global. He also had a meeting with Ali Akbar Safaee, Deputy Minister and Managing Director of Iran's Ports and Maritime Organisation, where they discussed the possibilities of unlocking

---

Raisi-addressing-21st-SCO-SummitSCO-can-turn-into-a-driving-force-for-global-multilateralism.

[72] *Ibid.*

[73] Aliasgary & Ekstrom (2021). *Op. cit.*

trade potential between Central Asian countries with South Asia, Southeast Asia, and even countries from the Far East like Japan and Korea.[74] Subsequently, Sonowal visited the UAE, where he held meeting with heads of shipping and freight companies. Later reports emerged that the Chabahar port operator IPGL is considering partnership with an entity based in Abu Dhabi, Dubai, or Sharjah, which would procure the equipment and facilitate their transfer to Chabahar.[75]

In parallel developments, China opened its first consulate in Bandar Abbas in December 2022. The choice of the location suggested that under the 25-year cooperation agreement with Iran, Beijing was considering a bigger role in the region that is home to Iran's biggest seaports and trading hubs, such as the islands of Kish and Qeshm, and Jask and Chabahar in the Gulf of Oman.[76] A month later in January 2023, China established its first direct shipping line to Chabahar after one of its container ships docked there.[77] In the same month, reports emerged that Iran's Valfajr Shipping Company had been operating regular container shipping lines from Chabahar to various ports of India, completing a total of 15 trips in the past three months.[78] Earlier, in May 2022, Iran's PMO had launched three direct container shipping lines from Chabahar Port to Nhava Sheva and Kandla ports in India and the Jebel Ali Port in the UAE. These

---

[74] *The Times of India.* (2022, August 20). Union minister Sonowal reviews development work at India-operated Chabahar port in Iran. https://timesofindia.indiatimes.com/india/union-minister-sonowal-reviews-development-work-at-india-operated-chabahar-port/articleshow/93683208.cms.

[75] *Construction World.* (2023, October 24). IPGL consider Gulf entities for equipment procurement for Chabahar Port. https://www.constructionworld.in/transport-infrastructure/ports-and-shipping/ipgl-consider-gulf-entities-for-equipment-procurement-for-chabahar-port/46031.

[76] Zhou, L. (2023, August 30). China's new consul general Xu Wei arrives in oil route hub Bandar Abbas as Beijing and Tehran strengthen ties. *South China Morning Post.* https://www.scmp.com/news/china/diplomacy/article/3232714/chinese-envoy-arrives-oil-route-hub-bandar-abbas-beijing-and-tehran-strengthen-ties.

[77] Statecraft Staff. (2023, January 2). China establishes first direct shipping Line to Iran's Chabahar Port. https://www.statecraft.co.in/article/china-establishes-first-direct-shipping-line-to-iran-s-chabahar-port.

[78] Sidharth, R. (2023, January 23). Chabahar takes up sea trade and between India and Iran up a notch with regular container shipping lines. *Logisticsinsider.* https://www.logisticsinsider.in/chabahar-takes-up-sea-trade-between-india-and-iran-up-a-notch-with-regular-container-shipping-lines/.

developments show that Iran after all is on the path to realize its vision of Chabahar as a deep-water port, which will not only save time and costs for goods headed to Iranian and Central Asian markets but also address Iran's dependence on the ports of its Arab neighbours on the southern side of the Persian Gulf. Iran's southern ports can only accommodate 100,000 Ton ships, meaning any ship above that capacity carrying goods for Iran has to dock in UAE ports such as Fujairah and Jabal Ali, whereupon their cargo is loaded onto smaller ships and brought to Iran.[79]

On future involvement of Afghanistan in Chabahar, experts have pointed out that Iran and Uzbekistan, which are neighbours of Afghanistan and have maintained their economic ties and political relations with the Taliban, have played a key role in maintaining the Chabahar Port Transit Project through Afghanistan.[80] But even Iranian and Uzbekistani ties with Taliban are on shaky grounds, as they have differences with the Taliban; in the past, they have also supported anti-Taliban forces in Afghanistan.[81] Further, Afghanistan and Uzbekistan have depended on each other for trade, transport, and connectivity to Central Asia and South Asia, respectively. Even after Taliban takeover, Tashkent has continued to support the idea of Trans-Afghan railway connecting Uzbekistan's and Pakistan's railway networks through Afghanistan. In July 2023, these three countries signed a tripartite agreement in Islamabad agreeing on a route and conducting feasibility studies to be shared with international financial institutions.[82]

However, there has been an uptick in interest in Chabahar from Central Asian countries following Russia's invasion of Ukraine and

---

[79] The Diplomat. (2010, July 09). Iran's Weakness? Its Ports. https://thediplomat.com/2010/07/irans-weakness-its-ports/.

[80] Kaleji, V. (2022, April 18). With Russian route blocked, Uzbekistan looks to Indian-Iranian-Afghan Chabahar Port project. *The Jamestown Foundation.* https://jamestown.org/program/with-russian-route-blocked-uzbekistan-looks-to-indian-iranian-afghan-chabahar-port-project/.

[81] Pannier, B. (2023, February 22). PANNIER: Uzbekistan's relations with Taliban start to fray. *Intellinews.* https://www.intellinews.com/pannier-uzbekistan-s-relations-with-taliban-start-to-fray-270778/.

[82] Ariana News. (2023, July 15). Afghanistan, Pakistan, Uzbekistan agree on route of trans-Afghan railway project. https://www.ariananews.af/afghanistan-pakistan-uzbekistan-agree-on-route-of-trans-afghan-railway-project/.

Chabahar: Geoeconomic Hopes and Geopolitical Games 139

comprehensive Western sanctions against Russia disrupted east-west transit corridor traversing Russian territory. The Northern Corridor (China–Kazakhstan–Russia–Belarus–Poland–Germany), which has been the primary artery of China–EU rail trade, is now considered a risky proposition. As a result, Central Asian states are increasingly turning to Iran to either protect or enhance their transit role by diversifying transport routes via Iran, whose overland transit networks offer connections to Turkey and Europe as well as to Iranian ports on the Persian Gulf and the Gulf of Oman.[83] In June 2023, Shavkat Mirziyoyev became the first Uzbek president to visit Iran in over 20 years. A key item on the bilateral agenda was to advance transit and transport cooperation. Iran's Supreme Leader in his meeting with Mirziyoyev noted that 'Iran has the capability to conveniently connect Uzbekistan to international waters through Turkmenistan and Afghanistan, while the fields of cooperation are beyond trade and transportation and can be achieved through various initiatives in the field of science and technology.'[84] Also, Russia, which now has a burgeoning trade with India, has stakes in realising the eastern branch of the INSTC connecting eastern and central regions of Russia through Kazakhstan and Turkmenistan to Chabahar. In July 2022, a rail freight from Russia traversed 4,000 kilometres through Kazakhstan and Turkmenistan, entering Iran through Sarakhs on the Iran–Turkmen border and then further 1,600 kilometres to Shaheed Rajaee Port in Bandar Abbas and further to India by sea.[85] Once the Chabahar–Zahedan railway is complete, Chabahar will likely become the key port in the eastern branch of the INSTC. In March 2022, the head of CDTIC, which is responsible for the Zahedan–Chabahar railway project noted that Iran was accelerating the project and that the track-laying operations were being done from both ends of the 628-kilometre line. He noted that since the project started in November 2020, the physical progress of the project was 57% and that Iran was

---

[83] Kaleji (2022). *Op. cit.*; Saraswat, D. (2022, July 19). Iran's Central Asia policy gains momentum amid Russia–Ukraine war. *Manohar Parrikar Institute for Defence Studies and Analyses.* https://www.idsa.in/issuebrief/iran-central-asia-policy-gains-momentum-dsaraswat-190722.

[84] *Tehran Times.* (2023, June 18). Restart for better future. https://www.tehrantimes.com/news/485923/Restart-for-better-future.

[85] *Mehrnews.* (2023, July 4). Iran, Russia, India hold meeting on INSTC. https://en.mehrnews.com/news/202777/Iran-Russia-India-hold-meeting-on-INSTC.

Conclusion

Over the last three decades, Iran has looked at Chabahar as crucial to raising the country's geoeconomic and strategic profile. However, reeling under international or Western sanctions for a better part of the period, Iran has sought to piggyback on the geopolitical designs of others, especially India in Afghanistan and increasingly its alignment with Russia in having a 'sanctions-free' north-south route to India. However, Tehran's dream of turning Chabahar into a 'gateway' connecting Eurasia and the Indian Ocean means that it must rise above the zero-sum geopolitical competition inherent to the connectivity projects spearheaded by great powers. Further, as Tehran sees the US sanctions as more or less a permanent reality and has turned to developing long-term trade and economic ties with China and Russia, but also wider Asia, it is determined to leverage the extant Eurasian connectivity dynamics shaped by the BRI and the INSTC to realise its own transit potential. Nevertheless, Iran remains conscious of the competing visions of Gwadar and Karachi as rival gateway ports to Chabahar. It is therefore safe to assume that India will remain a key actor in the geopolitical games and geoeconomics hopes of Chabahar.

---

[86] *Tehran Times*. (2022, March 4). Zahedan-Chabahar railway to be completed by March 2024. https://www.tehrantimes.com/news/470675/Zahedan-Chabahar-railway-to-be-completed-by-Mar-2024#:~:text=TEHRAN%20%2D%20Head%20of%20Iran%27s%20Construction,(March%2020%2C%202024).

Part III

Regional and External Dynamics

© 2025 World Scientific Publishing Company
https://doi.org/10.1142/9789811294709_0007

Chapter 7

The Strait of Hormuz and Iran's Active Deterrence Strategy

Alam Saleh and Zakiyeh Yazdanshenas

Introduction

Geography matters. Having been invaded several times in the past three centuries from its northern, southern, eastern, and western borders, Iran has learned vital lessons in how to use its geography as a strategic asset, employing geopolitical capabilities against powerful adversaries. The Islamic Republic of Iran has adopted a diverse mix of conventional and unconventional military tactics as deterring measures over the past four decades. Since the 2003 Iraq War, a range of external threats has surrounded Iran, in particular a heavy US military presence. Tehran has sought to ensure that a cost as great as possible will be imposed on adversaries should they invade the country.[1] Tehran's security strategy has combined military and non-military policies, complementing official

---

[1] In a virtual meeting with the cabinet members on 13 August, 2023, Iran's supreme leader, Ali Khamenei, said: 'You see that the enemy is scheming against you. They are constantly plotting against you. ... Well, you should devise schemes against theirs as well. You should not stay passive and silent, nor should you surrender because he is always plotting and we should not surrender in the face of his plots. ... If they intrigue against you — in other words if they conspire and plot against you — you should plot, scheme and intrigue against them as well.'

143

military strength with abundant investment in non-state actors such as Hezbollah in Lebanon and elements of the Iraqi Popular Mobilization Forces,[2] capable of bolstering Iranian interests.

Tehran has spared no effort in exercising ideological influence in the region in an attempt to delegitimise and disable the United States and its allies. By supporting and mobilising non-state armed groups, Tehran has been able to frustrate extra-regional forces and thwart their political objectives across the Middle East. Militarily, Tehran has advanced its capabilities, focusing particularly on missile and drone technologies. Given the country's physical proximity to a host of unstable, belligerent, or unreliable states, Tehran has also attempted to weaponise its geography as a critical component of its security doctrine. The threat of the closure of the Strait of Hormuz[3] is a potent policy option in this respect.

War determined by geography and strategies seeking to exploit geographical features are of course not new in the region or international politics at large. The various straits that line the Middle East and North Africa constitute pertinent examples. Egypt's nationalisation of the Suez Canal led to the Suez Crisis,[4] after which Israel, the United Kingdom, and France invaded the country in 1956.[5] Insecurity in Bab-el-Mandeb, caused

---

[2] On the history of Iran's support for non-state actors, see Ataie, M. Continuity despite revolution: Iran's support for non-state actors. *Middle East Brief*, Brandeis University. https://www.brandeis.edu/crown/publications/middle-east-briefs/pdfs/101-200/meb141. pdf.

[3] On the history of Iran's threat of closing the Strait, see Iddon, P. (2018, December 13). A history of Iranian threats to blockade Gulf oil exports. *The New Arab*. https://www.newarab.com/analysis/history-iranian-threats-close-hormuz-straits.

[4] On July 26, 1956, the Suez Crisis unfolded as an international crisis in the Middle East. It was triggered by the decision of Egyptian President Gamal Abdel Nasser to nationalise the Suez Canal, which was previously owned by the Suez Canal Company and was controlled by French and British interests. The crisis was a direct consequence of the American and British refusal to finance Egypt's construction of the Aswan High Dam due to Egypt's increasing ties with communist Czechoslovakia and the Soviet Union. In response, Nasser declared martial law in the canal zone and took control of the Suez Canal Company. Ultimately, Egypt emerged as the victor, with Nasser becoming a celebrated figure for Arab and Egyptian nationalism. As a result of the Suez Crisis, Britain and France experienced a significant decline in their influence in the Middle East. For more information, see Varble, D. (2008). *The Suez Crisis*. New York: The Rosen Publishing Group.

[5] On Suez Crisis, see Anthony, G. & Lewis, J. (2013). *The Suez Crisis*. Abingdon: Taylor & Francis.

by piracy and unrest led by the Houthis, has raised growing concern over the security of this strategically pivotal strait in the past two decades.[6] Several global and regional powers have sent in their navies to ensure free shipping routes as a response. The Bosporus Strait in Turkey, which has been demilitarised since World War I (1914–1918), was closed during World War II (1939–1945). These straits are critical to the global economy and international security, and their closure or interruption can lead to tangible global crises.

There has been extensive research done to determine whether Iran has the military capability to close the Strait of Hormuz and whether it would be in Tehran's best interests to do so. Considering Iran's acquisition of new asymmetric military capabilities[7] after the 8-year-long Iran–Iraq war (1980–1988), and given Iran's geopolitical dominance over the Strait, some experts like Hadi Ajili[8] take Iran's technical ability to close the Strait for granted.[9] Other scholars like Anthony Cordesman[10] and Peter Pham[11] highlight the undeniable military superiority of the United States and indicate the dire consequences Iran might face were it to close the strait, believing that they would deter Iran from implementing a blockade. Both arguments have valid backing, and the importance of the Strait of Hormuz and its role in Iran's security strategy are undoubted, but the future remains exposed to constant changes in regional power dynamics over the coming decade, so it is too early to identify one argument as having significantly greater weight behind it than the other. This chapter does not analyse Iran's ability to close the strait, nor does it run potential scenarios

---

[6] On Bab-al-Mandab's security situation see Al Ashwal, A. (2021, May 18). Yemen and the curse of geography: Bab-Al-Mandab disputed by great power. *Carnegie Edowment for International Peace (SADA)*. https://carnegieendowment.org/sada/84558.

[7] On Iran's asymmetrical capabilities, see Chubin, S. (2014). Is Iran a military threat? *Survival, 56*(2), 65–88.

[8] Ajili, H. & Rezaee, N. (2020). Iranian military capabilities and possibility of blocking Hormuz Strait by Iran. *Cywilizacja I Polityka.*

[9] For another example see Khan, S. (2010, January 20). Iranian mining of the Strait of Hormuz plausibility and key considerations. *Institute for Near East & Gulf Military Analysis*. http://www.inegma.com/admin/content/file-29122013113155.pdf.

[10] Cordesman, A. (2007, March 26). Iran, oil, and the Strait of Hormuz. *Center for Strategic and International Studies*. https://csis-website-prod.s3.amazonaws.com/s3fs-public/legacy_files/files/media/csis/pubs/070326_iranoil_hormuz.pdf.

[11] Pham, P. (2010). Iran's threat to the Strait of Hormuz: A realist assessment. *American Foreign Policy Interests, 32*(2), 64–74.

of conflict in the case of its closure. Instead, it focuses on how Iran has embedded the geographical significance of the strait into its defence strategy, enabling it to ensure its national security.

The main argument of this chapter revolves around Iran's ability to embed its geographic features including its control over the Strait of Hormuz in its defence-security doctrine. It first provides an overview of the strategic importance of the Strait of Hormuz for Iran and its significance in global energy security. Then it analyses the evolution of Iran's defence doctrine known as 'active deterrence' in light of regional developments. Finally, it explores how Iran effectively utilises the geographical features of the Strait of Hormuz to enhance its active deterrence strategy.

The Geostrategic Importance of the Strait of Hormuz

Persian Gulf countries are collectively the world's largest exporter of fuels, and the Strait of Hormuz — the only waterway leading out of the Persian Gulf — serves as the passage for all tankers transporting oil from its ports. According to current data, 48% of proven oil reserves are located in the Persian Gulf,[12] and seven countries in this sub-complex[13] (Bahrain, Iran, Iraq, Kuwait, Qatar, Saudi Arabia, and the UAE) produce nearly 30% of total crude oil.[14] There are a few alternative passages for transporting Persian Gulf crude oil, such as the Trans-Arabian Pipeline[15] or the

---

[12] Statistical Review of World Energy. (2021), 70th edn. https://www.bp.com/content/dam/bp/business-sites/en/global/corporate/pdfs/energy-economics/statistical-review/bp-stats-review-2021-oil.pdf.

[13] Based on Barry Buzan's regional security complex theory, the Persian Gulf is considered one of sub-complexes of the Middle East regional security complex. He argues that in the post-Cold War era, international conflicts and rivalries should be analysed in the context of sub-regional developments.

[14] Oil and Petroleum Products Explained: Where Our Oil Comes from, U.S. Energy Information Administration (eia) (2022). https://www.eia.gov/energyexplained/oil-and-petroleum-products/where-our-oil-comes-from.php#:~:text=In%202021%2C%20the%20seven%20countries,countries%20are%20not%20the%20same.

[15] The Editors of Encyclopedia Britannica, Trans-Arabian Pipeline (2016, January 28). *Britannica.* https://www.britannica.com/topic/Trans-Arabian-Pipeline.

Goureh–Jask crude oil transfer project,[16] but their export capacity is relatively small compared to that of the shipping route. As such, the Strait of Hormuz is one of the most significant chokepoints in terms of global energy security, which heavily relies on freedom of navigation in the strait.

Iran's coastline is 1,800 kilometres long, including the islands in the Persian Gulf, and also the Gulf of Oman. The Strait of Hormuz, approximately 45 kilometres wide at its narrowest point, connects the Persian Gulf and the Gulf of Oman. Iran controls the strait on the northern coast, and Oman and the UAE control the southern coast. With a length of merely 180 kilometres, it accommodates two shipping lanes for large vessels. Each channel is 3.2 kilometres wide, with a buffer zone of the same width between them. The northern channel is situated within a few dozen kilometres of the Iranian coast.[17]

The Strait of Hormuz has been a potential area of conflict for many decades, facing constant threats of closure by Iran since the Iran–Iraq War in the 1980s. Both Iran and Iraq have targeted tankers in each other's ports without consideration for their impartiality as commercial vessels. This period, referred to as the 'Tanker Wars', witnessed Iran repeatedly accusing Iraq of unfair intervention and threatening to shut down the strait. In April 1988, the strait became a battleground between the US Navy and Iran as part of the Iran–Iraq War. In the 1990s, Iran engaged in tense disputes with the UAE over the control of several small islands near the strait, once again contemplating closure as a strategic move.[18]

The three strategic islands of Abu Musa, Greater Tunb, and Lesser Tunb, located near the primary tanker routes in the Strait of Hormuz, have long been contentious points in relations between Iran and the UAE. Following Britain's withdrawal from the Persian Gulf in the early 1970s, Mohammad Reza Pahlavi claimed control over these islands, establishing

---

[16]Tasnim News Agency. (2021, July 20). New pipeline transfers oil to Iran's SE coast, Hormuz Strait circumvented. https://www.tasnimnews.com/en/news/2021/07/20/2541092/new-pipeline-transfers-oil-to-iran-s-se-coast-hormuz-strait-circumvented#:~:text=The%20pipeline%20starts%20at%20Goureh,system%20in%20late%20June%202020.

[17]Talmadge, C. (2008). Closing time: Assessing the Iranian threat to the Strait of Hormuz. *International Security*, *33*(1), 86.

[18]Sayin, Y. & Kilic, F. (2020). The Strait of Hormuz and Iran's international relations. *Eurasian Research Journal*, *2*(1), 34.

Iranian military presence on their soils. This control grants Iran the abilities to utilise the islands for potential military operations, increase its maritime borders, and make threats of closure or shipping disruption in the strait both tenable and dangerous.[19]

Iran's geographical features have historically acted as a double-edged sword in Iran's foreign policy.[20] On the one hand, they have limited Iran's power projection and involved it in great power competitions not necessarily of its own design, even leading to territorial occupation during the two World Wars. On the other hand, they have periodically served as a means of leverage for advancing Iran's national interests or expanding Iran's influence in the Middle East and beyond. Iran's dominance over the Strait of Hormuz is one of the most pertinent examples of the strategic ambiguity of the country's geography.[21]

As with other Persian Gulf countries, Iran's oil reserves are mainly concentrated in the Persian Gulf itself, and the most vital sea route for oil exports passes through the Strait of Hormuz. Iran's major ports and industrial centres are located along the Persian Gulf coast, making it commercially reliant on unhindered navigation through the strait. Law of the Sea and maritime regulations limit Iran's actions in the strait. The Strait of Hormuz is subject to Article 37 (section 2) of the United Nations Convention on the Law of the Sea (UNCLOS). The Strait of Hormuz also connects the exclusive economic zones of Iran with those of Oman and the UAE in the Gulf of Oman. According to Article 37 of UNCLOS, all ships and aircraft enjoy right of transit passage, and this shall not be impeded unless the criteria mentioned in Articles 39–42 are not met.[22]

---

[19]Cordesman, A. H. (2007, March 26). Iran, oil, and the Strait of Hormuz. *Center for Strategic and International Studies*, Arleigh A. Burke Chair in Strategy. https://www.csis.org/analysis/iran-oil-and-strait-hormuz.

[20]On pros and cons of Iran's geographical features for its foreign policy see Ehteshami, A. (2002). *The Foreign Policy of Iran*. Boulder, Co.: Lynne Rienner.

[21]Divsallar, A. (2002). Shifting threats and strategic adjustment in Iran's foreign policy: The case of Strait of Hormuz. *British Journal of Middle Eastern Studies*, 49(5), 874–887.

[22]Article 39–42 are about (1) duties of ships and aircraft during transit passage like refraining from any threat against sovereignty of states bordering the strait, (2) prohibition of marine scientific research surveys without the prior authorization of the states bordering straits, (3) states' authority to designate sea lanes and prescribe traffic separation schemes, and (4) laws and regulations of states bordering straits relating to transit passage. For more

The right of transit passage applies throughout the strait, although the territorial seas of the strait's various states overlap.[23]

Nevertheless, Iran's control over the Strait of Hormuz is a geopolitical asset in deterring external threats. While blocking the strait may be detrimental or impractical for Iran, merely harassing shipping or briefly closing the strait would suffice in disrupting the oil supply market.[24] In the long term, this would affect key investments in the region and lead to dramatic increases in the costs of insurance for oil tankers, other sector facilities, and oil or gas sites.

Iran's Growing Power and Potential Conflicts in the Persian Gulf Region

Closing in on the attainment of advanced nuclear technologies, and now with advanced missile and drone technologies, Iran's military capabilities are growing rapidly.[25] Tehran aims to develop its nuclear and military capabilities regardless of the accord or volatility of its relationships with the West and neighbouring countries, whether now or in the anticipatable future.

Iran's rapid and sustained military development coincides with its expanding influence in the region at large. The country's military progress and Tehran's assertive regional behaviour have in part been provoked and driven by a heavy US presence in the region. Since the

---

information, see Convention on the Law of the Sea, December 10, 1982, 1833 U.N.T.S. 397. https://www.un.org/depts/los/convention_agreements/texts/unclos/unclos_e.pdf.

[23] Lott, A. & Kawagishi, S. (2022). The legal regime of the Strait of Hormuz and attacks against oil tankers: Law of the sea and law on the use of force perspectives. *Ocean Development & International Law, 53*(2–3). https://doi.org/10.1080/00908320.2022.2096 158. It is worth mentioning that Iran has not officially agreed to the terms of UNCLOS and believes that some aspects of it are not binding and may not accurately represent customary practices.

[24] On different scenarios for the closure of the Strait of Hormuz see Talmadge (2008). *Op. cit.*, p. 88.

[25] On Iran's military capability, see U.S. Defense Intelligence Agency. (2019). *Iran Military Power: Ensuring Regime Survival and Securing Regional Dominance.* Washington: US Government Publishing Office. https://www.dia.mil/Portals/110/Images/News/Military_Powers_Publications/Iran_Military_Power_LR.pdf.

long-term survival of the political system and securing territorial integrity are the Islamic Republic of Iran's most pressing goals,[26] the effective reduction of the US influence in the region has been at the centre of its security strategy. Iran is a rising regional power; but can it ascend peacefully?

The 2003 Iraq War, the Arab Uprisings, and the US reluctance to be involved directly in the regional conflicts have enabled Iran to expand its influence across the region and challenge the previous security order in the Middle East.[27] The familiar regional dynamics established when the Cold War began in the mid-20th century have now been seismically transformed, and Iran plays a critical role in the new paradigm of Middle Eastern security.[28]

A state's rise in power generates security dilemmas of its own. Uncertainty as to whether Iran's rise in power will play out in defensive or offensive ways will lead to other regional powers preparing for the worst-case scenario. Iran's sudden growth in influence and capability will be considered a threat by definition, and Tehran will inevitably be confronted by other regional actors which seek to establish a sustainable balance of power, namely Israel, Saudi Arabia, and Turkey.[29] This is even more likely now because both Israel and Turkey are becoming more engaged in the Persian Gulf region in attempts to fill the security gap left behind by the United States. Iran's rise in power may have thus far been defensive, but in the longer term, the state's regional policy will likely shift into a more assertive and ambitious one.

---

[26] On Iran's defined National interests, see Katzman, K. (2020, January 30). Iran's foreign and defense policies. *Congressional Research Service* (R44017). https://crsreports. congress.gov/product/pdf/R/R44017/76.

[27] Saleh, A. & Yazdanshenas, Z. (2020, August 29). American's role in crafting Middle East security architecture. *The National Interest.* https://nationalinterest.org/feature/america% E2%80%99s-role-crafting-middle-east-security-architecture-168010.

[28] On Iran's relative gains in the Middle East in the 21st century, see Beck, M. (2020). The aggravated struggle for regional power in the Middle East: American allies Saudi Arabia and Israel versus Iran, *11*(1), 85.

[29] On Iran's growing reach and influence, see Loft, P. (2023, April 14). Iran's influence in the Middle East. *House of Common Library.* https://researchbriefings.files.parliament.uk/ documents/CBP-9504/CBP-9504.pdf.

Dramatic changes in the security architecture and political landscape of the region necessitate a new political model for checking power concentrations and containing threats.[30] The region, experiencing (often frequently reformulated) recalibrations of the security architecture, as it attempts to both comprehend and manage those changes, must produce a new model of stability to deal with major structural challenges. These include nuclear proliferation, the rise of great power politics (and the decline of *super*power politics), the increasingly important role of non-state actors, the growing interest China is showing in the region,[31] inter-state territorial disputes, and intra-state societal insecurity between ethnic and sectarian/religious factions.

Tehran, so far, has been benefiting from the constant and sporadic changes that have emerged in the Middle East's political security landscape. Exploiting opportunities to weaken rivals or strengthen allies, it has taken up all opportunities to advance its military technologies and enhance its influence further afield, from the Mediterranean to the Arabian Sea. The often-unpredictable waves of change in the region are occurring at three levels — the internal, the regional, and the international — and discrepancies, inconsistencies, and complexities in Iran's strategic capacity at these three levels prompt the question as to whether Iran can 'rise peacefully'.

When it comes to internal power, the Islamic Revolutionary Guard Corps (IRGC) has incrementally fortified its position, engendering a process of militarisation within the state apparatus and assuming significant influence across a range of security, political, and economic domains. The post-Khamenei era is envisioned to be characterised by a potent blend of militarism, nationalism, anti-imperialism, and Islamism. The trajectory of Iran's growing power suggests that Tehran aspires to reclaim its historical role. The revolutionary vision of the IRGC means that it exerts its power in both domestic affairs and external state relations, steering Iran's strategic orientation on multiple fronts.

---

[30] On new security architecture in the Middle East, see Colombo, S. & Dessi, A. (Ed.) (2020). *Fostering a New Security Architecture in the Middle East*. Rome: The International Spectator.

[31] On China's growing influence in the Persian Gulf, see Yazdanshenas, Z. & Saleh, A. (2023, April 5). Iranian-Saudi detente and 'Asianization' of the Persian Gulf: China fills the gap. *Middle East Institute*. https://www.mei.edu/publications/iranian-saudi-detente-and-asianization-persian-gulf-china-fills-gap.

After over two decades of regional conflicts, the Middle East is witnessing a hiatus of relative peace, with Iran normalising their relationships with Saudi Arabia,[32] the UAE, and Bahrain. US presence in the region is still receding, and China is becoming a far more influential agent in Middle Eastern politics than it has ever been. Other pockets of international relationships pervade the region, with the Russians still in Syria and the Taliban back in power in Afghanistan. The brewing tension in Caucasia looks set to intensify more, and Iran is watching events closely. Territorial disputes between Iran and the UAE, Kuwait, and Saudi Arabia are still alive, at times more visible than at others, but Iran feels more comfortable with its eastern and western borders, and it now focuses on its southern sea borders: the Persian Gulf and the Oman Sea.

Iran aims to develop its status into that of a *core state*, one able to define the security order of the region. Tehran's security doctrine is unwavering in its insistence that the Middle East be free of hostile non-regional actor interference and free of military threats from powers further afield. Tehran considers any Western military presence in the region, including that of Israel, as inherently hostile and as constituting an imminent threat to its national security. The complex and unstable balance of power in the region, now characterised by the reemergence of smaller powers such as Israel and Turkey in the Persian Gulf, increases the likelihood of conflict in the sub-regional security order.

Internationally, in the age of *deep pluralism* and the rise of multiple powers, regional powers such as Iran are coming to play a more important role in facilitating power transitions at the regional and global levels.[33] With its staunchly anti-hegemonic mindset, Tehran has fostered a close relationship with the West's two global rivals: China[34] and Russia. Global rivalries and contests between the West and its opposers will inevitably impact the Middle East, and Iran may come to comprise a Middle Eastern microcosm of what comprises a global conflict. Siding as Iran is with the

---

[32] On IRI-KSA rapprochement; *Ibid.*

[33] On Deep Pluralism, see Acharya, A. & Buzan, B. (2019). *The Making of Global International Relations: Origins of Evolution of IR at its Centenary* (pp. 261–284). Cambridge: Cambridge University Press.

[34] On Iran-China strategic Partnership and its regional impacts, see Saleh, A. & Yazdanshenas, Z. (2020, August 9). Iran's pact with China is bad news for the West. *Foreign Policy.* https://foreignpolicy.com/2020/08/09/irans-pact-with-china-is-bad-news-for-the-west/.

Eastern powers, Western interests in the region will be pursued using strategies that seek to contain, alienate, and vilify Iran.

Iran has ample experience of weakness, exclusion from the international community, and subjection to the interests of external powers, whether regional or global. Bitterness among the officials has festered after decades of economic sanctions, relentless containment of its nuclear ambitions, and the intrusion of the US on its borders. Iranian authorities hope for exploiting the gaps in power that characterised the perceived post-US era in the Middle East Iran will be considered a formidable threat to its adversaries once again. As long as there are belligerent nuclear powers at play, namely the US and Israel, which are perceived as a palpable threat by Tehran, Iran's leadership will likely pursue nuclear enrichment further. The combination of visceral embitterment within its upper ranks and the proliferation of fresh opportunities to empower the country suggest that Iran may well *not* rise peacefully.

The rise of Iran may concern all. Tehran adopts a worst-case scenario planning model in its defence doctrine, so its rivals in the region should do the same and its friends should remain vigilant. The recent relative pause in tensions and conflicts in the region, at least from a historical vantage point, does not mean that security dilemmas look set to abate.[35] In fact, a newly empowered Iran in the Middle East, free of the (albeit unwelcome) certainties afforded by the encroachment of a single superpower (the US), is ready to exploit any and every confusion, conflict, and alliance formation that it can.

Strait of Hormuz and Its Position in Iran's Security Discourse

The experience of the 8-year-long war between Iran and Iraq led Iranian policymakers to the conclusion that post-revolutionary Iran should use all means necessary to deter threats being posed by external forces in order to defend its territorial integrity and national security.[36] Tehran has

---

[35] On persistent security dilemmas in the Middle East, see Moshirzadeh, H. Threat perceptions and security dilemma in the Middle East. *Iranian Review of Foreign Affairs*. 20.100 1.1.20088221.2018.9.27.1.2.

[36] Tabatabai, A. M. (2019, October). Iran's national security: Implications for future U.S. — Iran negotiations. Rand Corporation, p. 18. https://www.rand.org/pubs/perspectives/PE344.html.

witnessed a number of inter-state and intra-state wars in the region over the past three decades or so. The Iraqi invasion of Kuwait in 1990, the US invasion of Afghanistan in 2001, the 2003 Iraq War, and the ongoing civil wars in Iraq, Syria, Libya, and Yemen have played a key role in shaping Tehran's security discourse since the Islamic Republic's establishment in 1979. Iranian officials have long been concerned about the potential for a significant rise in US military presence in the Persian Gulf. Leaders fear that neighbouring countries might allow the US to use their territories to target Iran's strategic installations.[37]

Iran continues to view the presence of the US in the Persian Gulf as a threat. According to the Supreme Leader, Ayatollah Ali Khamenei, the US of the Reagan and Bush eras was no different to today's America. He has stated that just as the US once considered it necessary to bombard Iran in the Persian Gulf out of grudge and anger, they would gladly do the same today if given the opportunity.[38] According to him, America has not changed its stance towards Iran nor shall it ever do so. Therefore, Iran has no choice but to prevent the United States from finding such an opportunity by enhancing its deterrence capabilities. Since the Republic has been under an arms embargo for decades and has been treated as a pariah state, it has formed a new model of deterrence based on asymmetric, multistage, and dynamic capabilities known as *active deterrence*. As Hassan Rouhani, the former Iranian president, said, 'The strategy of the Islamic Republic of Iran has always been based on active deterrence to help establish peace and security in the country and the region.'[39]

Passive or traditional deterrence relies solely on conventional military power and ostensibly serves to deter the enemy from military mobilisation. An international actor opting for traditional deterrence would avoid military action against adversaries as long as they have not taken any offensive action. In *active* deterrence, however, the ultimate goal is to dissuade all threatening forces from any possible action by raising the costs of military aggression in a number of ways to outweigh its

---

[37] Divsallar (2002). *Op. cit.*

[38] Khamenei, S. A. (2016, January 20). Leader's speech in meeting with the officials in charge of holding elections. https://english.khamenei.ir/news/3205/Iran-will-stay-committed-only-as-long-as-the-other-side-will.

[39] *Financial Tribune*. (2015, April 19). Military doctrine based on active deterrence. https://financialtribune.com/articles/national/14886/military-doctrine-based-on-active-deterrence.

anticipated benefits.[40] Traditional deterrence is a binary game that either succeeds (and the security of the actor is protected) or fails (and the actor must engage in military defence). But in *active* deterrence, if deterrence fails in the first stage, the actor implements a new set of threats to deter hostile threats. This process is played out at different levels until a sustainable state of deterrence is achieved. Unlike passive deterrence, active deterrence is not based on military superiority, but on asymmetric capabilities, such as the ability to escalate conflicts. This is where geopolitical features can serve as strategic advantages,[41] when geography is *weaponised*.

Active deterrence is based on threat assessment and preemptive actions. According to former Iranian Defence Minister, General Amir Hatami, Iran's defence doctrine is centred around this principle. Referring to Western officials and their stance on Iran's regional influence, he has said the following:

> They ask us why we are present in the region, and they mean that we need to leave to let them initiate threats against us, while this region belongs to us, and its security should be established by us and not those who have come from thousands of kilometers away.[42]

Iran's perception of the United States as *the* arch-foe has been ingrained into the national consciousness (at least among the state's powerful leaders and the portion of the citizenry committed to the anti-American ideology of the Republic), due to historical experiences of US interventions, US-backed conflicts, White House-sponsored sanctions, and sequestration from the international community. Iranian officials believe that the US has consistently sought to weaken, challenge, or overthrow the Islamic Republic and that America's dedication to achieving these objectives will not waver. They point to critical junctures in Iranian history, such as the

---

[40] In strategic studies, it is also called punitive deterrence. See Morgan, F. E. & Muller, K. P. (Eds.) (2008). *'Dangerous Thresholds' Managing Escalation in the 21st Century* (p. 22). Santa Monica: Rand Corporation.

[41] Jingjie, H. (2017). A secured Iran? Iran's independent active deterrence strategy. *Contemporary International Relations*, *5*, 132–133.

[42] Farw News Agency. (2021, February 8). DM: Iran's active deterrence doctrine to kill in bud any threats. https://www.farsnews.ir/en/news/13991120000735/DM-Iran%E2%80%99s-Acive-Deerrence-Dcrine-Kill-in-Bd-Any-Threas.

1953 coup d'etat against Mohammad Mosaddegh's democratically elected administration, US support for the former Shah, Mohammad Reza Pahlavi, and the provision of chemical weapons to Iraq during the Iran–Iraq war, in depicting a US that is anti-Iran in a fundamental and unswerving way.

Additionally, the removal of the Iranian dissident group Mujahedin-e-Khalq (MEK) from the US list of terrorist organizations, the establishment of military bases close to Iran, particularly in the Persian Gulf monarchies (such as the Isa Air Base in Bahrain, the Ali Al-Saleh and Kuwait airbases in Kuwait, and the Al-Udeid Airbase in Qatar),[43] along with the imposition of severe unilateral sanctions on Iranian trade have fostered inherent distrust and fed into a visceral hostility towards the United States *tout court*. The impression that the US has encircled Iran and may wage a war on Tehran, if and when US strategic strengths make invasion a plausible option, has been further strengthened by the events of the 2001 invasion of Afghanistan and the 2003 Iraq War.[44]

With anti-American ideology bored into Tehran's foreign policy discourse, and with the fact remaining that Iran cannot deter the US by relying on conventional military capabilities due to explicit and unquestionable US military superiority, Iranian officials have adopted a multipronged and more nuanced security strategy. According to the Supreme Leader, the US has historically sought to create insecurity in the Persian Gulf for Iran, but the presence of the Islamic Revolutionary Guard Corps Navy (IRGCN) in the Persian Gulf has made the region insecure for America's military. The Supreme Leader has insisted that IRGCN commanders and officials intimidate the enemy, as he believes that the US is an inherent aggressor.[45] Hence, intimidating adversaries and creating an insecure environment for American forces in the Persian Gulf are aligned with its active deterrence strategy.

---

[43] On US presence in the Middle East, see Benaim, D. & Hanna, M. W. (2019, August 7). The enduring American presence in the Middle East. *Foreign Affairs*. https://www.foreignaffairs.com/articles/middle-east/2019-08-07/enduring-american-presence-middle-east.

[44] Lotfian, S. (2011). Threat perceptions and Iran's national security policy. *Foreign Relations*, 3(9), 175–207.

[45] Khamenei, S. A. (2015, October 7). Leader's speech in meeting with commanders and personnel of Islamic Revolution Guard Corps. https://english.khamenei.ir/news/2194/Leader-s-speech-in-meeting-with-commanders-and-personnel-of-Islamic.

The Strait of Hormuz and Iran's Active Deterrence Strategy   157

Iran also exploits the geographical advantages of the Strait of Hormuz to advance its active deterrence by threatening to close the Strait of Hormuz and interrupting the free flow of energy. While Iranian officials have repeatedly declared that Iran has no intention of closing the Strait,[46] they assert their control over it as a means to safeguard their interests. According to Major General Mohammad Bagheri, Chief of Staff of the Iranian Armed Forces:

> The Iranian Armed Forces are in charge of the security of the Strait of Hormuz... If anybody is to make the Strait of Hormuz unsafe, we will certainly counter it, and if our oil is not to be shipped through the Strait of Hormuz, then the oil of others will definitely not go through the Strait either... This would not mean the closure of the Strait of Hormuz, we have no intention of closing it, unless the hostility of enemies reaches a point at which there is no other choice. That day, we will be fully capable of closing the Strait.[47]

In response to threats it perceives as requiring immediate attention and the ongoing political uncertainty and military insecurity in the region, Iran's strategy of active deterrence involves combining diverse tactics drawn from a range of strategic theories and types of conflict, including conflict zone expansion, conflict protraction, the diversification of retaliatory methods, and positive engagement with global rivals to the US.[48] This mix of strategies bolsters Iran's deterrence capabilities and escalates costs for

---

[46] For example, see Fars News Agency (2019, February 23). Fars News staff, top security official: Sealing Strait of Hormuz only one of Iran's several options to block oil exports from region. https://www.farsnews.ir/en/news/13971204000791/Tp-Secriy-Official-Sealing-Sai-f-Hrmz-Only-One-f-Iran39-s-Several. Ensaf News Staff. (2019, August 26). Zarif: No need to close the Strait of Hormuz. *Ensaf News*. http://www.ensafnews.com/18 6959/%D8%B8%D8%B1%DB%8C%D9%81-%D9%86%DB%8C%D8%A7%D8%B2%DB%8C-%D8%A8%D9%87-%D8%A8%D8%B3%D8%AA%D9%86-%D8%AA%D9%86%DA%AF%D9%87-%D9%87%D8%B1%D9%85%D8%B2-%D9%86%DB%8C%D8%B3%D8%AA/.

[47] Tasnim News Agency. (2019, April 28).Top general: Iran not intending to close Strait of Hormuz.https://www.tasnimnews.com/en/news/2019/04/28/1999238/top-general-iran-not-intending-to-close-strait-of-hormuz.

[48] On tactics of active deterrence, see Saleh, A. & Yazdanshenas, Z. (2023). China-Iran strategic partnership and the future of US hegemony in the Persian Gulf Region. *British Journal of Middle Eastern Studies*. https://doi.org/10.1080/13530194.2023.2215188.

potential adversaries. It is designed to deter the full ensemble of Iran's potential aggressors but more specifically tailored to deter its perceived arch-foe: the United States.

In terms of conflict zone expansion, Iran has expanded all its conflict zones, extending its reach into the Levant over to the Mediterranean, and into the Persian Gulf towards the Oman Sea. Recognizing the significance of the Oman Sea, the Supreme Leader has emphasized the need for an increased presence of army and navy forces, as well as the IRGCN, in this zone.[49] General Hatami, touching upon the geopolitical importance of Iran, has talked extensively about Iran's willingness to play a more active role in the Indian Ocean.[50]

The constant threat of the closure of the Strait of Hormuz by Iran has been the topic of intense discussion about global energy security. Disruption in the Persian Gulf oil supply could quickly scale up the scope of any local conflict and increase pressure on the US. With nearly 90% of Persian Gulf crude oil production relying on tankers passing through this waterway, prolonged closure or repeated disruption could lead to a serious supply shock in the energy market, causing prices to soar and global supply chains to freeze.

Irrespective of Iran's actual military strength or the likelihood that it will block the strait, the asymmetric capability-building and tactics of the Islamic Revolutionary Guard Corps Navy (IRGCN) could pose complex challenges for tanker passage through this narrow route. Even without completely halting maritime traffic, Iran has the potential to significantly impact the global energy market. This is one of the ways Iran seeks to pose a risk of critical strategic costs for the United States. The resulting instability in the oil supply market would internationalise the conflict and intensify pressure on the United States.[51]

In terms of conflict protraction, Iran aims to protract regional conflicts. Experiences of the disastrous repercussions — both locally and

---

[49] The development of Makran coast in the statements of the Supreme Leader. (2022, December 30). https://makran.isu.ac.ir/fa/news.php?rid=39.

[50] Farw News Agency. (2021). *Op. cit.*

[51] Wehrey, F., Thaler, D. E., Bensahel, N. *et al.* (2009). Asymmetric ambition and conventional reality: Iran's evolving defense strategy, doctrine, and capabilities. In *Dangerous but Not Omnipotent: Exploring the Reach and Limitations of Iranian Power in the Middle East* (p. 68). RAND Corporation. http://www.jstor.org/stable/10.7249/mg781af.11.

internationally — of prolonged and open-ended wars, particularly evident in the cases of Iraq and Afghanistan, mean that the US and other democratic nations are highly averse to direct involvement in Middle Eastern conflicts. By prolonging conflicts, Iran effectively raises the costs of aggression. For instance, it may selectively target American sites in the region at different intervals or launch attacks on US allies and partners, as exemplified by the 2019 assault on Saudi Aramco oil facilities.

Furthermore, Iran employs a policy of tactical diversification, applying new modes of warfare, as a means to realise its active deterrence strategy. While Washington would rely on limited airstrikes in the event of military action against Tehran, Iran would employ a more diverse range of methods of retaliation designed to escalate costs of conflict for potential adversaries. Leveraging its network of unofficial allies and friends in the region and capitalising on its asymmetrical military capabilities, such as drones, unmanned speedboats, mines, and anti-ship cruise missiles, Iran would be capable of expanding the theater of war and significantly increasing an adversary's expenses.

The unique geographical characteristics of the Strait of Hormuz give Iran an upper hand by constraining the movement of US maritime vessels and placing them within range of Iran's short-range maritime exclusion capabilities, including anti-ship cruise missiles (ASCMs), fast attack crafts (FACs), mines, and mini-submarines.[52] Initiating any attack from the Indian Ocean, or from US military bases in Europe, would significantly reduce the accuracy and impact of the air attack.

According to the US intelligence community's annual worldwide threat assessment, Iran possesses sufficient military capabilities for targeting US and European military assets in the region (or for disrupting traffic in the Strait of Hormuz to an extent that constitutes a significant threat to global energy security). It could deploy a number of technologies to achieve this, including ballistic missiles, naval mines, unmanned explosive boats, UAVs, anti-ship and land-attack cruise missiles, and submarines. It is worth mentioning that Iran has the largest stockpile of

---

[52] Gunzinger, M. & Dougherty, C. (2012, January 17). Outside-in: Operating from range to defeat Iran's anti-access and area denial threats. Center for Strategic and Budgetary Assess. https://csbaonline.org/research/publications/outside-in-operating-from-range-to-defeat-irans-anti-access-and-area-denial.

ballistic missiles in the region, some of which have a range of up to 2,000 kilometres.[53]

Lastly, Iran is engaging in strategically orientated relationship-building with major global rivals to the United States, namely Russia, and China, using strengthened relations as a balancing act to offset over-reliance on forging foreign policies solely geared to countering Western policies and to safeguard its interests both regionally and globally.[54] By cultivating alliances with these nations, Iran aims to craft an emerging role as *the* regional power, deterring threats from further afield while protecting its broader regional interests. As China's reliance on Gulf oil has grown, so too has its strategic interest in safeguarding security and stability in the Strait of Hormuz. The military presence of the United States and its allies in the Strait has encouraged China to expand its influence in the region and protect its commercial interests by forming shrewd alliances wherever possible. China's increasing willingness to interfere in the region will likely help Iran to initiate active deterrence tactics in the strait more confidently and with greater effect.[55] According to the United States Department of Defense's annual report, the Strait of Hormuz is one of several strategic places which China is looking at to potentially expand its military presence.[56]

Conclusion

Geography matters, and it matters very much to Iran. The country has been invaded from all sides in its centuries-old history, but in the

---

[53] Coats, D. R. (2019, January 29). Worldwide threat assessment of the US intelligence community. Office of the Director of National Intelligence of the US. https://www.dni.gov/files/ODNI/documents/2019-ATA-SFR---SSCI.pdf.

[54] On Iran Balancing act, see Ahmadian, H. (2021). Iran and the new geopolitics of the Middle East: Search of equilibrium. *Journal of Balkan and Near Eastern Studies, 23*(3), 458–472.

[55] Baabood, A. (2023, May 24). Why China is emerging as a main promoter of stability in the Strait of Hormuz. MALCOM H. KERR, Carnegie Middle East Center. https://carnegie-mec.org/2023/05/24/why-china-is-emerging-as-main-promoter-of-stability-in-strait-of-hormuz-pub-89829.

[56] The US Department of Defense. (2020). Military and security developments involves the People's Republic of China. https://media.defense.gov/2020/Sep/01/2002488689/-1/-1/1/2020-DOD-CHINA-MILITARY-POWER-REPORT-FINAL.PDF.

The Strait of Hormuz and Iran's Active Deterrence Strategy   161

contemporary era, Iranian officials are increasingly weaponising Iran's geographical characteristics as military and geopolitical assets. The Strait of Hormuz is one specific geographical feature which Iran has a great degree of control over. The strait's importance for commerce, its use as the transit route for a huge proportion of the world's oil (and gas) exports, as well as the vulnerability of the global energy market to events on the strait mean that Iran can weaponise the waterway as an integral component of a multipronged strategy for serving Tehran's interests in the region and beyond. Having the option of closing or disrupting the strait at its disposal could come to form one of the most powerful advantages for Iran moving forward, acting as a crucial leverage point in its overall strategy of active deterrence.

The Persian Gulf region has always been Tehran's main security concern. This is for several reasons. First, Iranian naval power has been relatively weak over the past four decades. Second, the United States, as the only superpower in the international arena to have been a dominant power in the Persian Gulf, is still present there. Since the removal of Saddam in 2003, and the withdrawal of US troops from Iraq, Iran perceives the major external threat to be located in the south, namely in the Persian Gulf and the Gulf of Oman.

In addressing this threat, Tehran has strengthened its naval power. It has also expanded its military reach from the Persian Gulf into the Gulf of Oman, and onwards to the Indian Ocean. Continuing in this trajectory will help Iran to push the opposing powers, the United States and its allies, further away, and to make the option of invasion less attractive. Tehran has also been developing new defence methods and techniques, such drones and speedboat technologies, to deter US naval assertiveness in the region.

And so, in the last instance, Tehran has made it clear that the closure of the Strait of Hormuz is an option that is always on the table. In explicitly declaring this, Tehrani officials seek to show that they can achieve three major goals with one action: (1) they can quickly internationalize any emerging conflict, (2) they can bring about such adverse effects on all other six countries in the Persian Gulf that they will be discouraged from supporting a large-scale US invasion, and (3) they can affect major crises in the global economy, from huge oil price hikes to critical supply chain disruptions, making it difficult for the US to consider a prolonged war.

Closure of the strait could be initiated rapidly and would be a remarkably effective tactic, so Iran rightly perceives the waterway as a geopolitical asset. This threat of closure is the jewel in the complex crown of Iranian active deterrence — closure could affect damage and confusion across markets worldwide and governments in every continent. Iran will continue to advance military capabilities, form alliances, and develop infrastructure to protect and exploit its power over its several geographical assets; the Strait of Hormuz is arguably the most valuable one.

© 2025 World Scientific Publishing Company
https://doi.org/10.1142/9789811294709_0008

Chapter 8

Comparing UAE and Oman *Beyond Hormuz* Security Strategies

Eleonora Ardemagni

Introduction

This chapter analyses the type of security strategies which the member states of the Gulf Cooperation Council (GCC) have adopted to circumvent the Hormuz Strait, focusing on the United Arab Emirates (UAE) and Oman. Security strategies refer here both to defence and commercial dimensions, with maritime infrastructures playing a role in the interplay between civilian and military goals. With respect to Hormuz, the UAE and Oman stand in a different geographical and geostrategic position. While most of the Emirati territory is placed *before* or *in* the strait (with the notable exception of the Fujairah emirate), the Sultanate can directly access the Indian Ocean, also sharing with Iran the responsibility for Hormuz's viability (through the Musandam Peninsula enclave in the UAE territory). After a framework on the 'Hormuz issue' in GCC states' history and politics, this chapter addresses 'the state of the strait' in Gulf monarchies' contemporary security strategies outlining, for instance, Saudi Arabia's increased pivot to the Red Sea as an alternative route for oil export. In a comparative way, this chapter then focuses on the Emirati and Omani security strategies to secure their passage through Hormuz, as well as in building alternative routes for navigation. Efforts are analysed taking

164   E. Ardemagni

the following into account: threat perception and political strategy, post-hydrocarbon economic diversification, naval defence build-up, and bilateral and multilateral diplomacy (e.g., relations with Iran and implications of the *Abraham Accords*). This chapter has the following structure: (1) framework: the 'Hormuz issue' in GCC states' history and politics, (2) the 'state of the strait' in contemporary security strategies, (3) the UAE (Fujairah), (4) Oman (Duqm), and (5) comparing UAE and Oman's Security Strategies: findings and conclusion.

Framework: The 'Hormuz Issue' in GCC States' Contemporary History and Politics

In the contemporary Persian Gulf, geopolitical tensions in the Hormuz area have significantly heightened after the British withdrawal from the region in 1971, when the Gulf monarchies' protectorates (Saudi Arabia, the United Arab Emirates, Qatar, Bahrain, Kuwait, and Oman) became independent states. The issue of the disputed islands between the UAE and Iran in the Hormuz Strait, Abu Musa, and the Greater and Lesser Tunb epitomises the level of threat the Gulf monarchies have perceived from Iran since the 1970s when the Pahlavi monarchy was still in charge.[1] In such an unstable context, the monarchies reacted with the founding of the Gulf Cooperation Council (GCC) in 1981: this regional alliance primarily aimed to counter-weight the Islamic Republic established in Tehran after the 1979 Iranian revolution. Since the 1970s, Hormuz has been perceived by the monarchies as a potential flashpoint for three reasons. The first is the confessional (Shia–Sunni) and the ethnic (Persian–Arab) divides, which have traditionally generated rivalry between Iran, Saudi Arabia, and the neighbouring monarchies. The second reason is the GCC states' economic dependency on oil and gas exports through the strait, as all their economies are founded on hydrocarbons. The third stands in the dual nature of the Islamic Republic, comprising elected and appointed institutions, and especially in

---

[1] These are strategic islands placed in the Hormuz Strait belonging, respectively, to the emirate of Sharjah (Abu Musa) and of Ras Al Khaimah (Greater and Lesser Tunb), seized by Iran in 1971 as the British were withdrawing from their protectorates in the Persian Gulf and the UAE wasn't formally established as an independent state yet. In these islands, the population is predominantly made of ethnic Arabs even though it speaks a Bandari dialect from Farsi, since the islands were dominated by the Persians for a long time.

the dual nature of its security sector, which is organised into regular armed forces and the paramilitaries of the Islamic Revolutionary Guard Corps (IRGC), both with a navy division.

As a matter of fact, conflict has not been absent in the post-1979 Persian Gulf thus affecting directly and indirectly maritime security around Hormuz, even though the strait has never been closed to navigation. Three Gulf wars were in fact fought: in 1980–1988 (Iran vs Iraq, the last symmetrical war combated in the Middle East so far), which also resulted in a 'tanker war' since Saddam Hussein's Iraqi regime targeted Iranian ships and then also international shipping transiting through the strait, thus pushing the US to organize a naval intervention in 1987; the invasion of Kuwait in 1990 by Iraq and the following US-led military intervention in 1991; and the Anglo–American invasion of Iraq in 2003 leading to the fall of Hussein's regime.

Moreover, Arab region's social and political unrest reached also the Persian Gulf in 2011, with the uprisings in Bahrain and Oman and, to a lesser extent, the protests of the Saudi Shia community in the Eastern region of the kingdom. More recently, geopolitical tensions have developed around the Persian Gulf and the Hormuz Strait, even though these haven't been translated into open, state vs state confrontation so far. Asymmetry is in fact the main feature marking the antagonism between Iran and Israel which also displays a maritime side. Since 2019, the shadow naval war between the Iranians and the Israelis — with Iranian actors seizing or attempting to seize oil tankers and commercial vessels, and Israeli agents striking against Iranian intelligence boats — sheds light on the saliency of the plausible deniability factor. In many cases, attacks occur in the Hormuz Strait and off the coasts of the UAE and of Oman. This has contributed to keep GCC states' security focus on the Hormuz chokepoint as a flashpoint.

In the Islamic Republic's propaganda, closing the Hormuz Strait is an 'all season threat' that has returned, in the official rhetoric, since the 2018 American unilateral withdrawal from the JCPOA (the Joint Comprehensive Plan of Action) or nuclear deal. A threat mitigated by the re-establishment of diplomatic relations between Saudi Arabia and Iran in March 2023, a Chinese-brokered deal marking a de-escalation phase in the Persian Gulf, especially thanks to previous negotiation efforts by Iraq and Oman. However, this menace is improbable: the closure of Hormuz would be first of all detrimental to Iran since it exports more than 90% of its goods — especially oil — through the strait while importing only 13%

through it.[2] Therefore, for the Islamic Republic, the Hormuz's closure would be, if, really the final weapon only in case of war. Instead, the disruption of freedom of navigation through the strait — with attempts to seize and the seizing of oil tankers in Hormuz and Gulf of Oman by both the IRGC Navy and the Artesh (regular) navy — is a bargaining chip that puts rivals under political pressure and has proved to be much more feasible than the closure hypothesis in terms of political strategy.

This adds to Iran's gradual militarisation of the Persian Gulf islands, comprising Jask and the occupied islands, and to the rise, since 2003, of the Iranian-related and mostly Shia militias surrounding the Persian Gulf and the Arabian Peninsula. This network, including Hezbollah in Lebanon, pro-Assad regime militias in Syria, the Hashd al-Shaabi in Iraq, and the Houthis in Yemen, is a nuanced constellation of armed groups with varied degrees of dependency and alliance with Tehran: some of them, especially the Houthis and to a lesser extent Hezbollah, have also developed maritime capabilities in the Bab-el-Mandeb and Southern Red Sea sub-region (Houthis) and in the Mediterranean Sea (Hezbollah), thus endangering maritime security in other areas surrounding the GCC states and their direct neighbourhood. This risk has become a global security issue since late 2023, due to the Houthis' attacks against international navigation in the Southern Red Sea, the Bab-el-Mandeb Strait and the Gulf of Aden, in the context of the Israel-Hamas war.

This also highlights the rising interdependence level between Hormuz and other regional chokepoints due to the presence of Iranian-related actors and activities, first of all arms smuggling. The GCC states' post-hydrocarbon diversification efforts reorganise their economic priorities: however, Hormuz's viability remains crucial to their economies for three main reasons. First, the persisting centrality of oil and gas revenues to finance the post-oil and gas transition, shaped by the 'Visions', the national programs drafted by each of the GCC states to design the trajectory towards post-hydrocarbon economies. Second, most of the oil and gas exported by the GCC states is directed towards Asia, with particular regard to China, India, and Japan, so the Hormuz export route still appears as the first choice. Third, the rise of non-oil trade sectors as well as infrastructures, logistics, tourism, and big events, all require Persian Gulf's stability, also at a maritime level, to allow economic prosperity.

---

[2] For data, see Dolatabadi, A. B. & Kamrava, M. (2022). Iran's changing naval strategy in the Persian Gulf: motives and features. *British Journal of Middle Eastern Studies*, 4.

In the last decades and especially since the 2010s, geopolitical balances around Hormuz have evolved due to the activism of Middle Eastern and international powers. In 1995, the US returned to the Persian Gulf with the reactivation of the Fifth Fleet in Bahrain, France opened in 2009 a permanent military base in the UAE strengthening its ties with the Arab powers in the Persian Gulf, the UK returned 'East of Suez', establishing two military bases in Bahrain and Oman (2018), and Turkey opened its first military base abroad in Qatar in 2016, sending stationed troops in 2017. New geopolitical balances in the Persian Gulf and around Hormuz are also the outcome of the rise of the GCC states as ambitious middle powers (Saudi Arabia, the UAE, and Qatar), with interventionist foreign policies[3] and of shifting power relations in the region.

In 2017, the intra-GCC crisis between Qatar and its Saudi, Emirati, and Bahraini neighbours resulted in Doha's blockade and boycott. For this reason, Qatar had to rely on alternative re-import and re-export routes, so leaning on Kuwait and most of all Oman to circumvent the direct passage through Hormuz under the Qatari flag. The *Abraham Accords*, the diplomatic normalisation process signed between the UAE, Bahrain, and Israel in 2020, also contributed to alter the consolidated status quo of the Hormuz area. In fact, blossoming defence cooperation among the Emiratis, the Bahrainis, and the Israelis unprecedentedly provided Israel with a strategic window in the Persian Gulf, just in front of Iran. In 2022, Bahrain and Israel also signed a security cooperation agreement.

In terms of naval defence, GCC navies, especially Emirati and Saudi ones, are working to improve maritime defence capabilities, with equipment and most of all indigenous expertise: from 2014 to 2022, the number of GCC states' vessels grew from 512 to 621. Navy is the defence dimension the GCC states have traditionally underdeveloped because of their reliance on the American security umbrella: for instance, the Peninsula Shield Force doesn't have a naval component. Joint drills and defence cooperation with regional and international partners are also part of navies' modernisation. The main GCC states' purpose is to focus on deterrence through denial, and by detection in regional waters, also to develop blue-water navies.[4]

---

[3] Young, K. E. (2013, December). The emerging interventionists of the GCC. *London School of Economics and Political Science*, LSE Middle East Centre Paper Series/02.

[4] See Thievon, K. (2023, June 5). New ambitions at Sea: Naval modernisation in the Gulf States. *The International Institute for Strategic Studies (IISS)*, Research Paper.

From an international perspective, the Persian Gulf and the Hormuz chokepoint have turned into a key hub first due to the 2000s' globalisation process, with the Dubai corridor linking Europe to Asia and Africa and then with the rise of Asian powers in global economy also as top oil and gas importers from the Persian Gulf. This has occurred especially since the launch of the Chinese *Belt and Road Initiative* in 2013 and with the Indian commercial and geopolitical expansion towards the Persian Gulf also to counterweight Beijing's politics. Such a context has accelerated the shift from a post-1989 US-dominated unipolar order to a multipolar world in which middle regional powers from the Persian Gulf (Saudi Arabia, the UAE, Qatar, and Iran) also exercise an inter-regional influence and want to play a role. In this evolved scenario, Hormuz regains a prominent role, becoming a global security point: 76% of oil barrels per day passing through Hormuz are destined for Asia.[5]

The Hormuz Strait's relevance for both Western and Asian economies has prompted major powers, especially since 2019, to organise and join naval multinational missions aimed to protect freedom of navigation, as well as to invest in joint maritime drills. The key date in Hormuz's balances is 2019: Saudi Aramco's plants in the Eastern Region of Saudi Arabia were heavily attacked by Iran and, across the same year, a number of oil tankers were seized, or their navigation was threatened, between Hormuz and the Gulf of Oman. International players partnered with GCC and regional states to organise naval multilateral missions. The US launched in late 2019 the International Maritime Security Construct ('Operation Sentinel'), amid the Arabian Sea and the Southern Red Sea. In 2020, the French initiative EMASOH (European-led Maritime Awareness Strait of Hormuz), based in the UAE, involved European and regional players in the Persian Gulf, the Hormuz Strait, and the Gulf of Oman. In 2024, the EUNAVFOR Aspides was launched by some EU countries (as Greece, Italy, Germany and France) to protect commercial navigation in the Red Sea. The mission has an area of operation ranging from the Bab-el-Mandab Strait and the international waters in the Red Sea, the Gulf of Aden, the Arabian Sea, to the Hormuz Strait, the Gulf of Oman, and the Persian Gulf.

The US also launched two new task forces as part of the Combined Maritime Forces based at the Fifth Fleet in Bahrain: the CTF-153,

---

[5]Barden, J. (2019, June 20). The Strait of Hormuz is the world's most important oil transit chokepoint. *U.S. Energy Information Administration*.

deployed in 2022 between the Red Sea, the Bab-el-Mandeb and the Gulf of Aden to counter smuggling activities, with particular regard to weapons, and, in 2023, the CTF-154 focused on training to advance local maritime forces' capabilities. As part of this sub-regional effort around Hormuz, the Americans also established *Task Force 59* at the Fifth Fleet in Bahrain, with a hundred drones (aerial, sub-surface, and surface) able to communicate and coordinate with the regional allies. The Western Indian Ocean is now an area of open geopolitical rivalries displayed by country alignments and counter-alignments: for instance, Iran, Russia, and China have been holding naval drills and wargames together in the Gulf of Oman since 2019, thus challenging a traditionally US-influenced area neighbouring the GCC states.

However, neither multinational missions nor the de-escalation path between Saudi Arabia and Iran re-started in 2022 are deterring Iranian-related attacks on freedom of navigation: this means that ongoing efforts are not enough to build a stable maritime security framework so far. Whatever kind of political scenario prevails — escalation or de-escalation — building alternative routes which can complement the Hormuz Strait is a long-term interest for Middle Eastern powers, starting from the GCC states, as well as for global energy and trade security.

The 'State of the Strait' in Contemporary Security Strategies: Saudi Arabia and the Red Sea

Differently from the UAE and Oman, Saudi Arabia's geographical territory can rely upon two distinct maritime waterways: the Persian Gulf–Hormuz and the Red Sea–Bab-el-Mandeb. This favours Saudi efforts to find alternative maritime routes which can complement Hormuz. However, the security of the Red Sea and of the Bab-el-Mandeb area has been significantly affected by the war in Yemen because of Yemen's Houthis armed militancy, also at maritime level: this means that even this complementary waterway presents some security risks now, dramatically emphasised by the Houthis' attacks against international navigation since late 2023. In the framework of *Vision 2030*, Saudi Arabia's security strategy aims to develop alternative routes to Hormuz, its risks and uncertainties: a strategy corroborated by the 2019 attacks against Aramco plants and the oil tankers.

The search for alternative routes occurs just while the kingdom is focused on the development of its Western Red Sea coast. The traditional

Saudi oil export route develops in fact from the Eastern Region, where Saudi oilfields are mainly located: this is home to a Saudi Shia minority (about 10% of the whole kingdom's population) and close to Hormuz. Currently, the Red Sea has acquired a new prominence in Saudi national security and foreign policy. This is mainly due to the need to protect the kingdom from the Houthis' maritime and drone attacks occurring in the Southern Red Sea and against the Saudi South-Western coast (national security dimension) and the attempts to influence and coordinate the Red Sea sub-region as a way to secure *Vision 2030* projects (national security), develop and influence trade corridors, strengthen food security (e.g., Saudi agricultural lands in Sudan), and Saudi power projection towards Africa, especially the Horn (foreign policy dimension).

From a geopolitical perspective, Saudi Arabia tried to build a Saudi-led forum for Red Sea security governance with the 'Red Sea Alliance', i.e., the Council of Arab and African States Bordering the Red Sea and the Gulf of Aden, a 2020 initiative that however hasn't resulted in any significant outcome so far. From a strictly infrastructural perspective, Riyadh has succeeded in developing oil exports from the Red Sea waterway, thus bypassing Hormuz: most of the oil exported through the Red Sea is directed to the EU and the US although this can't involve most of the Saudi exported oil: the majority of Saudi oil heads to Asia. The East-West Pipeline, also known as Petroline (a 1,200 kilometres pipeline), brings Saudi oil from the Abqaiq oilfields (Eastern region) to Yanbu on the Red Sea: more than 2 million barrels per day are currently exported through Petroline. Saudi Arabia exports about 7 million barrels each day: the goal is to export from Yanbu about 5 million barrels (estimated capacity).[6]

The search for alternative export routes and the creation of new export corridors beyond Hormuz stand also behind Riyadh's role in the redrawing of maritime balances in the Red Sea. For instance, sovereignty over Tiran and Sanafir, two small and uninhabited islands guarding the entrance to the Gulf of Aqaba, was ceded by Egypt to Saudi Arabia in 2017: the kingdom has claimed rights to the islands since ancient times. As the Straits of Tiran connect the Red Sea with the Gulf of Aqaba, this change allows Riyadh to control not only the northern section of the Red Sea and its maritime balances — crucial to the security of *Vision 2030* projects — but also the kingdom's strategic projection towards the Levant

---

[6]Perkins, R. (2019, May 14). Factbox: Escalating attacks raise risk on Saudi oil supply. *S&P Global.*

and the Mediterranean Sea. In terms of feasibility, the growing interdependence between Hormuz's balances and Bab-el-Mandeb's ones produces obstacles to the Saudi security strategy. The presence of the Houthis, i.e., Iranian-related actors, undermines Saudi short to medium-term plans for safe alternative export routes to Hormuz. As a matter of fact, the Southern Red Sea and the area close to the Bab-el-Mandeb are no longer as safe as it was before the 2015 Yemen war: this means that freedom of navigation in two of the chokepoints surrounding the Arabian Peninsula can't be taken for granted, thus troubling the Saudi security strategy.

The UAE (Fujairah)

The Emirati security strategy about Hormuz builds upon four dimensions: the improvement of naval defence capabilities, guarantees and cooperation with regional and international allies, quite constant neighbourhood relations with Tehran regardless of heightened geopolitical tensions, and the creation of an alternative maritime export route (Fujairah). Moreover, the Emirati Federation has designed a remarkable geostrategic presence amid the Bab-el-Mandeb and the Red Sea, especially due to the Yemen War, thus carving out an indirect maritime corridor. The UAE has traditionally perceived Iran as a direct threat to its territory. This is primarily due to factual reasons, i.e., the disputed islands issue, as well as to security perceptions. Geographically, the large majority of the Emirati territory is placed before Hormuz — comprising 90% of the oil and gas fields in the Abu Dhabi emirate — so the federation fears the strait can turn, in times of strong tensions, into a 'bottleneck'.

The Hormuz Strait is vital for the Emirati economy, which is an export-oriented country and bases its national security on reliable trade routes. The current Emirati foreign policy aims to increase the economic potential of the federation, as for the 'Principles of the 50' document: the goal is the further opening of the domestic economy to foreign investors, markets, goods, and people, especially from Asia. The UAE displays a networked perception of the world order, in which cross-regional initiatives and connectivity drive economic and energy choices.[7] This posture

---

[7]On the Emirati approach to foreign policy, refer to Young, K. E. (2014). *The Political Economy of Energy, Finance and Security in the United Arab Emirates: Between the*

is accentuated by the Emirati post-hydrocarbon economic diversification and by the growing reality of a multipolar international economy. Given this background, the UAE acknowledges that it cannot prosper in a highly polarised and conflictual system, especially at the regional level.

This is why the Emirati government has struggled to maintain a relationship of good neighbourliness with Iran even in the worst phase of the geopolitical escalation among Iran, the GCC states, and the US after 2018. This was primarily aimed to preserve the Emirati reputation as a safe country with safe waters, trying to mitigate the Hormuz 'bottleneck' risk. With this purpose, the UAE tried to capitalise on the Dubai emirate's good ties with Tehran, due to the community of Persian expats living in Dubai, trade and economic exchanges, thus balancing Abu Dhabi's stance which is traditionally more hawkish *vis-à-vis* Iran. At the same time, the president of the UAE and ruler of Abu Dhabi Mohammed bin Zayed Al Nahyan has subtly worked to reduce informal economic networks between Iran and the emirates of Ras al-Khaimah and Fujairah, 'albeit with limited success'.[8]

The 2019 Iranian attacks that targeted Saudi Aramco and then against the oil tankers between Hormuz and the Gulf of Oman pushed the UAE to intensify diplomatic contacts with the Islamic Republic despite tensions. Maritime security was the first issue the UAE addressed, re-engaging Iran in a bilateral dialogue on border security and navigation in shared waters through technical teams at coast guard level.[9] In mid-2022, the UAE resent its ambassador to Iran, a few months before the Chinese-brokered deal re-established diplomatic relations between Saudi Arabia and Iran in March 2023. Despite multilateral naval missions and diplomatic de-escalation, the UAE has perceived that it is better to invest in a security strategy which also entails a route alternative to Hormuz, in order to disempower persisting security risks. Naval missions and diplomatic de-escalation in fact are not enough to ensure maritime security, as Iranian attacks against tankers and disruption activities against freedom of navigation have continued despite the proliferation of naval operations and the

---

Majilis and the Market. Palgrave MacMillan, and to Baharoon, M. (2022, April 5). The keys to reading the UAE's strategic map. *The Middle East Institute.*

[8]Salisbury, P. (2020). Risk perception and appetite in UAE foreign and national security policy. *Chatham House*, Research Paper, 15.

[9]Vahdat, A. & Batrawy, A. (2019, July 31). UAE and Iran hold rare talks in Tehran on maritime security. *Associated Press.*

re-start of Saudi–Iranian diplomatic relations. For this reason, the UAE is investing in naval build-up, searching also for security guarantees from allies, and it is shaping alternative trade routes to Hormuz.

In terms of naval defence, the Emiratis bought corvettes to conduct anti-surface, sub-surface, and surveillance operations, in order to patrol their territorial waters. On the diplomatic side, the UAE expects to sign with the US a defence deal comprising guarantees in case of attack, although it is quite clear the Americans will no longer be the GCC states' defence umbrella that they used to be. The lack of military reaction by the US after the attacks against Saudi Aramco (2019) and those against the UAE (2022), respectively, under the Trump and Biden opposed presidencies, contributed to corroborate this conviction, so pushing the UAE to accelerate on multipolar relations, especially at East. With regard to alternative export routes, the UAE is mainly focused on the development of oil export and storage from Fujairah, the only emirate which stands 'beyond Hormuz', so naturally projected into the Indian Ocean.

Not by chance, Abu Dhabi — the main oil and gas producer emirate in the federation — is driving investments in Fujairah. In 2012, the Hasban–Fujairah pipeline was opened: it connects Abu Dhabi's oilfields directly with the Indian Ocean through the Gulf of Oman. The pipeline can transport about 2 million barrels of oil daily, which is about 75% of the Emirati daily oil exports. The UAE aims to transform Fujairah into the regional hub for storage and bunkering, putting the emirate in direct competition with Oman's Duqm. However, also the Fujairah 'beyond Hormuz' route reveals some risks. Since 2019, the radius of maritime insecurity has gradually moved in fact from Hormuz to the Gulf of Oman enlarging the area of insecurity, due to seizing and attempts to seize oil tankers by Iranian actors occurring close to the Emirati and the Omani coasts, in the Gulf of Oman. This means that even the alternative route bypassing Hormuz can't be taken for granted.

Since 2015, the UAE has also significantly committed to maritime security in the Red Sea–Bab-el-Mandeb waterway, given the rising Emirati military and commercial interests in Yemen and the Horn of Africa. The federation has struggled to balance the geostrategic gains coming from its military presence in Yemen (2015–2019), and from its enduring ties with Yemeni Southern actors and militias, with global security concerns about freedom of navigation. In 2019–2021, the UAE recalibrated its foreign policy in the Red Sea and Bab-el-Mandeb area, shifting from a season of 'power projection' to one of 'power protection' in the sub-region, epitomised by its direct military involvement in Yemen.[10] For this reason and to mitigate over-exposition, the UAE reduced its military footprint in the Horn of Africa, reconsidering the outpost in Berbera (Somaliland), turning it into a civilian airport project, and downsizing its presence in the Assab base (Eritrea) between 2020 and 2021.

Instead, the Emiratis stepped up their military positioning — directly and indirectly with the support of Yemen's Emirati-backed forces — in Yemeni coasts and islands, just in the Red Sea–Bab–Aden complex, in areas where the Emiratis don't have to face direct competitors and can rely on local allies: Perim island and Mocha city in the Bab-el-Mandeb, Aden and Mukalla in Hadhramawt, and Socotra island close to the Somali coast. These islands and ports, which are currently held by Yemeni groups backed by the UAE, could potentially become, in the medium to long term, hypothetical linchpins for Emirati-controlled export of Yemen's energy resources and goods, thus indirectly carving out a new oil route with respect to Hormuz. The UAE's military adjustment in the Red Sea and the Bab-el-Mandeb is focused on securing maritime waterways from Iranian-related threats to trade and energy transit. This goal is also shared by Israel, as both the countries who signed the *Abraham Accords* in 2020 are building their cooperation mixing geo-economic and geo-strategic interests.

Oman (Duqm)

Oman's security strategy, strictly tied to the Hormuz issue, is a mix of formal and informal diplomacy centred on a direct and friendly relation-ship with Iran, cooperation with regional and international players, and consolidated naval capabilities. However, the Sultanate is also developing alternative routes to Hormuz and the north of the country (e.g., Duqm), since even the Gulf of Oman has turned into a quite risky area for com-mercial navigation since 2019. Geographically placed between the Persian Gulf world and the Indian Ocean, not far also from Africa's coasts, the Sultanate of Oman used to cultivate friendly relations with Iran, before and after the 1979 revolution. Both Muscat and Tehran are the *de facto*

---

[10]Ardemagni, E. (2021, April 19). The UAE's military adjustment in the Bab El-Mandeb: From power projection to power protection. *Italian Institute for International Political Studies*, ISPI Commentary.

guardians of Hormuz and, unlike the Emirati-Iranian relations, there are no disputed lands to complicate the relationship.

Oman stands in front of the Hormuz Strait because of Musandam, the peninsula which is an Omani enclave in the UAE, with Khasab as the epicentre of informal economy and smuggling activities between the Omani and the Iranian coasts. In Musandam (Oman), which is the Southern and Arabian side of the Hormuz Strait, the Khasab Port is in fact the epicentre, since 1979, of smuggling activities from Omani coasts to the Iranian ones, despite the peninsula hosting many of Oman's military outposts. Dhows (small boats) led by Iranians, as well as fishing boats, arrive daily, with goods smuggled from Southern Iran, especially through the island of Qeshm, leaving the Omani shores in the evening with other goods, often shipped from Dubai. The local government of Musandam has regulated this activity, collecting commercial taxes, organising deliveries, and thus institutionalising this informal practice which is not illegal for Muscat, given the historical connections between these countries and routes.[11]

Besides the geographical factor, the Sultanate has a foreign policy tradition of neutrality *vis-à-vis* regional crises, comprised of those emanating from Iran.[12] It is a GCC member — and thus is loyal to the unity of the monarchies' organisation — but it has never ceased to pursue a good neighbourhood policy with Tehran. Specifically, informal diplomatic skills have transformed Oman into the number one mediator between Iran and the US, and among Iran, Saudi Arabia, and Yemen's Iranian-backed Houthis. Oman has also deepened economic ties with Qatar during Doha's blockade in 2017–2021, allowing the emirate to rely upon the Omani ports for trade and re-export activities, thus bypassing the Saudi, Bahraini, and Emirati boycott.

The Sultanate has a strong interest in preserving its reputation of stability through mediation power but, at the same time, it is also a country which

---

[11] Historically, trade and marriage drive intra-Gulf linkages between Musandam and the Iranian Southern coast. Language is also a unifying factor: the Kumzari dialect, a syncretic language mixing Farsi, Arabic, Portuguese and Hindi, is still spoken in Oman's Musandam and in neighbouring Iranian islands.

[12] On the Omani historical approach to foreign policy, with particular regard to the maritime domain, refer to Jones, J. & Ridout, N. (2012). *Oman, Culture and Diplomacy*. Edinburgh: Edinburgh University Press, and to Al Salimi, A. & Staples, E. (Eds.) (2016). *A Maritime History*. Verlag (see especially Beatrice Nicolini's chapter).

spends a lot on defence procurement. Specifically, Oman is the GCC state that traditionally invests more in the naval dimension to keep a modern and capable navy, building upon its glorious past of maritime empire. With the purpose of also preserving its maritime safety, Muscat cultivates an array of defence relations. For instance, Oman and Iran perform joint drills for security in the strait, and the Sultanate hosts a British military base (opened in 2019), providing defence access — also at the naval level — to the US and India. China's navy frequently docks at Salalah port, 480 kilometres southwest of Duqm in the Arabian Sea, as also the Russian navy does. Despite this effort, Oman is also developing alternative routes to Hormuz and the north of the Sultanate, since the Gulf of Oman — and not only the strait — has become since 2019 a quite risky area for commercial navigation.

In this way, the Sultanate aims to chart a trade and oil route directly in the Indian Ocean. Currently, Oman's oil export passes in fact through the Mina Al Fahal terminal, which is close to the capital Muscat, in the north of the country. Since 2022, Oman has started to expand oil exports from the terminal of Ras Markaz, placed in the special economic zone of Duqm, in the Arabian Sea, to transform it into a regional hub. Therefore, the newly constructed port of Duqm is planned to become an alternative to Hormuz for oil export and storage, thus openly competing with the Emirati Fujairah's hub. This is primarily due to Oman's post-hydrocarbon diversification plans, known as 'Vision 2040', as well as its increasing oil and gas exports to China.

Not by chance, Duqm represents a kaleidoscope of competing influences by regional and international powers, on whom the Sultanate seeks to strike a balance to strengthen its own security. For instance, Saudi Arabia and Kuwait invested in Duqm's industrial and refinery projects, as also China did. Moreover, Oman signed a series of agreements with the UAE to build a railway connection between the Sultanate and the Emirati Federation. This is going to carve out another trade route for the Sultanate: the port of Sohar, in the north of the country, could especially benefit from this.

Comparing UAE and Oman's Security Strategies: Findings and Conclusion

Both committed to maritime security and freedom of navigation in the Hormuz Strait, the UAE and Oman display nuanced policy stances on this issue. In terms of security strategies, the main difference is that the UAE tends to address Hormuz with a preventive posture embodied by defence build-up, especially naval, pragmatic dialogue with Tehran and regional and cross-regional cooperation with partners. Conversely, Oman addresses security threats from Hormuz mainly through a direct relationship with Iran, promoting bilateral communication and collaboration with Tehran. In terms of threat perception, the UAE conceptualises Hormuz as a direct menace to national security while Oman, although interested in waterways security, doesn't perceive Hormuz as a direct threat against its national security, and it mainly focuses on the overall Persian Gulf stability. This difference is primarily related to geography, as the UAE perceives some sort of entrapment in the Persian Gulf's waters differently from Oman, which is also naturally projected into the Arabian Sea and the Indian Ocean.

In terms of foreign policy, the UAE tends to focus on multiple partnerships and the shaping of cross-regional and mini-lateral formats (for instance, the I2U2 with the US, India, and Israel and the Trilateral Initiative with India and France) and frequently joins naval multinational missions as in the case of the US-led Combined Maritime Forces.[13] In this framework, as threats from Iran and its non-state allies and proxies raised, the Emirati Federation has multiplied joint military drills, especially at a maritime level. Examples are several: the UAE's joint naval drills with the US, Bahrain, and Israel after the *Abraham Accords* in 2021, followed in 2022 by a larger naval drill ('The International Maritime Exercise') in 2022, also comprising Saudi Arabia and Oman in the Western Indian Ocean.

In 2021, the UAE had also joined France and the QUAD (US, India, Japan, and Australia) for the first time in a joint naval exercise between the Persian Gulf and the Gulf of Oman. In 2023, there were also the first-ever bilateral naval exercise with Israel off the coast of Abu Dhabi, the first edition of the UAE–India–France Maritime Partnership Exercise in the Gulf of Oman as part of the Trilateral Cooperation Initiative, and the UAE–India joint naval drill ('Zayed Talwar') close to the Emirati coast to enhance shared capabilities, since India considers the Persian Gulf regions

---

[13] It is not by chance that the UAE opted in 2023 for the withdrawal of its forces from the US-led task forces of the CMF just to emphasise its disappointment regarding the American role in assuring maritime security in the Persian Gulf's region.

'as its immediate neighbourhood'.[14] With regard to the Sultanate, Oman tends instead to opt for a mediation-oriented foreign policy which prioritises good neighbourliness and dialogue on assertiveness and projection, which marked on the contrary the Emirati foreign policy in the 2010s. Differently from the UAE's approach to maritime security, Oman seems more focused on bilateral cooperation and naval exercises rather than on multilateral initiatives, although it joins the US-led task forces of the Combined Maritime Forces. The Sultanate has a privileged bilateral partnership with the UK (as the UAE has with France), although its cooperation with the US and India is strong. For instance, Oman and India regularly hold joint military exercises between their navies, and Muscat conducts annual bilateral drills with Iran's navy. This occurs as part of the Omani–Iranian Military Friendship Committee, and the exercises are centred on search and rescue activities, in the framework of the Sultanate's training plans 'with friendly countries'.[15]

More recently, the UAE is undergoing naval build-up to improve its defence capabilities, thus moving in the framework of the integrated deterrence outlined by the Americans, as for the *US National Defense Strategy 2022*.[16] Under the leadership of Sultan Haitham bin Tariq Al Said (who ascended to the throne in 2020), the Sultanate has continued the traditional attention to the naval dimension given its past of naval power

---

[14]Kumar, S. (2023, August 12). India, UAE conclude joint Arabian Gulf naval exercises. *Arab News*.

[15]*Oman News Agency*. (2021, December 16). Oman, Iran conduct naval exercise.

[16]Integrated Deterrence is a framework for working across warfighting domains, theaters and the spectrum of conflict, in collaboration with all instruments of national power, as well as with U.S. allies and our partners. U.S. Department of Defense. (2022, March 4). Integrated Deterrence at Center of Upcoming National Defense Strategy. The broader vision behind defense integration echoes what the US Central Command (CENTCOM) commander, Michael 'Erik' Kurilla, called the 'People, Partnerships, and Innovation' strategic approach to the region. For the GCC states and especially the UAE 'defense integration means supporting autonomy-oriented foreign policies — and staying ahead with technological innovations- without scaling-back from the multipolar choice in international relations. For the US, promoting defense integration is a chance to strike a strategic balance between retrenchment and presence in the Middle East, reducing spaces for Chinese and Russian military penetration. Instead of building new military bases, the Americans want to build coalitions able to handle regional security'. Ardemagni, E. (2023, February 24). Defense integration refashions the US-GCC alliance. *Italian Institute for International Political Studies*, ISPI Commentary.

and has accelerated on the road towards defence modernisation. The country is also less inclined than the UAE to advertise neighbours and media about procurement and skills: Muscat can rely upon three frigates and two corvettes of UK origin as of 2021 and the UAE on seven corvettes mostly from France.[17]

Another difference in the Emirati and Omani's security strategies is that while the UAE is also building indigenous defence capabilities for the navy, Oman can rely upon a consolidated group of national militaries willing to serve the navy. Moreover, the UAE and Oman also differ regarding security guarantees from allies. In fact, the UAE seeks security guarantees and external protection especially from the US, while Oman seems less focused on receiving external protection and more interested in implementing a dialogue-oriented foreign policy aimed to prevent potential crises. For instance, the UAE signed a defence agreement with France and is working to obtain security guarantees from Washington. This has become a real strategic priority for the UAE since the country was attacked three times by the Houthis with drones and missiles, in January and February 2022. In that event, three states actively supported the Emirati security: the US, France, and Israel.[18]

Against this backdrop, the UAE is likely to strengthen defence cooperation with these states, also with regard to maritime security and freedom of navigation through the Hormuz Strait. Without any doubt, a specific Emirati–Israeli cooperation on Hormuz would be a highly sensitive issue *vis-à-vis* Iran and, in that case, wouldn't be publicly announced, at least in the short term. Nevertheless, the blossoming UAE–Israel defence cooperation — which continues despite the Israel–Hamas war in Gaza — and the Pentagon's choice to move Israel under CENTCOM's area of responsibility in 2021 reveal this strategic direction. Despite Hormuz's security being a long-time issue for the stability of the Persian Gulf and its

---

[17] International Institute for Strategic Studies. (2022, March 5). The defence policy and economics of the Middle East and North Africa. Study presented at the *IISS Riyadh Defense Forum 2022*.

[18] The US intercepted some missiles and drones with the Patriot and the THAAD system placed at the Al Dhafra military base, close to Abu Dhabi. Washington sent later some F-22 and deployed the warship USS Cole off the Emirati coasts. France supported the UAE in the protection of the Emirati airspace through the Rafale fighter jets. Israel sent intelligence agents, also selling to the UAE the SPYDER system to intercept low-altitude threats, such as drones and cruise missiles.

neighbourhood, new regional and international dimensions (e.g., the rise of China and India's dependence on hydrocarbons, the Abraham Accords, and the growing geopolitical assertiveness of the GCC states) are contributing to re-shape the balance of power around Hormuz, transforming the strait into a global security issue. Something that impacts regional powers' security strategies, starting from the UAE and Oman.

© 2025 World Scientific Publishing Company
https://doi.org/10.1142/9789811294709_0009

Chapter 9

The People's Republic of China Strategic Imperatives in Oman's Port of Duqm

Mohammed Al-Hajri

Introduction

This chapter analyses the strategic imperatives guiding China's involvement in the Port of Duqm in the Sultanate of Oman. The overarching question guiding this analysis is the apparent disparity between the anticipated deepening of China's strategic and commercial presence at Duqm and the limited current outcomes. Despite shared economic interests and the early stages of the Belt and Road Initiative (BRI), why has China encountered challenges in establishing a more pronounced foothold at the Port of Duqm?[1]

China adopts a Port-Park-City (PPC) paradigm in Duqm, mirroring its approach in various African and East Asian countries.[2] This model seeks to develop industrial projects complemented by a Chinese-managed port to facilitate exports. However, the outcomes of China's overseas PPC projects vary significantly, ranging from effective operations to complete

---

[1] See among others Chaziza, M. (2018). The significant role of Oman in China's Maritime Silk Road Initiative. *Contemporary Review of the Middle East, 6*(1), 44–57.

[2] Bräutigam, D. & Xiaoyang, T. (2012). Economic statecraft in China's new overseas special economic zones: Soft power, business or resource security? *International Affairs, 88*(4), 805.

dissolution. In Duqm, Chinese presence at the port is notably limited, marked only by a loan from the Asian Infrastructure Investment Bank (AIIB) and setbacks in the progress of the Sino–Omani Industrial Park: the project's park component.

This chapter contends that the diverse outcomes of China's overseas projects are linked to the interactions among multifaceted actors in host countries and China, each with distinct interests and capacities to navigate implementation challenges. Therefore, understanding the state capacities of host countries becomes crucial, encompassing their ability to offer compelling investment incentives, deliver strategic and commercial returns, and strategically balance traditional security alliances. The geopolitical competition in the Western Indian Ocean involving extra-regional powers such as the United States and India, alongside China, holds profound strategic implications for smaller states like Oman and shapes the trajectory of Sino–Omani security cooperation in Duqm. As such, this chapter underscores the paramount importance of evaluating the capabilities of Chinese actors entrusted with overseas Port-Park-City (PPC) projects, particularly under China's 'hands-off' approach. The success of these firms in establishing projects and overcoming challenges hinges on their internal resource access and support from the host country.

To address the deficiencies in regional port projects with potential strategic significance, China embraces a 'quasi-mediation diplomacy' role in Middle East security issues. An illustrative example is China's recent mediation in the Iran–Saudi Arabia rivalry, reflecting its efforts to mitigate geostrategic challenges in the Persian Gulf and Strait of Hormuz. This chapter first addresses the conceptual discussion of the geostrategic/geoeconomic imperatives of China's overseas port construction. It then scrutinises China's tangible economic and strategic contributions in the Port of Duqm while examining the primary challenges and opportunities shaping Sino–Omani port cooperation.

Conceptualising the Imperatives of Chinese Overseas Port Construction

The discourse surrounding the People's Republic of China's (PRC) motivation for constructing overseas ports has garnered significant scholarly attention over the past decade, particularly since the inception of the BRI. The maritime facet of the BRI, known as the '21st Century Maritime Silk

Road (MSRI)', is commonly perceived as a strategic tool serving China's geopolitical interests, with ports playing a pivotal role in advancing both commercial and naval objectives. However, the narratives encompass a nuanced spectrum, oscillating between arguments that emphasise a geostrategic rationale for China's global rise[3] and an acknowledgement of the imperative to address developmental challenges in impoverished Chinese regions and economic growth issues stemming from industrial overcapacities.[4] Despite the perception of a comprehensive 'grand strategy' behind China's contested ports, the actual investments vary across different ports, contingent on the degree of the PRC's state involvement in each project.[5] Therefore, while geopolitical narratives might occasionally overemphasise China's overseas port construction for strategic purposes, it is crucial to empirically evaluate the extent of engagement by Chinese stateowned enterprises (SOEs) in managing, owning, and operating these ports and to discern the specific goals they seek to achieve and how they are able to overcome potential challenges in the implementation process.[6]

Furthermore, the foreign policy approach of the PRC in overseas port construction is characterised as 'fragmented', shaped by diverse actors including policy makers from the party-state, provincial governments, and private firms, often diverge in their objectives and levels of internal coordination.[7] The fragmentation of the implementation of the BRI is a manifestation of China's domestic political economy. An analytical misconception that scholars of China foreign policy in the Middle East

---

[3] See among others Blanchard, J.-M. F. & Flint, C. (2017). The geopolitics of China's Maritime Silk Road Initiative. *Geopolitics, 22*(2), 223–245; Niblock, T. (2018). Situating the Gulf in the changing dynamics of the Indian Ocean region. In Niblock, T., Ahmad, T. & Sun, D. (Eds.), *The Gulf States, Asia and the Indian Ocean: Ensuring the Security of the Sea Lanes* (pp. 5–32). Gerlach Press.

[4] See Sun, D. (2018). China's seaport diplomacy: Theories and practice. *China Economist, 13*(6), 34–48; Zou, Z. (2021). China's participation in port construction in the Western Indian Ocean region: Dynamics and challenges. *Asian Journal of Middle Eastern and Islamic Studies, 15*(4), 489–504.

[5] Jones, L. & Zeng, J. (2019). Understanding China's 'Belt and Road Initiative': Beyond 'Grand Strategy' to a state transformation analysis. *Third World Quarterly, 40*(8), 1415–1439.

[6] Kardon, I. B. & Leutert, W. (2022). Pier competitor: China's power position in global ports. *International Security, 46*(4), 9–47.

[7] Jaros, K. A. & Tan, Y. (2020). Provincial power in a centralizing China: The politics of domestic and international 'development space'. *The China Journal, 83*(1), 79–104.

often make is treating the state as unitary actor.[8] Also, they consider the BRI as the starting point for China's overseas investment in ports and free zones in the Middle East and Africa.[9] Another misreading is to analyse the success and failure of such Chinese Port-Park-City (PPC) projects solely from the prism of US–China geopolitical competition and the influence of the former on the agency of host-countries.[10] Thus, Lee (2017) contends against the generic term of 'Chinese firm', suggesting instead to unpack the interests of different kinds of Chinese capital as they tend to act differently in the pursuit of various benefits.[11] This approach highlights the economic and political interests that drive specific Chinese firms to invest, irrespective of their ownership status, thus providing a more nuanced understanding of China's multifaceted role in overseas port development.

The involvement of China's central government in the development of ports and free zones varies significantly across different cases. Prominent scholars focusing on China in Africa propose that the Chinese government adopts a 'hands-off' approach in the creation of overseas PPCs, serving primarily as a diplomatic facilitator between private stakeholders and host countries.[12] This perspective, however, does not undermine the central government's strategic role in policymaking or its function as a driving force to encourage diverse Chinese firms to embark on global ventures, addressing critical issues such as industrial overcapacity and the development of western regions.

Between the economic and strategic imperatives guiding Chinese overseas port construction, location emerges as a critical variable in this complex equation. The Strait of Hormuz, designated as one of the pivotal geostrategic chokepoints, holds paramount significance for the 'developmental interests' safeguarding the People's Republic of China's (PRC) national security, drawing considerable attention within Chinese

---

[8] Salman, M., Pieper, M. & Geeraerts, G. (2015, October 27). Hedging in the Middle East and China-U.S. competition. *Asian Politics & Policy, 7*(4), 575–596.

[9] Chaziza (2018). *Op. cit.*, 45.

[10] Matar, L. & Kadri, A. (2023). China against US imperialism in the Arabian Sea: The case of Oman. *Middle East Critique, 32*(2), 285–303.

[11] Lee, C. K. (2017). *The Specter of Global China: Politics, Labor, and Foreign Investment in Africa* (pp. 4–5). Chicago: University of Chicago Press.

[12] Bräutigam, D. & Xiaoyang, T. (2011). African Shenzhen: China's special economic zones in Africa. *The Journal of Modern African Studies, 49*(1), 27–54.

The People's Republic of China Strategic Imperatives in Oman's Port of Duqm   185

party-state policymaking circles.[13] Despite this emphasis, Middle Eastern scholars largely converge on the notion that the PRC plays a limited role as a regional security provider in the Middle East, raising questions about its willingness and capacity to expand its position.[14] An additional perspective suggests that the PRC has, in fact, functioned as a 'free rider', benefiting from the United States' security umbrella in the Persian Gulf without the imperative to augment its security footprint.[15] Instead, China has opted for diplomatic engagement in addressing security issues in the Middle East.[16] While the Middle East holds escalating economic importance for China, it does not claim the apex position in the party-state's regional security concerns, which accord higher geopolitical priorities to East, Southeast, and South Asia.[17] However, recent shifts in the Middle East's regional order, influenced by the US's debated security commitments and announcements of potential military presence, have prompted extra regional powers like China to consider assuming a more substantial role in the evolving geopolitical dynamics of the region.[18]

Nevertheless, while establishing a comprehensive naval presence may be deemed impractical, the possibility of China leveraging its overseas commercial ports for military purposes is constrained yet progressively feasible. Kardon & Leutert (2022) present three primary criteria for evaluating the People's Liberation Army Navy (PLAN) utilisation of overseas ports: geographical proximity to critical chokepoints and strategic sea

---

[13]Andrea, G. (2021). *Protecting China's Interests Overseas* (p. 55). Oxford: Oxford University Press.

[14]Andrea, S. (2018). China's search for security in the Greater Middle East. In James R.-A. (Ed.), *The Red Star and the Crescent: China and the Middle East* (pp. 13–36). Oxford: University of Oxford Press; Tim, N. (2021). The Middle East in China's global strategies. In Fulton, J. (Ed.) *Routledge Handbook on China–Middle East Relations* (pp. 29–47). London: Routledge.

[15]Degang, S. (2018). China's military relations with the Middle East. In James, R.-A. (Ed.), *The Red Star and the Crescent: China and the Middle East* (pp. 83–84). Oxford: University of Oxford Press.

[16]Janardhan, N. (2020). Belt and Road initiative: China's diplomatic-security tool in the Gulf? *Asian Journal of Middle Eastern and Islamic Studies, 14*(1), 1–17.

[17]Fulton, J. (2022, September 20). Cooperative Security in the Middle East: A role for China? *Kalam: Chatham House.* https://kalam.chathamhouse.org/articles/cooperative-security-in-the-middle-east-a-role-for-china/.

[18]Fulton, J. (2022). Systemic change and regional orders: Asian responses to a Gulf in transition. *The International Spectator, 57*(4), 1–19.

lines of communication, the extent of operational control by Chinese state firms, and the physical capacity to accommodate large PLAN vessels. From this standpoint, commercial ports meeting these criteria could potentially serve Chinese naval operations.[19]

Furthermore, the significance of the Strait of Hormuz extends beyond its role as a pivotal energy chokepoint, encompassing a vital line for Chinese exports to the region. The level of overseas port ownership by key Chinese central government seaport companies, such as COSCO and China Merchant Group (CMG), is highlighted as a factor increasing the likelihood of potential naval utilisation. However, this potential is contingent upon the presence of requisite infrastructural capabilities, including deep berths, Roll-on/Roll-off (RO-RO) equipment, and ample fuel resources to support large PLAN vessels.[20] Also, the capacity of the PLA Navy to deploy these commercial ports for extensive military operations remains limited. While such ports might contribute to peacetime operations, the security considerations of host countries must be taken into account. Balancing the dual roles of commercial ports and military interests requires a nuanced approach that acknowledges both the economic and strategic dimensions at play, emphasising the importance of collaboration and diplomacy in navigating these complex considerations.[21]

The increasing presence of China's People's Liberation Army Navy (PLAN) operations in the Indian Ocean underscores Beijing's commitment to addressing emerging threats to its interests in the region. These threats emanate from both states, such as India and the United States, and non-state actors, including sea piracy and terrorism. Given China's limited capacity for large-scale naval operations, fostering positive diplomatic relations with regional countries and investing in the construction and operation of port facilities are essential measures to achieve its security goals.[22] Since the late 2000s, the People's Republic of China (PRC) has conducted naval exercises and anti-piracy operations in the Western Indian Ocean, particularly around the Strait of Bab-el-Mandab and the

---

[19] Kardon & Leutert (2022). *Op. cit.*, 21.

[20] *Ibid.*

[21] Logan, D. C. *et al.* (2023). Correspondence: Debating China's use of overseas ports. *International Security, 47*(3), 174–179.

[22] D. Sun & Zoubir, Y. (2018). China's participation in conflict resolution in the Middle East and North Africa: A case of quasi-mediation diplomacy? *Journal of Contemporary China, 27*(110), 224–243.

Gulf of Aden. These efforts culminated in the establishment of the first overseas Chinese base in Djibouti in 2017.[23] The Djibouti example has led many observers to speculate that China may pursue similar initiatives to address challenges in the Strait of Hormuz, often referring to locations such as Gwadar, Abu Dhabi, and Duqm.[24]

Discussions surrounding the geopolitical implications of China's 'String of Pearls' strategy have triggered concerns about great power competition, particularly with the United States and its allies, notably India.[25] However, while structural developments are crucial to understanding China's strategic initiatives, these analyses often overlook the impact of host countries' political dynamics and their ability to shape the overall extent of Chinese engagement.[26] Recognising the agency of host countries in influencing the trajectory of Chinese involvement is paramount for a comprehensive understanding of the evolving geopolitical landscape in the Indian Ocean region. These dynamics exhibit variations from the perspectives of host countries regarding the economic and political benefits derived from their relationships with China. Simultaneously, Chinese investments are guided by the pursuit of projects that are both commercially and strategically viable, with their progress contingent on the institutional and economic capacities of the recipient nations.[27] It is crucial to consider the security perceptions of Gulf capitals and their strategic alignments with Western powers as influential factors in this complex landscape.

Certain scholars posit that Gulf states are adopting hedging strategies, attempting to sustain positive strategic ties with longstanding Western allies while concurrently capitalising on economic opportunities with

---

[23] Styan, D. (2019). China's maritime Silk Road and small states: Lessons from the case of Djibouti. *Journal of Contemporary China, 29*(122), 191–206.

[24] Kardon, I. B., Kennedy, C. M. & Dutton, P. A. (2020). China Maritime Report No. 7: Gwadar: China's Potential Strategic Strongpoint in Pakistan.

[25] Brewster, D. (2016). Silk Roads and Strings of Pearls: The strategic geography of China's new pathways in the Indian Ocean. *Geopolitics, 22*(2), 269–291.

[26] Kuik, C.-C. (2022). Interlude: Locating host-country agency and hedging in infrastructure cooperation. In Schindler, S. & DiCarlo, J. (Eds.), *The Rise of the Infrastructure State*. Bristol, UK: Bristol University Press.

[27] Blanchard, J.-M. F. (2021). Belt and Road Initiative (BRI) blues: Powering BRI research back on track to avoid choppy seas. *Journal of Chinese Political Science, 26*, 235–255.

China.[28] This perspective is grounded in the notion that Gulf states are hesitant to strengthen security partnerships with China if such collaboration might adversely affect their relations with the West. However, this assumption presupposes a shared interest between China and the Gulf in upholding the status quo of the US-led security structure, all while intensifying economic and diplomatic cooperation. In the realm of overseas port construction, Chinese motivations can significantly differ, oscillating between the pursuit of commercial gains and the need to address security challenges. The proximity to crucial chokepoints may shape the selectivity rationale for Chinese state firms, yet the successful execution of such endeavours is contingent upon the state capacities of host countries. The widespread adoption of China's 'Shekou model',[29] involving the development of ports and industrial parks, holds particular appeal for developing nations in the Middle East and Africa. This trend is especially noticeable among Gulf Cooperation Council (GCC) states that aspire to diversify their economies beyond hydrocarbons. Despite the growing prevalence of the 'Shekou model', whether the People's Republic of China (PRC) can leverage its strategic position in the Persian Gulf and utilise these commercial ports for power projection remains uncertain.

The Port of Duqm: China's Arab 'Port-Park-City' Project, The Asian Infrastructure Investment Bank, and the Limited Outcomes

The establishment of the Port of Duqm by the government of Oman initially aimed to support the Sultanate's economic diversification efforts. With the assistance of foreign investments, the goal was to create a Special Economic Zone (SEZ) to stimulate a diverse range of industrial activities. The Special Economic Zone Authority at Duqm (SEZAD) was established in 2011 through Royal Decree 119/2011 to oversee the

---

[28]Hamdi, S. & Salman, M. (2020). The hedging strategy of small Arab Gulf states. *Asian Politics & Policy, 12*(2), 127–152.

[29]The Shekou model was firstly developed by the Shekou Industrial Zone in Shenzhen symbolising a port-park-city project: 'A port in the front, an industrial zone in the middle and a city at the back.' Liu, Z., Dunford, M. & Liu, W. (2021). Coupling national geopolitical economic strategies and the Belt and Road initiative: The China-Belarus Great Stone Industrial Park. *Political Geography, 84*, 102296.

development of the free zone.[30] Rapidly gaining momentum, SEZAD has become one of the largest free zone projects in the Middle East, encompassing 2,000 square kilometres of reserved land. The strategic location of Duqm is considered Oman's greatest asset, leveraging its proximity to vital sea lines of communication in the Arabian Sea and Western Indian Ocean, as well as its strategic position near the Strait of Hormuz and Bab-el-Mandab. The concept of developing Duqm into a secure haven for hydrocarbon exports, circumventing the Strait of Hormuz, traces back to the first Gulf War between Iran and Iraq when Saudi Arabia and Oman conceived the idea of constructing an oil pipeline.[31]

SEZAD authorities actively promote Duqm as an alternative logistical hub, providing a strategic bypass to the geopolitical uncertainties associated with the Strait of Hormuz. Energy-centric projects, including oil storages, refineries, and petrochemical plants, constitute a central focus of Duqm SEZ. Additionally, its proximity to abundant mineral resources positions the Port of Duqm as a primary export point. While aligned with Omani objectives for economic diversification, these measures also reflect a broader trend in Gulf Cooperation Council (GCC) states towards 'late-rentier' economic reform, where energy-driven projects remain pivotal.[32] The geostrategic location and economic opportunities in Duqm align well with the strategic imperatives of the People's Republic of China (PRC), offering potential collaboration avenues and emphasising the intersection of economic and geopolitical interests in the region.

The presence of Chinese investments in Duqm reflects the application of the 'Shekou model' of port-park city projects, although its tangible outcomes are still in the making. The Port of Duqm is an Omani state-led initiative, with its inception predating the establishment of the Special Economic Zone Authority at Duqm (SEZAD). The project initially took shape with plans to construct a ship-repair yard by South Korea's Daewoo

---

[30] Sultanate of Oman, Royal Decree 119/2011 establishing the special economic zone authority at Duqm and promulgating its system. Released October 26, 2011. https://decree.om/2011/rd20110119/.

[31] Gulf International Forum. Saudi-Omani partnership: Economic and security ties deepen. GIF. https://gulfif.org/saudi-omani-partnership-economic-and-security-ties-deepen/.

[32] Gray, M. (2011, August 11). A theory of 'late Rentierism' in the Arab States of the Gulf. *CIRS Occasional Papers*.

Shipbuilding and Marine Engineering in 2006.[33] Managed by the Ministry of Transport and Communication, the Port of Duqm underwent various tendering processes and feasibility studies between 2007 and the establishment of the Port of Duqm Company (PDC) as a joint venture with the Belgian Consortium Antwerp Port (CAP) in 2012.[34] CAP officially received the concession to operate, manage, and develop the port through a Royal Decree in July 2015.[35] Funding sources for the port's construction were diverse, encompassing contributions from the state, regional, and international banks. Regional entities such as the Arab Fund for Economic and Social Development and the Kuwait Fund for Arab Economic Development provided partial loans in the project's early stages.[36]

Controversy arose when the China-led Multinational Development Bank (MDB), the Asian Infrastructure Investment Bank (AIIB), granted a US\$265 million concessional loan in 2016, covering 75% of the US\$349 million total cost for the first phase construction of the Port of Duqm.[37] This sparked debates about China's expanding influence in the region through its involvement in port development projects. While SEZAD authorities have announced the completion of the first phase, the port has yet to commence full-capacity commercial operations,

---

[33] Offshore Energy. (2006, September 25). Daewoo shipbuilding in Oman deal. *Offshore Energy*. https://www.offshore-energy.biz/httpwww-worldmaritimenews-comarticle shipbuilding5579daewoo-shipbuilding-in-oman-deal/.

[34] Offshore Energy. (2014, March 21). CAP to run the port of Duqm for next 28 years. *Offshore Energy*. https://www.offshore-energy.biz/cap-to-run-the-port-of-duqm-next-28-years/.

[35] Royal Decree 28/2015 promulgating the law granting the concession for the development management and operation of the Port of Duqm and approving the agreements relating to it, issued on July 12. https://decree.om/2015/rd20150028/.

[36] Arab Fund for Economic and Social Development. Al Duqm Port. https://www.arabfund.org/blog/projects/al-duqm-port/; https://www.arabfund.org/default.aspx?pageId=359&pId=571; Kuwait Fund for Arab Economic Development. Projects information for Oman up to 27-07-2023. https://www.kuwait-fund.org/ar/web/kfund/table?p_auth=Kk11pTcU&p_p_id=kfundloanstable_WAR_KFundPortletsportlet&p_p_lifecycle=1&p_p_col_id=column-5&p_p_col_count=2&_kfundloanstable_WAR_KFundPortletsportlet_country Code=137&p_p_state=normal&p_p_lifecycle=0&p_p_col_id=column-4&_kfundloanstable_WAR_KFundPortletsportlet_javax.portlet.action=setSectorsLoansDetailPage.

[37] The Asian Infrastructure Investment Bank. Oman: Duqm Port commercial terminal and operational zone development. https://www.aiib.org/en/projects/details/2016/approved/Oman-Duqm-Port-Commercial-Terminal-and-Operational-Zone-Development.html.

The People's Republic of China Strategic Imperatives in Oman's Port of Duqm   191

leaving the project's overall impact and success still unfolding. The role of the Asian Infrastructure Investment Bank (AIIB) in serving Chinese strategic imperatives and the interests of the BRI remains a subject of debate.

Early discussions cantered around whether the AIIB represents a 'revisionist' or 'status quo' initiative in the global governance of the liberal order. While China played a significant role in establishing the AIIB, the organizational design of the Multinational Development Bank (MDB) suggests that it serves as a 'soft and normative' attempt to further Beijing's foreign policy objectives with limited intent to undermine existing global norms.[38] The AIIB follows a policy of maintaining a high market valuation, aiming for an 'A' plus rating status.[39] It actively collaborates with other MDBs in project financing and seeks to avoid ventures deemed overly risky. Despite the Port of Duqm being labelled as a Maritime Silk Road Initiative (MSRI) project, reports indicate that the AIIB's involvement in financing the BRI is comparatively limited when compared to other Chinese banks such as the China Development Bank (CDB) and Export–Import (Exim) Bank.[40] Nevertheless, the energy-based and geographical opportunities presented by Duqm might have influenced the AIIB's decision to finance the Port, serving the interconnected purposes of the PPC project. As of now, Chinese contributions to the Port of Duqm have not extended beyond the AIIB loan. The operation of port facilities remains under the control of the Special Economic Zone Authority at Duqm (SEZAD) and Antwerp Port.[41]

Following the criteria set by Kardon and Leutert for the potential People's Liberation Army Navy (PLAN) use of China's overseas commercial ports, the Port of Duqm seems to meet the requirements of geographical proximity to important maritime routes and the physical capacity to support large naval vessels.[42] However, the critical factor of operational control is notably absent. The Port of Duqm is located within

---

[38] Hameiri, S. & Jones, L. (2018). China challenges global governance? Chinese international development finance and the AIIB. *International Affairs, 94*(3), 573–593.

[39] Haga, K. Y. (2021). The Asian Infrastructure Investment Bank: A qualified success for Beijing's economic statecraft. *Journal of Current Chinese Affairs, 50*(3), 391–421.

[40] *Ibid.*

[41] Oman Observer Newspaper. (2022, February 4). Duqm Port officially opens. *Oman Observer.* https://www.omanobserver.om/article/1113711/business/economy/duqm-port-officially-opens.

[42] Kardon & Leutert (2022). *Op. cit.*, 21.

400 nautical miles of the crucial Strait of Hormuz and is strategically positioned near vital sea lines of communication. While other ports in Oman, such as the Port of Sohar (within 110 nautical miles), might offer closer proximity to the Strait of Hormuz, the distance from Duqm is still considered adequate for potential PLAN operations.

Furthermore, the infrastructural capacity of the Port of Duqm includes a dedicated terminal of approximately 10 hectares for naval services, along with additional reinforcement facilities such as roll-on/roll-off (RO-RO) infrastructure, deep berths, and warehousing.[43] Despite these capabilities, PLAN vessels have not yet utilised these facilities due to the absence of Chinese operational control. The dynamics might shift as the Port of Duqm initiates the tendering process for multinational terminal operations, potentially opening the door for Chinese state port companies to compete for acquisition.[44] However, it is crucial to note that PLAN operations do not rigidly adhere to this discussed paradigm. Historical evidence indicates that Chinese navies made frequent port calls to Salalah between 2008 and 2015, totaling 25 visits.[45]

The People's Republic of China's (PRC) most significant contribution to the development of Duqm is marked by the establishment of the Sino–Omani Industrial Park in 2017. This initiative, led by a consortium of private Chinese companies from the Ningxia Autonomous Region, saw the Special Economic Zone Authority at Duqm (SEZAD) allocating 11.7 square kilometres to Oman Wangfang, the principal developer of the industrial park.[46] The Chinese industrial park was designed to include energy-intensive projects categorised into multilevel industries, petrochemical complexes, and a smaller section dedicated to tourism projects. Initial reports suggested that Oman Wangfang committed to generating US$10 billion worth of Chinese investments in the park over the first ten years of the project.[47] Since 2017, the Chinese industrial park in Duqm has

---

[43] Port of Duqm. Port terminals. https://portofduqm.om/terminals/#.

[44] Oman Observer Newspaper. (2021, July 17). Oman lunches tender for new container terminal at Duqm Port. *Oman Observer*. https://www.omanobserver.om/article/1104001/business/economy/oman-launches-tender-for-new-container-terminal-at-duqm-port.

[45] Andrea (2021). *Op. cit.*, 227.

[46] The Special Economic Zone Authority at Duqm. (2017, January 22). *The Seventh Issue of Quarterly Magazine. SEZAD*. https://duqm.gov.om/en/sezad/media/publications.

[47] Oman Observer Newspaper. (2017, April 19). $10 bn investments pledged. *Oman Observer*. https://www.omanobserver.om/article/83653/Main/10-bn-investments-pledged.

The People's Republic of China Strategic Imperatives in Oman's Port of Duqm   193

faced setbacks, and its progress has been limited, with only a single pipe-line factory established by 2021.[48] The reasons for these delays are not entirely clear, but they are commonly attributed to challenges within the host country, as well as perceived weaknesses in the administrative capabilities of Oman Wangfang, the principal developer. Issues such as the overall slow development of Duqm Special Economic Zone (SEZ), bureaucratic hurdles, and a lack of essential resources, including electricity and gas crucial for operating heavy industries, have contributed to the challenges faced by the industrial park.[49]

Despite these obstacles, the role of the Chinese state in the industrial park remains limited. The management is primarily entrusted to provincial-level private entities, driven by commercial interests and reliant on incentives provided by host countries. This 'hands-off' approach is consistent with China's strategy in other overseas free zone projects.[50] It reflects a pragmatic and commercially oriented approach to overseas investments, aligning with the broader theme of China's 'Western Development Program.' This approach acknowledges the complex challenges inherent in overseas ventures and emphasises the role of private entities in navigating and overcoming specific challenges while pursuing economic opportunities.

The prospects for China's economic expansion in Duqm remain contingent on the development of adequate infrastructure in the zone. Among the significant projects in Duqm Special Economic Zone (SEZ), the refinery and oil storage projects hold particular importance for China's energy security imperatives. The China Petroleum Pipeline Engineering Company, a subsidiary of the Chinese state-owned firm China National Petroleum Corp (CNPC), secured a US$320 million construction bid in 2018 for the Duqm Ras Markaz Oil storage.[51] This project is managed by Oman Tank Terminal Company (OTTCO), a subsidiary of the Omani state-owned

---

[48] Oman Observer Newspaper. (2021, October 21). Oman's first polyethylene pipe factory set for launch. *Oman Observer.* https://www.omanobserver.om/article/1108551/business/markets/omans-first-polyethylene-pipe-factory-set-for-launch.

[49] Gnana, J. (2017, September 10). China's refinery in Duqm plans at Duqm faces delays. *MEED.* https://www.meed.com/exclusive-chinas-refinery-plans-at-duqm-face-delays/.

[50] Bräutigam & Xiaoyang (2011). *Op. cit.*

[51] China Global Investment Tracker. Chinese investments & contractors in Oman (2005–2023). *American Enterprise Institute.* https://www.aei.org/china-global-investment-tracker/.

enterprise OQ. The oil storage facility has a capacity of up to 25 million barrels of crude and is connected to the Port of Duqm.[52]

In addition, the Duqm refinery is a major collaboration between OQ and Kuwait Petroleum International (KPI), which is intended to be the largest in Oman with a capacity of 230,000 barrels per day and an estimated cost of US$7 billion.[53] The refinery project encountered setbacks due to OQ's financial difficulties, stemming from the decline in oil prices post-2014 and state austerity measures to mitigate fiscal burdens.[54] However, recent reports indicate that the project is nearing completion and is expected to be operational by the end of 2023. The energy-intensive opportunities in Duqm suggest the potential for increased Chinese interest, particularly as these petrochemical projects and the port begin functioning.[55] Nonetheless, the prospects of Chinese investments in Duqm are subject to the multifaceted dynamics of the political economy in host countries and broader systemic changes at the regional level. The success and trajectory of these projects will likely be influenced by the evolving economic, political, and geopolitical landscape in the region.

The Economic Realities for the Implementation of China's Port-Park-City Project in Duqm

The commercial aspects of Chinese investments underscore the necessity for economically viable opportunities and high levels of state capacity to achieve desired outcomes. The economic challenges faced by Oman, including the post-2014 decline in oil prices and the repercussions of the COVID-19 pandemic, alongside the abundance of port projects in the

---

[52] OTTCO. Ras Markaz terminals. https://ottco.om/terminals/ras-markaz.

[53] Prabhu, C. (2021, January 18). Oman's Duqm refinery is rebranded as OQ8. *Oman Observer*. https://www.omanobserver.om/article/5061/Business/omans-duqm-refinery-is-rebranded-as-oq8.

[54] Ingram, J. (2022, November 18). Oman's Duqm refinery set for end-2023 start-up. *MEES*. https://www.mees.com/2022/11/18/news-in-brief/omans-duqm-refinery-set-for-end-2023-start-up/450f2f40-673f-11ed-b106-d371154556d8.

[55] Zawaya. (2023, September 22). Oman's Duqm refinery completes start-up, sees commercial ops by year-ends. https://www.zawya.com/en/business/energy/omans-duqm-refinery-completes-start-up-sees-commercial-ops-by-year-end-qp0k1ynk.

Gulf region, have collectively impacted the pace of development in the Chinese-led PPC project in Duqm.

The extent of engagement by the central state of the PRC, through its various state institutions, is a crucial factor to consider. This engagement reflects the strategic imperatives to participate in ventures that may involve inherent risks. Chinese state-owned enterprises (SOEs), sitting at the top of the strategic hierarchy, are generally more willing to engage in potentially precarious investments to achieve both commercial and diplomatic/strategic gains.[56] In contrast, provincial-level and private Chinese companies typically have less access to central government resources and must compete with various actors for state incentives. Consequently, the latter tends to be more self-sufficient and pursue developmental opportunities aligned with their own interests, dependent on the economic realities of host countries.[57]

The decline in oil prices after 2014 significantly impacted Oman's fiscal situation, affecting state developmental spending. Three years after the establishment of the Duqm Special Economic Zone (SEZ) mega-project in 2011, the cost of crude oil dropped from US$103 to US$56 in 2015.[58] Given that hydrocarbon revenues constituted up to 60% of the Omani state budget, the decline in oil prices led to increasing deficit burdens that needed to be addressed through various structural adjustment policies.[59] While borrowing and issuing debt were direct solutions, the debt-to-GDP ratio grew considerably from 5% in 2014 to 60% in 2019, affecting Oman's credit rating scores, important measures for evaluating the risks of borrowing.[60] Yet, since the ascendance of Sultan Haitham bin Tariq in January 2020, important austerity measures and governance restructuring were undertaken, such as the Medium-Term Fiscal Plan

---

[56]Liu, Z., Schindler, S. & Liu, W. (2020). Demystifying Chinese overseas investment in infrastructure: Port development, the Belt and Road initiative and regional development. *Journal of Transport Geography, 87,* 1–10.

[57]Jaros & Tan (2020). *Op. cit.*

[58]National Centre for Statistics and Information. *Statistical Yearbook 2016* (p. 196). Sultanate of Oman.

[59]Ennis, C. A. & Al-Saqri, S. (2021). Oil price collapse and the political economy of the post-2014 economic adjustment in the Sultanate of Oman. In *Oil and the political economy in the Middle East.* Manchester, England: Manchester University Press.

[60]Ministry of Finance. Medium-term fiscal plan 2020–2024. Sultanate of Oman. https://www.mof.gov.om/MediumTermFiscalPlan.

(2020–2024), aiming to rationalise state expenditure to achieve fiscal balance.[61] These measures affected many state-led projects in Duqm, reflecting the challenging domestic economic situation. The delays in the operational opening of the Duqm Port and refinery serve as examples illustrating the impact of the broader economic challenges on specific developmental projects.

Furthermore, the implications of the declining Chinese economy and the COVID-19 lockdowns have led to a slowdown in the inflow of overseas Chinese investments. The initial enthusiasm for China's investments in Oman, and the Middle East in general, appears to have diminished after 2017, with investment decreasing from over US$5.2 billion in 2016 to US$100 million in 2020.[62] According to the China Global Investment Tracker, the total BRI investments in Oman, a decade after its establishment, amounted to US$2.2 billion in 2023, which includes US$1 billion from Ningxia Wangfang in Duqm in 2017.[63] The challenging domestic economic situation, along with efforts to review various underperforming BRI-related projects amid lockdown hurdles, has significantly impacted the ability of both Chinese state and subnational enterprises to access privileged resources necessary to 'go global.'[64]

Given that the companies based in Ningxia involved in the Chinese industrial park project in Duqm are privately owned, the aforementioned economic dynamics have had a substantial impact on the project implementation process. Nevertheless, the availability of alternative regional investment opportunities that may be perceived as more commercially competitive could also influence the investment decisions of Chinese entities. Such lucrative locations might exist in other Gulf states like the United Arab Emirates that provide both attractive investment incentives and available resources. The shifting economic landscape and uncertainties brought about by the global economic downturn and the pandemic have prompted a reassessment of investment priorities and risk considerations by Chinese investors, affecting the trajectory of projects such as the one in Duqm.

---

[61] Baabood, A. & Chay, C. (2021, April 16). Respite for reform: Sultan Haitham stamps his mark on Oman. *ISPI.* https://www.ispionline.it/en/publication/respite-reform-sultan-haitham-stamps-his-mark-oman-30092.

[62] Herrero, A. G. (2022, February 9). How China's investment in Middle East is evolving. *Asia Times.* https://asiatimes.com/2022/02/how-chinas-investment-in-middle-east-is-evolving/.

[63] See China Global Investment Tracker (2023). *Op. cit.*

[64] Shi, W. & Ye, M. (2021). Chinese capital goes global: The Belt and Road initiative and beyond. *Journal of East Asian Studies, 21*(2), 173–192.

Despite the geographical advantages of Omani ports in terms of both access to and bypassing the Strait of Hormuz, the development of port and free zone projects is more advanced in other parts of the Persian Gulf. The United Arab Emirates (UAE) has strategically positioned itself as the region's logistical hub, boasting extensive experience in managing ports and free zones.[65] China has already utilised Dubai's Jebel Ali as a key trading entrepôt in the region, fostering economic and investment cooperation. Furthermore, the Khalifa Port and Industrial Zone in Abu Dhabi (KIZAD) has emerged as a significant BRI location in the Persian Gulf, implementing a similar PPC paradigm.[66] The China–UAE Industrial Capacity Cooperation Demonstration Zone (ICCDZ), led by Jiangsu Overseas Cooperation and Investment Company (JOCIC), was established between 2015 and 2017.[67] Additionally, the Chinese state-owned enterprise (SOE) COSCO Shipping Ports inaugurated the container terminal at Khalifa Port in 2018, aiming to be a key regional hub for the BRI in the Middle East.[68] Despite Khalifa Port's location in Abu Dhabi after the Strait of Hormuz, its close proximity to the chokepoint (within 160 nautical miles) aligns with Kardon and Leutert's model, with operational control under COSCO. Commercially, Abu Dhabi's abundance of energy resources, attractive business regulations, and stable economic situation have all contributed to the pace of development.[69]

The Gulf region already witnesses competition among privately owned Global Network Terminal Operators (GNTs) that are often profit-driven.[70] Despite China's attempts to establish a cooperative mechanism between BRI ports in the Gulf, particularly between UAE's Khalifa Port, Oman's Duqm Port, and Saudi Arabia's Jizan Port, through the 'Industrial

---

[65] Henderson, C. (2017). The UAE as a Nexus State. *Journal of Arabian Studies, 7*(1), 83–93.

[66] Fulton, J. (2019). China-UAE relations in the Belt and Road era. *Journal of Arabian Studies, 9*(2), 253–268.

[67] Yumul, J. (2023, July 28). Industrial pact with Beijing reaches new highs. *China Daily.* https://www.chinadaily.com.cn/a/202307/28/WS64c31c43a31035260b819074.html.

[68] Abu Dhabi Ports. (2018, December 18). COSCO shipping ports partners with Abu Dhabi ports to create regional trading hub and Middle East gateway for Belt and Road. https://www.adports.ae/cosco-shipping-ports-partners-with-abu-dhabi-ports-to-create-regional-trading-hub-and-middle-east-gateway-for-belt-and-road/.

[69] Fulton (2019). *Op. cit.*

[70] Ziadah, R. (2017). Constructing a logistics space: Perspectives from the Gulf cooperation council. *Environment and Planning D: Society and Space, 36*(4), 666–682.

Park–Port Interconnection, Two-Wheel and Two-Wing' initiative, the implementation remains unclear.[71] Achieving such coordination is challenging as private foreign investments, including those from China, prioritise commercial benefits and seek to avoid risky ventures. However, with the recovery of oil prices and the global economy, the prospects for Chinese investments may change. Recent reports from the Omani Ministry of Finance indicate positive financial performance due to rising oil prices since the end of 2021, driven by the global energy market's growth amid the Russian War on Ukraine. This positive development led to the conclusion of the Medium-Term Fiscal Plan (MTFP) before its 2024 deadline, a decline in the debt-to-GDP ratio to 40%, improved credit ratings, and the resumption of suspended projects in Duqm and elsewhere.[72] Moreover, the Omani government signed promising new deals with the UAE in September 2022 to build railway projects connecting the Ports of Abu Dhabi and Sohar, aiming to circumvent the risks associated with the Strait of Hormuz and promote Gulf Cooperation Council (GCC) integration.[73]

The Securitisation of Duqm and the Strategic Narrative in the Persian Gulf and Western Indian Ocean Region

The analysis of structural-level changes in the presumed transformation of the regional order and increased securitisation in the Persian Gulf and the Western Indian Ocean region reveals profound strategic dilemmas that influence the decision-making options of all stakeholders involved. The

---

[71] Ministry of Foreign Affairs of the People's Republic of China. (2018, July 10). Wang Yi: China and Arab states should jointly forge the cooperation layout featuring Industrial Park-Port Interconnection, Two-Wheel and Two-Wing approach. https://www.fmprc.gov.cn/eng/gjhdq_665435/2675_665437/2903_663806/2905_663810/201807/t20180712_536469.html.

[72] Reuters. (2023, April). Oman repays 29 billion loans in Q1 — Finance ministry. *Reuters*. https://www.reuters.com/world/middle-east/oman-repays-29-billion-loans-q1-finance-ministry-2023-04-11/.

[73] Oman Observer Newspaper. (2022, September 28). Agreement signed for 303km Suhar-Abu Dhabi railway network. *Oman Observer*. https://www.omanobserver.om/article/1125923/oman/his-majesty/agreement-signed-for-303km-suhar-abu-dhabi-railway-network.

The People's Republic of China Strategic Imperatives in Oman's Port of Duqm 199

rise of China's security interests in the Western Indian Ocean, coupled with the perceived potential strategic decline of the US, has prompted rising powers like India to be more cautious about potential 'encirclement' in what is considered by New Delhi as its own backyard.[74] Concurrently, while significant great power competition remains limited, smaller regional states are acutely aware of the geopolitical environment and seek hedging policies to maximise both strategic and economic gains.[75] Therefore, the developments in the geostrategic rivalry between major powers and the abilities of regional states to astutely pursue hedging strategies impact the range of available choices. Oman's strategic approach, attempting to maintain its alignment with Western powers such as the United States and the United Kingdom while simultaneously fostering economic ties with China, plays a pivotal role in shaping the potential for Sino-Omani relations beyond energy trade. This nuanced diplomatic stance reflects Oman's effort to navigate the complex and evolving geopolitical landscape, balancing between different actors to safeguard its national interests and maintain stability in the region.[76]

The strategic importance of the port of Duqm for China and the limited capacity to establish a regional 'strongpoint' align with the broader security narrative discussed earlier. An analysis of the implications of China's 'String of Pearls' strategy in the Western Indian Ocean, coupled with potential Chinese interest in Duqm, has triggered a strategic response from Oman's security allies — the United Kingdom and the United States — as well as India, seeking to balance Beijing in this strategically located port.[77] The UK's military presence in Duqm is notable, marked by the establishment of the UK Joint Logistics Support Base in 2017.[78]

---

[74] Huwaidin, M. B. (2022). China and India's soft rivalry in the Gulf region. *Journal of the Indian Ocean Region, 18*(1), 6–20.

[75] Kuik, C.-C. (2021). The twin chessboards of US-China rivalry: Impact on the geostrategic supply and demand in post-pandemic Asia. *Asian Perspective, 45*(1), 157–176.

[76] Al-Hajri, M. & Fulton, J. (2023). Navigating asymmetry in the Indian Ocean region: Oman in the US-India-China strategic triangle. *Journal of the Indian Ocean Region, 19*(1), 6–20.

[77] Grare, F. & Samaan, J.-L. (2022). *The Indian Ocean as a New Political and Security Region* (p. 44). Switzerland: Palgrave Macmillan.

[78] Ministry of Defence. (2017, August 28). Defence secretary strengthens ties between UK and Oman. *Gov.UK*. https://www.gov.uk/government/news/defence-secretary-strengthens-ties-between-uk-and-oman.

This presence is further complemented by a multimillion-pound joint venture between the British defense company Babcock and the Oman Drydock Company, providing engineering and training facilities for Britain's Royal Navy. In a similar vein, the US signed an agreement with the government of Oman in March 2019 to expand access to facilities and ports in Duqm and Salalah.[79] While both the US and the UK have not explicitly stated an intention to counter China's presence, emphasising the imperative to address non-state threats like piracy, terrorism, and illicit trafficking, the timing of these initiatives suggests a geostrategic narrative.

India's agreement for access to the port of Duqm, resulting from Indian Prime Minister Narendra Modi's visit to Oman in February 2018, has sparked controversial geostrategic debates on the potential for regional competition between India and China.[80] This move reflects India's proactive stance in response to perceived Chinese strategic interests in the Indian Ocean region. The evolving strategic landscape in the Western Indian Ocean underscores the complex interplay of interests and alliances among major powers, regional actors, and smaller states, each seeking to safeguard its own security concerns in this geopolitically significant area.

The competition between China and India for influence in the ports of the Western Indian Ocean has intensified since the announcement of the BRI in 2013. India's strategy of 'evasive balancing' towards China, involving both strengthening ties with the US and regional powers while reassuring Beijing of its non-intention for 'hard balancing',[81] has resulted in the establishment of new minilateral regional security and connectivity initiatives such as the India, Israel, United Arab Emirates, and United States (I2U2) and the 'Arab-Mediterranean Corridor.'[82] Both

---

[79] U.S. Embassy in Oman. (2019, March 24). U.S. statement on the signing of the strategic framework agreement. https://om.usembassy.gov/u-s-statement-on-the-signing-of-the-strategic-framework-agreement/.

[80] Panda, A. (2018, February 14). India gains access to Oman's Duqm Port putting the Indian Ocean geopolitical contest in the spotlight. *The Diplomat.* https://thediplomat.com/2018/02/india-gains-access-to-omans-duqm-port-putting-the-indian-ocean-geopolitical-contest-in-the-spotlight/.

[81] Rajagopalan, R. (2020). Evasive balancing: India's unviable Indo-Pacific strategy. *International Affairs, 96*(1), 75–93.

[82] Tanchum, M. (2021, August). India's Arab-Mediterranean corridor: A paradigm shift in strategic connectivity to Europe. *South Asia Scan*, Issue No. 14. Singapore: Institute of South Asian Studies.

The People's Republic of China Strategic Imperatives in Oman's Port of Duqm   201

initiatives consider the UAE and Israel as key port locations connecting India's economic and strategic imperatives. However, the differing perceptions of the UAE and Israel towards the People's Republic of China (PRC) as an important partner impede efforts to build a strong coalition effectively countering Beijing.[83] This underscores the importance of considering regional security perspectives and their role in shaping the contours of strategic engagement.[84] Moreover, the politics of 'zero-sum' games becomes complicated as the strategic interests of the concerned stakeholders are deeply intertwined, and consensus is difficult to achieve. The cautious incremental steps of China's strategic footprint in the Gulf and the wider Western Indian Ocean also reflect this particular dilemma and the significant costs of antagonising various stakeholders.

Oman's 'omni-enmeshment' approach towards regional security often seeks to involve all strategic stakeholders with delicate measures to avoid upsetting existing alignment ties.[85] Mogielnicki suggests that the late Sultan Qaboos bin Said (1970–2020) was apprehensive about the opportunities presented by Chinese investments in Duqm and the potential strings attached to their financial support.[86] While the accuracy of this statement is unclear, it reflects the general 'neutrality' of Oman's foreign policy approach towards regional security issues. This neutrality is notably evident in Oman's maritime security doctrine, where it regularly conducts naval exercises with both rival powers and allied states, including Iran, GCC states, Pakistan, India, and frequently hosts Chinese naval vessels through port calls in Salalah. Oman's neutral stance has led some scholars to speculate about the potential for Duqm to play a role similar to Djibouti, hosting multiple naval bases from various countries.[87] Furthermore, despite recent rumours suggesting China's intention to establish a military base in Duqm, and the US expressing discomfort,

---

[83] Al-Hassan, H. & Solanki, V. (2022, November 11). The I2U2 minilateral group. *IISS*. https://www.iiss.org/online-analysis/online-analysis//2022/11/the-minilateral-i2u2-group.

[84] Gray, M. (2023). The rise of minilateralism, the Indo-Pacific context, and the Arab Gulf States. *Journal of the Indian Ocean Region, 19*(1), 40–56.

[85] Al-Hajri & Fulton (2023). *Op. cit.*

[86] Mogielnicki, R. (2021). *A Political Economy of Free Zones in Gulf Arab States* (p. 121). Cham: Palgrave Macmillan.

[87] Grare & Samaan (2022). *Op. cit.*, pp. 45–46.

202   M. Al-Hajri

there have been no official statements confirming this plan.[88] Nevertheless, Oman shares the imperative of securing the supply of energy to China, given its heavy dependence on the Chinese oil market, where it purchased up to 81% of its total exported oil in 2022.[89]

Therefore, while Chinese commercial investments in the ports of GCC states have grown considerably over the past decade, adopting a 'quasi-mediation diplomacy' is one way to address complicated security issues.[90] However, Ghiselli reflects on Chinese commentators' views that the latest mediation role in the Saudi Arabia and Iran peace deal suggests a 'paradigm shift' in the PRC's security approach to the Middle East.[91] The de-escalation efforts made by China reflect the difficulty of achieving security objectives in the Persian Gulf and Strait of Hormuz through the construction of physical strongpoints. While Chinese port projects in Duqm and Pakistan's Gwadar are still under development with ambiguous prospects in playing important strategic roles for China, Saudi–Iranian rapprochement serves valuable benefits to Beijing's security concerns in the region. Moreover, the deal is interpreted as a manifestation of China's broader 'international mediator' role, reflecting the framework of its newest Global Security Initiative (GSI) aiming to provide an alternative global security order.[92] Whether the brokered deal indicates a new precedence in Chinese engagement in Middle East security issues or not, the permanence of the agreement depends on the ability of both Saudi Arabia and Iran to address their complex security issues. For now, diplomacy is the coin to the PRC's strategic achievements in the region.

---

[88] Bloomberg. (2023, November 7). Biden briefed on Chinese efforts to put military base in Oman. *Bloomberg.* https://www.bloomberg.com/news/articles/2023-11-07/biden-briefed-on-chinese-effort-to-put-military-base-in-oman?embedded-checkout=true.

[89] National Centre for Statistics and Information. *Statistical Yearbook 2023* (p. 155). Sultanate of Oman.

[90] Sun & Zoubir (2018). *Op. cit.,* 224.

[91] Ghiselli, A. (2023, July). Interpreting China's changing approach to security issues in the Middle East. *China Trends by Institut Montaigne.* https://www.institutmontaigne.org/en/publications/china-trends-16-chinas-diplomatic-coup-middle-east-facts-behind-hype.

[92] Jash, A. (2023, June). Saudi-Iran deal: A test case of China's role as an international mediator. *Georgetown Journal of International Affairs.* https://gjia.georgetown.edu/2023/06/23/saudi-iran-deal-a-test-case-of-chinas-role-as-an-international-mediator/.

Conclusion

In conclusion, the Port of Duqm stands as a geostrategically significant location for extra-regional powers, yet China's limited footprint raises questions about its prospects for increased presence. This chapter explored the factors contributing to China's limited involvement in Duqm. Despite initial intentions from both Oman and China to develop Duqm as a Port-Park-City (PPC) project, a combination of host-country political economy dynamics, inadequate Chinese capacities, and geopolitical concerns from the US and India have shaped the minimal outcomes.

Oman, grappling with fiscal constraints since the oil price decline in 2014, faces challenges in expanding spending on ambitious developmental projects like the Port of Duqm and the Special Economic Zone (SEZ). The unpreparedness of Duqm's facilities, such as the port and refinery, insufficient energy supply like gas, and bureaucratic hurdles in mobilising resources from both Oman and China have significantly influenced the trajectory of these projects. While Duqm holds immense potential as a strategic location to mitigate risks associated with chokepoints like the Strait of Hormuz and Bab-el-Mandab, the ability of China and Oman to overcome these challenges remains uncertain.

The chapter highlights the diminishing outlook of Chinese industrial investments in Duqm and their meagre role in the port operations. The concurrent military presence of the US, the UK, and India further complicates China's potential role in the near future. The evolving dynamics in Duqm underscore the complexities of navigating geopolitical interests and economic imperatives in the strategically vital Western Indian Ocean region.

© 2025 World Scientific Publishing Company
https://doi.org/10.1142/9789811294709_bmatter

Index

1+2+3 cooperation pattern, 40
21st Century Maritime Silk Road, 42, 106, 183

A
Abu Dhabi, 173
active deterrence, 154
Ajili, Hadi, 145
Alexander the Great, 99
Anglo–Russian rivalry, 123
anti-ship cruise missiles (ASCMs), 159
Antwerp Port, 191
Arab–Israel War, 12
Arab-Mediterranean Corridor, 200
Asia, 19
Asian Development Bank, 28
Asian Infrastructure Investment Bank (AIIB), xxii, 182, 190–191
asymmetry, 165

B
Bab-el-Mandeb, 13
Bagheri, Mohammad, 157
Balochistan, 94
Belt and Road Initiative (BRI), xiv, xix, 4–5, 32, 41, 86–87, 95, 106–108, 168, 182

Biden, Joseph (Joe), 6, 75–76, 78
Black Sea Grain Initiative, 65
Blinken, Antony, 79
Bosporus Strait, 145
Brewster, David, 125
Buledi, Pasand Khan, 17

C
Carter's State of the Union Address, 38
CENTCOM, 178–179
Chabahar, 13–14, 119–140
Chabahar Agreement, xviii
China, 21–22, 31–46, 105
China Harbour Engineering Company Limited, 23
China–India competition, xvii, 72
China–Iran, 70, 92
China Merchant Group (CMG), 186
China Merchants Port Holdings Company Limited (CM Port), 28
China–Myanmar Economic Corridor (CMEC), 18
China National Petroleum Corp (CNPC), 193
China–Oman relations, 85

206 *Index*

China–Pakistan Economic Corridor (CPEC), 16, 41, 94–95, 106, 108–112, 131
China Petroleum Pipeline Engineering Company, 193
China's People's Liberation Army Navy (PLAN), 186
China's State Council Information Office, xiv
chokepoints, 69–92
civilisation approach, 63
Cold War, 3–4, 31, 150
collective security, 38–39
Collective West, 51
Combined Maritime Forces (CMF), 38
conflict zone, 158
Consortium Antwerp Port (CAP), 190
Construction, Development of Transport Infrastructure Company (CDTIC), 130
contemporary security strategies, 169–171
Corbett, Julian S., 10
Cordesman, Anthony, 145
COSCO, 186
COVID-19 pandemic, 53
Cyclone Phet, 115

D
debt trap, xiv, 28
deep pluralism, 152
domino effect, 50
Doval, Ajit, 85
dry climate, 97
Duqm Industrial Park, 85, 87

E
Energy Triangle, 56
Enhanced Defense Cooperation Arrangement (EDCA), 19
Eurasian Customs Union, 52

Eurasian Economic Community, 52
Eurasian Economic Union (EAEU), 51
European-led Maritime Awareness Strait of Hormuz (EMASOH), 168
European Union (EU), 8
evasive balancing, 200

F
fast attack crafts (FACs), 159
foreign policy concept, 52
free trade-industrial zones, 119

G
G-20 Summit, 20
Gaddis, John Lewis, 61
Garlick, J., 17
geography, 98
geopolitical sensitivity, 81
geopolitical shock, 48
Global Coalition to Defeat ISIS, 39
Global Network Terminal Operators (GNTs), 197
Global Security Initiative (GSI), 202
Greater Eurasia, xviii, 54, 64
Greater Eurasian Partnership (GEP), 51–52
Gulf Cooperation Council (GCC), xx–xxi, 42, 163, 166, 188–189
Gulf of Thailand, 23
Gwadar Port, 16, 93–117

H
Haifa Port, 7
'hands-off' approach, 182, 193
Hatami, Amir, 155
Hormozgan, 122
Hu Jintao, 16

I
imperial powers, 102
India, 71–80

India–Central Asia Dialogue, 134
India–China competition, 31
India–GCC relations, 44
India–Gulf dynamics, 43
India–Iran cooperation, 132
India–Middle East-Europe Economic
 Corridor (IMEC), xiv, 6–7, 27
Indian Ocean region (IOR), xiii, xxi,
 96
Indian Ports Association (IPA), 129
Indian Railway Construction Limited
 (IRCON), 128, 130
India Oman Joint Statement, 85
India Ports Global Private Limited
 (IPGPL), 130
integrated deterrence, 178
International Defense Exhibition
 (IDEX), 61
International Maritime Security
 Construct, 168
International Monetary Fund (IMF),
 73
International North–South Trade
 Corridor (INSTC), 48, 54–55, 64,
 122, 139
International Transit and Transport
 Corridor, 129
Iran, 71–80, 126–129, 153–162
Iranian Armed Forces, 157
Iran–Iraq war, 124, 145, 147
Iran's Active Deterrence Strategy,
 143–162
Iraq war, xx, 150
Islamic Republic, 165
Islamic Republic of Iran, 35, 143
Islamic Republic of Iran Navy
 (IRIN), 34
Islamic Revolution, 32
Islamic Revolutionary Guard Corps
 (IRGC), 128, 151, 165
Islamic Revolutionary Guard Corps
 Navy (IRGCN), 34, 156, 158

J
Joint Comprehensive Plan of Action
 (JCPOA), 33, 76

K
Kahl, Colin, 39
Kardon, I. B., 185
Khalifa Port and Industrial Zone in
 Abu Dhabi (KIZAD), 197
Khamenei, Ayatollah Ali, 54,
 126
Khan, Nasir, 101
Khan of Kalat, 101
Khatami, Mohammed, 126
Kra Canal, 23

L
Laskar, R. H., 14
Leutert, W., 185
littoralisation, 94
Lobito Corridor, 8
Look East policy, 121

M
Mackinder, Halford J., 123
Mahan, Alfred T., 9–10, 123
Makran Coastal Range, 97
Malik, Ammar A., xiv
Maritime Silk Road Initiative
 (MSRI), xxi, 86
Medieval sources, 101
Medium-Term Fiscal Plan (MTFP),
 198
memorandum of understanding
 (MoU), xiv, 7
Middle East, xvii, 79, 83
Middle East Force (MEF), 37–38
Milani, Mohsen, 127
mines, 159
mini-submarines, 159
Mirziyoyev, Shavkat, 139
Mitra, D., 20

208 *Index*

Modi, Narendra, 129, 134, 200
Mohammadi, Narges, 75
Mosaddegh, Mohammad, 156
Mujahedin-e-Khalq (MEK), 156
Multinational Development Bank (MDB), 190–191
Musandam, 175

N

Nasser, Gamal Abdel, 11
National Defense Strategy, 39
National Iranian Oil Company (NIOC), 57
NATO, 53, 55
natural resources, 98
naval defence, 167
Naval Forces Central Command (NAVCENT), 37
New Delhi Declaration, 126
Ningxia, 196
Non-Aligned Movement Summit, 128–129
non-traditional chokepoint, 81
Northern Corridor, 139

O

Obama, Barack, 53
Oman, 81, 163–180
Omani rule, 101
Oman Tank Terminal Company (OTTCO), 193
One Belt One Road (OBOR), 4, 106
Ottoman Empire, 49
overseas port construction, 182–188

P

Pahlavi, Reza Khan, 124
Pakistan, 102, 114
Partnership for Global Infrastructure and Investment (PGII), 6
passive deterrence, 154

People's Liberation Army Navy (PLAN), 185, 191–192
People's Republic of China (PRC), 181–203
Persian Gulf, xx, 15, 35–37, 40–41, 47–67, 198–202
Petroline, 170
Pham, Peter, 145
Port and Maritime Organisation (PMO), 133
Port of Duqm, 69–92
Port of Duqm Company (PDC), 190
Port-Park-City (PPC), 181, 184, 188–198
Price, Ned, 79
Project Mausam, 26
punitive deterrence, 155
Putin, Vladimir, 50–51, 58

Q

Quadrilateral Security Dialogue (QUAD), xiv, 5–6, 29, 45
quasi-mediation diplomacy, 202

R

Red Sea Alliance, 170
Regional Comprehensive Economic Partnership (RCEP), 45
Regional Security Complexes (RSCs), 18
Rezaei, Mohsen, 135–136
Ruble Crisis, 50
Russia, 47–67
Russian Foreign Policy Concept, 52
Russian World, 58
Russo–Iranian partnership, xvii, 54
Russo–Ukrainian war, xvii, 48, 61

S

Saudi Arabia, 15
Saudi Aramco, 173
Saudi Shia community, 165

Sea Lane of Communications (SLOCs), 3
Second World War, 11
Security and Growth for All in the Region (SAGAR), 25
Shah, Mohammad Reza, 147
Shekou model, 189
Shia Islamic rule, 74
Silk Road Economic Belt, 106
Sino–Omani Industrial Park, xxi
Sino–Pakistani realization, 118
Sino–Pakistan nexus, 114
Sistan-Baluchestan provinces, 122
Skyline Duqm, 84
South China Sea (SCS), 19
Soviet Union, 18, 35, 37, 49–50
Special Economic Zone (SEZ), 80, 82, 188, 193, 195
Special Economic Zone Authority at Duqm (SEZAD), 13, 188–189, 191–192
State of the Strait, 169–171
state-owned enterprises (SOEs), 183, 197
State-run India Ports Global Limited, 14
Status of Forces Agreement (SOFA), 21
Strait of Hormuz, xiii, xvi–xvii, xix, 12–13, 15, 31–46, 81, 89, 143–162
Strait of Malacca, 16
Strategic Framework Agreement, 87
'string of pearls' strategy, 187
Suez Canal, 11–13
Suez Crisis, 144
Sultanate, 175–176
Sultan, Said bin, 101
symbol of cooperation, 135–140
Syria, 59
System of the Bank of Russia (SPFS), 54

T
Tanker Wars, 147
Thailand, 22
traditional deterrence, 154
Trans-Arabian Pipeline (TAPLINE), 15, 146
Transport Corridor Europe-Caucasus-Asia (TRACECA), 124
Trilateral Agreement, 121, 129
Trump, Donald, 133
tsunamis, 95

U
UAE–India–France Maritime Partnership Exercise, 177
Ukraine, 47
United Arab Emirates (UAE), 53, 163–180
United Nations Convention on the Law of the Sea (UNCLOS), 148
United Nations Security Council, 4
United States of America (USA), xiii, 71–80
UN World Food Programme, 134
US–China rivalry, xvii
US–GCC Defense Working Groups, 39
US–India, 70, 92
US Institute of Peace, 75
US–Iran asymmetrical rivalry, 87
US National Security Strategy, 75

V
Vietnam, 20
Vision 2030, 169–170
Vision 2040, 176

W
Western Container Terminal (WCT), 24
Western Indian Ocean Region, 198–202

210   *Index*

Westernism, 58
white paper, 28
World Bank, 28
World Island, 51
World War II, 145

X
Xi Jinping, 4, xiv

Z
zero-sum approach, 124

www.ingramcontent.com/pod-product-compliance
Lightning Source LLC
Jackson TN
JSHW011605180225
79191JS00002B/18